DECENTRALIZATION
and
DEVELOPMENT

DECENTRALIZATION
and
DEVELOPMENT

Policy Implementation in Developing Countries

Edited by

G. Shabbir Cheema
Dennis A. Rondinelli

Published in cooperation with the
United Nations Centre for Regional Development

SAGE PUBLICATIONS
Beverly Hills / London / New Delhi

For information address:

SAGE Publications, Inc.
275 South Beverly Drive
Beverly Hills, California 90212

SAGE Publications India Pvt. Ltd.
C-236 Defence Colony
New Delhi 110 024, India

SAGE Publications Ltd
28 Banner Street
London EC1Y 8QE, England

Printed in the United States of America

Library of Congress Cataloging in Publication Data

Main entry under title:

Dencentralization and development.

"Published in cooperation with the United Nations Centre for Regional Development."
1. Underdeveloped areas—Politics and government—Addresses, essays, lectures. 2. Underdeveloped areas—Decentralization in government—Addresses, essays, lectures.   I. Cheema, G. Shabbir.   II. Rondinelli, Dennis A.   III. United Nations Centre for Regional Development.
JF60.D42   1983   350.007'3'091724   83-3051
ISBN 0-8039-1988-3

FIRST PRINTING

CONTENTS

FOREWORD

One of the most crucial and recurring debates in the developing world is about the degree of control that central governments can and should have over development planning and administration. Thus, it should not be surprising that as the directions of development strategy have shifted over the past two decades, new questions about the most appropriate forms of planning and administering development policies have arisen in so many developing countries.

During the 1970s many governments in Asia, Latin America, and Africa began experimenting not only with new approaches to economic and social development, but also with new political and administrative arrangements for implementing development programs and projects. The increasing interest in decentralizing authority for planning and administration to state, regional, district and local agencies, field units of central ministries, local governments, and special-purpose organizations, as well as to nongovernment institutions and private associations, arose from three converging forces. First, it emerged from disillusionment with the results of highly centralized planning and control of development activities during the 1950s and 1960s. Second, it arose from the implicit requirements in the growth-with-equity policies of the 1970s for new ways of managing social development programs. Finally, it evolved from the growing realization among policy analysts during the early 1980s that as societies become more complex and government activities expand, it is increasingly difficult to plan and administer all development activities effectively and efficiently from the center.

However, many of the decentralization policies that are now being tried in developing countries either have been ineffectively implemented or have produced disappointing results. Relatively little attention has been given in many developing nations to formulating policies in a way that improves their chances of being implemented effectively.

This book is a collection of essays by development planners and administrators who gathered under the auspices of the United Nations Centre for Regional Development (UNCRD) in Nagoya, Japan. The mandate of UNCRD is to assist the developing countries in building up and strengthening their capabilities in regional planning and development by serving as a training and research center, providing advisory services, and disseminating relevant information to institutions in developing countries.

In this book, the authors review the variety of decentralization policies and programs that have recently been introduced in developing nations; examine the experience with implementing them; and identify the social, economic, political, and administrative factors that seem to influence the success or failure of decentralization policies. In addition, they explore alternative approaches to designing and administering decentralized development projects and prescribe ways implementation can be strengthened and improved.

Different forms and concepts of decentralization, and their advantages and disadvantages, are explored throughout the book. Relationships among decentralization, socially equitable economic growth, participation in decision making, and administrative capicity are examined in each chapter. The authors draw on experiences from East and Southeast Asia, South America, and East and North Africa.

The editors and I are thankful to the contributors to this volume for their willingness to revise the original versions of their papers for publication in the present form and to UNCRD staff for their comments and suggestions. Thanks are also due to Mitsuhiko Hosaka, Reasearch Associate, UNCRD, for proofreading some of the chapters and to Kuniko Kondo for diligently typing several drafts of the manuscript.

I am confident that the volume will be of great interest to planners, scholars, and development practitioners concerned with regional and local development in the Third World countries and will lead to a better understanding of the process of implementing decentralization policies and programs.

Hidehiko Sazanami
Director, UNCRD

CHAPTER 1

IMPLEMENTING DECENTRALIZATION POLICIES
An Introduction

Dennis A. Rondinelli and G. Shabbir Cheema

The structure of government in all countries changes constantly, sometimes rapidly and dramatically through administrative reforms and reorganization, sometimes slowly and imperceptibly through the interaction of social, administrative, and political forces. But the results of those changes are often most visible and profound in developing nations, where the government plays a dominant role in guiding development. There has emerged, therefore, a growing awareness of the relationships between political and administrative organization and the pace and direction of social and economic progress. It has become clear that the impacts of changes in political and administrative organization are rarely neutral: They advance the interests of some groups in society over those of others, alter the patterns of resource allocation among regions and localities, change the distribution of income and wealth, expand or contract the scope of political influence, and increase or restrict citizens' access to policymakers and to decision-making processes. Thus, no proposal for administrative reform or political change, even in unitary or totalitarian states, escapes debate.

One of the most crucial and recurring debates in the developing world is about the degree of control that central governments can and should have over development planning and administration. Thus, it should not be surprising that as the directions of development strategy shifted over the past two decades, questions about the most appropriate forms of planning and administering development policies should have arisen in so many developing countries.

During the 1970s, many governments in Asia, Latin America, and Africa began to experiment not only with new approaches to development, but also with new political and administrative arrangements for planning and managing development programs and projects. The increasing interest in decentralizing authority for planning and administration to state, regional, district and local agencies, field units of central ministries, local governments, and special purpose organizations arose from three converging forces: first, from disillusionment with the results of central planning and control of development activities during the 1950s and 1960s; second, from the implicit requirements for new ways of managing development programs and projects that were embodied in growth-with-equity strategies that emerged during the 1970s; and third, from the growing realization that as societies become more complex and government activities begin to expand, it becomes increasingly difficult to plan and administer all development activities effectively and efficiently from the center.

CHANGING APPROACHES TO DEVELOPMENT POLICY AND ADMINISTRATION

Since the early 1950s, control over development activities in most Third World countries has been centralized in national government ministries and agencies. Central control was compatible with the major theories of economic development that emerged in the late 1940s. Capital-intensive industrialization policies that were aimed at maximizing gains in gross national product were advocated by economic development theorists during the 1950s and 1960s. They required strong intervention in investment and production processes by national governments and called for centrally conceived, comprehensive, plans for national development. Central planning was introduced in most developing countries in the 1950s as a means of providing rational and coherent policies for using scarce resources effectively to promote rapid growth in industrial output. Central planning was prescribed by international assistance agencies, such as the World Bank, as a way of promoting "modernization," accelerating social and political change, generating employment, and mobilizing capital for further investment. It would allow the state, as Mydral noted, to "initiate, spur and steer economic development."[1] National plans would not only direct public resource allocation, but also guide private investment and the activities of parastatal organizations. The benefits of industrial investment, concentrated in one or two major metropolitan centers, would "trickle down" and spread throughout the economies of developing nations to alleviate poverty and generate income and savings. The capital mobilized through savings would be reinvested, thereby expanding production and employment, raising incomes, drawing larger numbers of people into productive activities, and eventually pushing poor societies into a stage of self-sustaining economic growth. Regional disparities would gradually be lessened, and the majority of people would benefit from continued growth and development.[2]

Central planning and administration were considered necessary to guide and control the economy and to integrate and unify nations that were emerging from long periods of colonial rule. Moreover, central control was implicit in the requirements of the international assistance agencies that were providing large amounts of capital during the 1950s and 1960s. They insisted that borrowers have comprehensive and long-term plans for the investment of external capital.

But by the end of the 1960s it was widely recognized hat central planning had not achieved these goals. Economic growth remained sluggish in most developing countries during the 1950s and 1960s; even where growth rates were high, only a small group usually benefited from increased national production. Income disparities between rich and poor, and among regions, widened in many countries. The living standards of the poorest groups in the least developed nations declined, and the numbers of people living in what World Bank officials called "absolute poverty" were increasing.[3] Many development planners and administrators began questioning the effectiveness of strategies based primarily on increasing industrial output and challenging theories calling for maximum economic growth regardless of the patterns of income distribution. Much of the interest in decentralization undoubtedly came from the realization during the 1970s that central control and management of the economies of developing nations did not ensure rapid economic growth and that few countries could easily follow the prescriptions made by economic theorists and international assistance organizations for comprehensive and long-range planning.

In most developing countries it was difficult to mobilize support for centrally planned courses of action even among the national leaders who officially endorsed the plans. Ministries and agencies in most countries continued setting and following their own priorities and pursuing their own interests, or at least pursuing their own interpretation of the national interest. The plans were produced usually only for international consumption — to satisfy the requirements of international lenders or to impress other countries with an image of unity and control over national economic and political destinies. But the plans were often useless in guiding internal decisions: Their goals were stated in vague and amorphous terms; the objectives were grandiose; they failed to disaggregate goals into programs and projects that could be carried out; they often lacked cost estimates, ignored limits on resources, and failed to consider the differing needs and conditions of various regions of the country or groups within society. The methods of macroeconomic analysis that were adopted from industrialized countries by national planners were difficult or impossible to apply without more accurate and abundant data than were available in poor countries. The results, even when the data were available, were often irrelevant, inappropriate, and perverse. High population growth rates within developing nations and adverse fluctuations in the world economy often wiped out the meager gains from investment schemes. Implementation of the plans, moreover, was usually impeded by internal weaknesses in administrative capacity. Private institutions with significant amounts of financial and managerial resources were rarely involved in plan formulation. The low levels of administrative skill within central ministries and in local governments made planned activities difficult to carry out even if they were well conceived.[4]

Many of the basic premises of development theory came into question during the 1970s, and the directions and priorities of development policy shifted drastically. The very concept of development was stretched beyond that of maximizing gains in gross national product and, indeed, beyond ecomonic growth as a primary objective. Planners and policymakers began to recognize that development requires a basic transformation in social, economic, and political structures that enables poor people to help themselves to increase their productivity and incomes. The market structures that seemed to be so effective in promoting development in industrial countries rarely worked in most poor countries; poverty would not be ameliorated "automatically" through trickle-down and spread effects. But it was also found that deficiencies in market mechanisms were not necessarily overcome by central planning. In many countries central control simply substituted one set of obstacles to equitable growth for another. Policies had to be fashioned deliberately and carefully to spread the benefits of growth to increasing numbers of the poor in developing nations, and ways had to be found to increase their participation in decisions affecting them.

Governments of developing countries and international development organizations began giving much more attention to providing for the basic needs of the poor so that they could become more productive participants in the development process, and to increasing the income and purchasing power of the rural population to build stronger and more self-reliant domestic economies. These growth-with-equity policies reflected social and political values that had not been apparent in previous economic development strategies and had fundamental implications for the ways development planning and administration were organized. Greater equity in the distribution of income and wealth, many development theorists argued, required wider participation in the economic, social, and political processes through which wealth was generated and distributed. The new strategies, as Keith Griffin has pointed out,

> cannot easily be centrally planned. Consequently the shift of thinking in favor of agriculture and mobilization of local human and material resources has been accompanied by a reduced emphasis on national planning and a growing awareness of the need to devise an administrative structure that would permit regional decentralization, local autonomy in making decisions of primary concern to the locality and greater local responsibility for designing and implementing development programs. Such changes, evidently, are not just technical and administrative; they are political. They involve a transfer of power from the groups who dominate the center to those who have control at the local level.[5]

Central planning was not only complex and difficult to implement, but may also have been inappropriate for promoting equitable growth and self sufficiency among low-income groups and communities within developing societies. Through central planning, it was charged, an elite group of political leaders, economists, technicians, and administrators attempted to preempt decision making and prescribe for government agencies, private organizations, and local communities courses of action that reflected their own values and priorities. They used central planning to set the criteria that others would follow rather than to promote and facilitate courses of action that would be planned and carried out by those who were to benefit from development.

The growth-with-equity policies adopted in many countries during the 1970s highlighted the inconsistencies between central control over planning and administration and the widespread participation and equitable distribution of benefits they were attempting to generate. New structures and procedures were needed to elicit the participation of lower-income groups and communities in rural areas in promoting greater self-sufficiency in regional economies. In some Latin American countries, governments established regional development corporations to stimulate local investment and greater agricultural production, and many African governments set up provincial, district, and regional planning committees. In Asia, there was a rapid proliferation of frontier-region resource management agencies, regional planning and development offices, provincial development programs, integrated rural development schemes, and financial aid programs for district and village administrative units.

THE RATIONALE FOR
DECENTRALIZATION POLICIES

The growing interest in decentralized planning and administration is attributable not only to the disillusionment with the results of central planning and the shift of emphasis to growth-with-equity policies, but also to the realization that development is a complex and uncertain process that cannot be easily planned and controlled from the center. Advocates of decentralization have offered a long list of reasons for transferring more responsibility for development planning and administration to local governments, voluntary organizations, and regional authorities. Rondinelli had identified the variety of arguments that have been made for decentralizing development planning and administration in Third World countries[6]:

(1) Decentralization can be a means of overcoming the severe limitations of centrally controlled national planning by delegating greater authority for development planning and management to officials who are working in the field, closer to the problems. Decentralization to regional or local levels allows officials to disaggregate and tailor development plans and programs to the needs of heterogeneous regions and groups.[7]

(2) Decentralization can cut through the enormous amounts of red tape and the highly structured procedures charcteristic of central planning and management in developing nations that result in part from the overconcentration of power, authority, and resources at the center of the government in the national capital.[8]

(3) By decentralizing functions and reassigning central government officials to local levels, these officials' knowledge of and sensitivity to local problems and needs can be increased. Closer contact between government officials and the local population would allow both to obtain better information with which to formulate more realistic and effective plans for government projects and programs.

(4) Decentralization could also allow better political and administrative "penetration" of national government policies into areas remote from the national capital, where central government plans are often unknown or ignored by the rural people or are undermined by local elites, and where support for national development plans is often weak.[9]

(5) Decentralization might allow greater representation for various political, religious, ethnic, and tribal groups in development decision making that could lead to greater equity in the allocation of government resources and investments.[10]

(6) Decentralization could lead to the development of greater administrative capability among local governments and private institutions in the regions and provinces, thus expanding their capacities to take over functions that are not usually performed well by central ministries, such as the maintenance of roads and infrastructure investments in areas remote from the national capital. It could also give local officials the opportunity to develop their managerial and technical skills.

(7) The efficiency of the central government could be increased through decentralization by relieving top management officials of routine tasks that could be more effectively performed by field staff or local officials. The time released from routine administration would free political and administrative leaders to plan more carefully and supervise more effectively the implementation of development policies.[11]

(8) Decentralization can also provide a structure through which activities of various central government ministries and agencies involved in development could be coordinated more effectively with each other and with those of local leaders and nongovernmental organizations within various regions. Regions, provinces, or districts provide a convenient geographical base for coordinating the myriad

specialized projects that many governments in developing countries are undertaking in rural areas.[12]

(9) A decentralized governmental sructure is needed to institutionalize participation of citizens in development planning and management. A decentralized government structure can facilitate the exchange of information about local needs and channel political demands from the local community to national ministries.[13]

(10) By creating alternative means of decision making, decentralization might offset the influence or control over development activities by entrenched local elites, who are often unsympathetic to national development policies and insensitive to the needs of the poorer groups in rural communities.

(11) Decentralization can lead to more flexible, innovative, and creative administration. Regional, provincial, or district administrative units may have greater opportunities to test innovations and to experiment with new policies and programs in selected areas, without having to justify them for the whole country. If the experiments fail, their impacts are limited to small jurisdictions; if they succeed, they can be replication in other areas of the country.[14]

(12) Decentralization of development planning and management functions allows local leaders to locate services and facilities more effectively within communities, to integrate isolated or lagging areas into regional economies, and to monitor and evaluate the implementation of development projects more effectively than can be done by central planning agencies.

(13) Decentralization can increase political stability and national unity by giving groups in different sections of the country the ability to participate more directly in development decision making, thereby increasing their "stake" in maintaining the political system.

(14) By reducing diseconomies of scale inherent in the overconcentration of decision making in the national capital, decentralization can increase the number of public goods and services — and the effeciency with which they are delivered — at lower cost.[15]

But it has also become clear from experience with attempting to implement decentralization policies that not all of the alleged benefits materialize and that few developing countries have been highly successful in carrying out their decentralization programs. Simply creating decentralized structures for development decision making and announcing new procedures for participation in development planning and administration do not guarantee that they will be effective or that they will generate economic growth with greater social equity.

Little attention has been given to identifying the appropriate functions that governments can and should decentralize, to the capacity of local organizations and administrative units to assume larger roles in development planning and management, or to the obstacles to implementing decentralization policies and programs.[16] As the authors of the following chapters point out, decentralization is not an end in itself; the obstacles to administrative reorganization in nearly all developing nations are often overwhelming. Even the strongest advocates of decentralization recognize that it is not a panacea for the social and economic ills of the poor and will not alone change political and social relationships that have obstructed greater participation in development planning and administration in the past. Griffin, for example, emphasizes that

> it is conceivable, even likely in many countries, that power at the local level is more concentrated, more elitist and applied more ruthlessly against the poor than at the centre. Thus, greater decentralization does not necessarily imply greater democracy let alone "power to the people." It all depends on the circumstances under which decentralization occurs.[17]

Thus, the chapters of this book focus on a number of issues: They review the variety of decentralization policies that have recently been introduced in developing nations; examine the experience with implementing them; identify social, political, economic, and administrative factors that influence the success or failure of decentralization programs; explore alternative approaches to designing and administering decentralized development projects; and prescribe ways in which the implementation of decentralization policies can be strengthened and improved. Some of the authors are enthusiastic advocates of greater decentralization; others are more skeptical of its desirability or feasibility. But from the diversity of views comes a more balanced and objective examination of the relationships between decentralization and development and a detailed assessment of the factors that seem to be important for improving implementation in those countries that have committed themselves to decentralizing their development-planning and administrative procedures.

The remainder of this chapter explores the concepts of and alternative approaches to decentralization and outlines a conceptual framework for examining the implementation of decentralization policies, the elements of which are referred to recurringly in the chapters that follow.

THE CONCEPT OF DECENTRALIZATION

Decentralization means different things to different people, and a variety of motivations can be uncovered for the recent attempts to decentralize planning and administration in developing countries. Decentralization is defined quite broadly in this book to mean the transfer of planning, decision-making, or administrative authority from the central government to its field organizations, local administrative units, semi-autonomous and parastatal organizations, local governments, or nongovernmental organizations. Different forms of decentralization can be distinguished primarily by the extent to which authority to plan, decide, and manage is transferred from the central government to other organizations and the amount of autonomy the "decentralized organizations" achieved in carrying out their tasks.

Forms of Decentralization

Although the authors of various chapters in this book use different terms to identify different degrees or forms of decentralization, all agree that the differences are important. They refer to four major forms of decentralization: deconcentration, delegation to semi-autonomous or parastatal agencies, devolution to local governments, and transfer of functions from public to nongovernment institutions.[18]

Deconcentration

Deconcentration involves the redistribution of administrative responsibilities only within the central government. At one extreme, what is often called decentralization in some countries is merely the *shifting of workload* from a central government ministry or agency headquarters to its own field staff located in offices outside of the national capital, without also transferring to them the authority to make decisions or to exercise discretion in carrying them out. Fesler argues that shifting workload may not really be decentralization at all: "To move workload out of the capital may be efficient and convenient for the public and may even promote a feeling that government is close to the people," he notes. "But it may not involve any decentralization of power, that is, it may not provide the opportunity to exercise substantial local discretion in decision making."[19] Although the observation is valid and probably true for most Western nations, in highly centralized governments in developing nations even the shifting of workload from central offices to staff outside the capital can has an impact on development. It may be a crucial first step that highly centralized governments must take toward more extensive deconcentration later.

A greater degree of deconcentration can be achieved through *field administration*. As opposed to merely shifting workload from central government offices in the capital city to those in other locations, creation of a system of field administration implies the transfer of some decision-making discretion to field staff, allowing them some latitude to plan, make routine decisions, and adjust the implementation of central directives to local conditions, within guidelines set by the central ministry. Under a system of field administration, even though government officers are working within local jurisdictions that may have semi-autonomous or delegated powers, field staff are employees of a central ministry and remain under its direction and control.

A useful distinction can also be made between field administration and *local administration*. Local administration is a form of deconcentration in which all subordinate levels of government within a country are agents of the central authority, usually the executive branch. Regions, provinces, districts, municipalities, and other units of government are headed by leaders who are either appointed by or are responsible directly to a central government agency, usually a ministry of local government or ministry of the interior. Local functions are performed under the technical supervision and control of central ministries, and the heads of the local administrations serve at the pleasure of the nation's chief executive. Two types of local administration are found in most developing countries: integrated and unintegrated.

Integrated local administration is a form of deconcentration in which field staff of central ministries work within a local jurisdiction under the supervision or direction of a chief executive of that jurisdiction, who is appointed by and responsible to the central government. In some African countries, for instance, the province commissioner has the power to supervise and coordinate the work of various ministry staff working within the province. Although the field staff may be hired, paid, trained, promoted, and transferred by the central ministry, field officers act as a technical staff to the province commissioner and are accountable to that person for the efficient performance of their duties.

Unintegrated local administration is an arrangement by which field staff of central ministries and administrative staff of local jurisdictions operate independently of each other. Both sets of officials are responsible to central authorities, but they have little or no formal power over each other. Each technical officer is responsible to his or her own ministry in the national capital, and the administrative staff of the local jurisdiction are supervised by its chief executive, who has little or no control over central ministry personnel. Coordination takes place informally, if at all, and each technical officer operates in accordance with guidelines prepared by supervisors in the national capital.

Although deconcentration does not transfer authority to plan, decide, or manage to individuals or organizations that are outside of the structure of the central government, officials of the United Nations Technical Assistance Program argue that if administration is brought closer to the people, citizens "will have a better understanding of what government proposes. Through this understanding they will be more likely to adopt the new ideas and practices, use the services offered, contribute their own effort and resources to the programme, give vitality to new institutions and make constructive adjustments in their lives.[20]

*Delegation to Semi-Autonomous
or Parastatal Organizations*

Another form of decentralization is the delegation of decision-making and management authority for specific functions to organizations that are not under the direct control of central government ministries. Often the organizations to which development functions are delegated have semi-independent authority to perform their responsibilities and may not even be located within the regular government structure. Delegation of functions from the central government to such organizations as public corporations, regional planning and area development authorities, multipurpose and single-purpose functional authorities, and special project implementation units represents a more extensive form of decentralization than administrative deconcentration. Delegation implies the transfer or creation of broad authority to plan and implement decisions concerning specific activities — or a variety of activities within specific spatial boundaries — to an organization that is technically and administratively capable of carrying them out without direct supervision by a higher administrative unit.

The response of many governments and most international lending institutions to the severe limitations on public administration in much of the Third World has been to delegate more functions to public corporations, special authorities, and semi-autonomous project implementation units. The practice of designating separate project implementation units gained strength after World War II, partly from the realization that certain innovative or high-priority projects had to be isolated from the routine political and bureaucratic conflicts that are pervasive in developing countries and partly because of the insistence by international lending organizations, especially the World Bank, that semi-autonomous implementation units be created to prevent revenues from income-earning ventures from being "comingled" with general budget funds. Mason and Asher, in their history of the World Bank, note that it has, "so far as possible, used its influence to assure that income of public revenue-producing entities be kept separate from other government revenues and be used, when needed, for the expansion of the organization's own facilities."[21] Creating special organizations, especially for integrated rural development projects, was also seen as a way of ensuring that the projects would be better managed and that the lenders would be repaid. The World Bank has used its lending powers to exert "leverage" on borrowing governments to improve administrative capacity within project implementation organizations.

Public corporations and regional development authorities have been used extensively in both Asia and Africa to execute development schemes. During the 1950s and 1960s the creation of public corporations was an integral part of Western public administration theorists' prescription for administrative reform and modernization and was seen by some political leaders as a way to "short-circuit the normal government machinery and endow it with developmental drive, coherence and authority to plan and pursue economic development by such means as seen fit to it."[22] Administrative theorists argued that public corporations or regional development authorities — most used the Tennessee Valley Authority in the United States as the implicit model — had distinct advantages over regular government agencies in that they could make decisions more expeditiously, free from the red tape and political maneuvering found in bureaucracies in most developing nations, and could operate outside the constraints raised by procurement regulations and civil service requirements. Moreover, a seperate and usually higher-level salary scale, the prestige of a corporate image, and the ability to use "business procedures" within these special authorities would attract the most highly qualified personnel and motivate them to perform more efficiently. Most of the public corporations and regional development authorities have been organized to undertake commercial projects in sectors in which the government maintains a vital interest or in which the private sector is weak. Public corporations and special authorities have been used extensively in Asia and Africa to finance, construct, and manage physical infrastructure projects such as highways, dams, hydroelectric facilities, railroads, and transportation systems and to organize and manage large-scale agricultural activities and integrated rural development projects.

Devolution

Another form of decentralization seeks to create or strengthen independent levels or units of government through devolution of functions and authority. Through devolution the central government relinquishes certain functions or creates new units of government that are outside its direct control.[23]

Devolution, in its purest forms, has certain fundamental characteristics. First, local units of government are autonomous, independent, and clearly perceived as separate levels of government over which central authorities exercise little or no *direct* control. Second, the local governments have clear and legally recognized geographical boundaries within which they exercise authority and perform public functions. Third, local governments have corporate status and the power to secure resources to perform their functions. Fourth, devolution implies the need to "develop local governments as institutions" in the sense that they are perceived by local citizens as organizations providing services that satisfy their needs and as governmental units over which they have some influence. Finally, devolution is an arrangement in which there are reciprocal, mutually beneficial, and coordinate relationships between central and local governments; that is, the local government has the ability to interact reciprocally with other units in the system of government of which it is a part. The concept implies, as Sherwood argues, that "local governments discharge obligations as part of a national political system and not as dependent elements of a central hierarchy. The concept of devolution is non-hierarchical in the sense that it posits a number of governments having a coordinate, systems relationship with one another on an independent, reciprocating basis."[24]

Although these specifications for devolution may be valid from a theoretical or even a legal perspective, in most developing nations actual requirements are less stringent. Devolution is usually seen as a form of decentralization in which local government units are given primary responsibility for some functions over which the central government often retains some supervisory powers and in which it may play an important financial role. Even where most of the theoretical conditions for devolution are met, however, central governments often attempt to make local governments act consistently with national development policies and plans in performing their functions, and certain formal or informal controls are often maintained to accomplish that goal. Few developing nations have a system of formal devolution meeting all of the conditions noted earlier, but some national constitutions devolve specific powers and responsibilities to local governments or give them residual powers that are not claimed by the central government. The United Nations Technical Assistance Program's study of decentralization notes that national governments exercise supervisory control over nationally funded programs carried out by local governments and sometimes even over purely "local" programs, even in a decentralized system. Among the "positive" measures for guiding local activities are:

— formulating national programs, with targets, timing, and costs classified, insofar as practicable, on an area basis;

— issuing general directives and guides from time to time, including the setting of technical and other standards by circulars, handbooks, and model ordinances;

— training local authority staff and, where advisable and practicable, councilpersons in order to convey information and to develop their capabilities;

— providing technical help readily to individual authorities from field units or from central offices, on request or as the need becomes clear;

— specifying minimum qualifications for technical and professional officers to be employed by local authorities, including, for some categories, the possession of a certificate or license issued by the central government.[25]

When programs or projects carried out by local governments are funded or supported by the national government, the central ministries may have more direct controls or engage in more direct supervision through spot checks on performance by inspectors from the ministries, by requiring progress reports on programs and projects, through budgetary and financial regulations, by exercising administrative powers when local governments default or carry out programs ineffectively, by approving bylaws and procedures of local governments, and through judicial remedies.[26]

For development purposes, however, the capacity of local governments to carry out programs and projects effectively and through reciprocal relationships with other organizations may be more significant than their legal status as independent units. Indeed, Uphoff and Esman have pointed out that "local autonomy by itself provides little leverage for development." They argue that it is the network of interaction — the linkages that local governments have with other organizations — that determines their ability to provide services and generate development. "What makes the most difference," they argue, "are systems or networks of organization that make local development more than an enclave phenomenon."[27]

Transfer of Functions from Government
to Nongovernment Institutions

Finally, decentralization takes place in many countries through the transfer of some planning and administrative responsibility, or of public functions, from government to voluntary, private, or nongovernment institutions. In some cases, governments may transfer to "parallel organizations" — such as national industrial and trade associations, professional or ecclesiastical organizations, political parties, or cooperatives — the right to license, regulate, or supervise their members in performing functions that were previously controlled by the government.[28] In other cases, governments may decentralize by shifting responsibility for producing goods or supplying services to private organizations, a process often called "privatization." In some countries, "self-management" arrangements have been created to allow workers in public enterprises or production cooperatives to plan and manage their own activities without strong central intervention and control. More often, government transfers responsibilities to or shares them with organizations that represent various interests in society and that are initiated and operated by members of those organizations: farmers' cooperatives, credit associations, mutual aid societies, village development organizations, trade unions, or women's and youth clubs. Moreover, decentralization may be implicit on the concept of "debureaucratization," that is, allowing decisions to be made through political processes that involve larger numbers of political interests, rather than having the decisions made exclusively or primarily by government through legislation, executive decree, or administrative regulation. In Chapter 2, Friedman discusses these and other forms of transferring responsibility from government to nongovernment institutions, and in Chapter 7, Cheema describes the role of voluntary organizations in decentralized development planning and administration in more detail.

Each of these forms of decentralization has different implications for organizational structure, the degree of power or authority to be transferred, the amount of citizen participation involved, preconditions for successful implementation, and advantages and disadvantages for different groups within society. But even though these forms of decentralization differ in their characteristics and implications, they are not mutually exclusive. In reality, all governments use some combination of these forms of decentralized planning, decision making, and administration. The highly centralized governments in developing countries have experimented with nearly all of these forms of decentralization in the past few years, with greater emphasis in most on deconcentration and delegation. But they have had great difficulty in many cases even deconcentrating development planning and administrative functions, and where they have succeeded in setting up decentralized arrangements they have not always generated the intended benefits.[29]

As the authors of various chapters in this book point out, any change in political and administrative structure or procedures in developing nations quickly meets severe constraints during implementation, and thus it is to the factors that influence policy implementation that most of the analyses are addressed. The chapters focus on different aspects of administration and give different weights to the various factors that influence successful policy implementation. Thus, before reviewing experience with decentralization policy in developing countries, it is important to provide an overview of the kinds of factors that are likely to promote or inhibit successful implementation in developing countries.

ANALYZING THE IMPLEMENTATION OF
DECENTRALIZATION POLICIES

Policy provides guidance for action. Public policies are incorporated in public documents such as the constitution, long- and medium-range plans, and annual budgets, and they are usually expressed most explicitly through government statements on specific issues. The scope of public policies can range from broad statements of intended goals, to guiding principles for public action, to specific schemes for achieving objectives. In reality, however, making public policies is not what a government intends to do, but what it actually does. A program is a collection of related activities that is designed to harmonize and integrate actions by government agencies and other organizations for achieving policy objectives. Implementation is the execution or carrying out of a program or project aimed at achieving specific policy objectives. Implementation has been defined as a "process of interaction between the setting of goals and actions geared to achieving them."[30] The literature on policy implementation identifies two competing views of the process: the "compliance" approach and the political approach.[33] The first assumes that implementation is a technical, routine, apolitical process of carrying out predetermined plans and that administrators or implementors are subordinates who comply with guidelines established by political leaders. The second approach views administration as an integral part of the policymaking process in which policies are refined, reformulated, or even abandoned in the process of implementing them, thus making implementation complex and unpredictable.

The factors that influence policy implementation have not been given adequate attention in developing countries, because many of those who formulate decentralization policies hold the "compliance" view of administration. They assume that once policies are announced they will be implemented by subordinate administrators and that the intended results will be achieved in a nonpolitical and technically competent way. However, all of the experience with decentralization in developing countries, and with other programs and policies as well, indicates that implementation is not merely a technical process of carrying out preconceived plans, but is a dynamic and somewhat unpredictable process of political interaction. A variety of political, social, behavioral, economic, and organizational factors influence the degree to which policies are implemented as they were intended and the degree to which they achieve their intended goals.

Figure 1.1 depicts four sets of factors that seem to influence the implementation of decentralization policies in developing countries that are discussed in greater detail in the chapters that follow: environmental conditions, interorganizational relationships, available resources, and the characteristics of implementing agencies. The factors presented in each of these sets are suggested variables, and their relative significance would vary from one situation to another.

Environmental Conditions

Policies emerge from a specific and complex socioeconomic and political environment that shapes not only the substance of policies but the patterns of interorganizational relationships and the characteristics of implementing agencies, as well as determining the amounts and types of resources available for carrying them out. An understanding of the social, economic, and political setting from which policies emerge is crucial to understanding the constraints on and opportunities for implementing organizations to translate policies into action. A nation's political structure, its dominant ideology, and the processes through which its policies are formulated all influence the pace and direction of implementation. Moreover, the characteristics of local power structures, social and cultural characteristics of groups involved in policymaking and administration, and the degree to which beneficiaries are organized also play a role in policy implementation, as does the adequacy of the physical infrastructure for distributing the benefits. As will be seen in the chapters that follow, and especially in Rondinelli's analysis of decentralization in East Africa and Nellis's study of the Magreb States of North Africa, these environmental conditions have been crucial factors both in initiating decentralization and in constraining its successful implementation.

Interorganizational Relationships

Successful policy implementation requires the interaction and coordination of a large number of organizations at different levels of government, on complementary actions by local, regional, and national agencies, and on cooperation by nongovernment organizations and groups of intended beneficiaries. As a recent World Bank study points out, "in the newer multisectoral projects success is determined

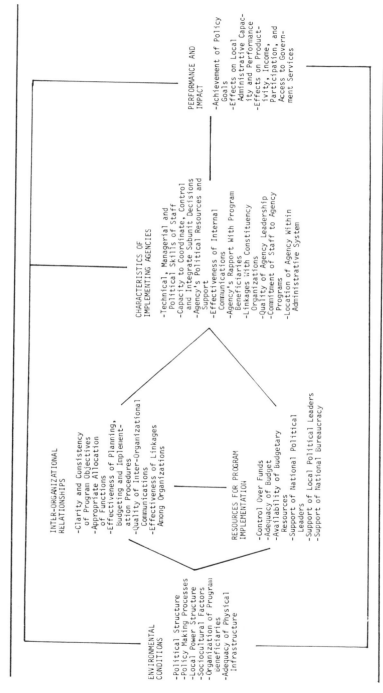

INTER-ORGANIZATIONAL RELATIONSHIPS

-Clarity and Consistency of Program Objectives
-Appropriate Allocation of Functions
-Effectiveness of Planning, Budgeting and Implement- ation Procedures
-Quality of Inter-Organizational Communications
-Effectiveness of Linkages Among Organizations

RESOURCES FOR PROGRAM IMPLEMENTATION

-Control Over Funds
-Adequacy of Budget
-Availability of budgetary Resources
-Support of National Political Leaders
-Support of Local Political Leaders
-Support of National Bureaucracy

ENVIRONMENTAL CONDITIONS

-Political Structure
-Policy Making Processes
-Local Power Structure
-Sociocultural Factors
-Organization of Program beneficiaries
-Adequacy of Physical Infrastructure

CHARACTERISTICS OF IMPLEMENTING AGENCIES

-Technical, Managerial and Political Skills of Staff
-Capacity to Coordinate, Control and Integrate Subunit Decisions
-Agency's Political Resources and Support
-Effectiveness of Internal Communications
-Agency's Rapport With Program Beneficiaries
-Linkages With Constituency Organizations
-Quality of Agency Leadership
-Commitment of Staff to Agency Programs
-Location of Agency Within Administrative System

PERFORMANCE AND IMPACT

-Achievement of Policy Goals
-Effects on Local Administrative Capac- ity and Performance
-Effects on Product- ivity, Income, Participation, and Access to Govern- ment Services

Figure 1.1: Factors Affecting Implementation of Decentralization Policies

not so much by the most logical or efficient arrangements of internal organization and resources but by an appropriate coalignment with external agencies."[32] Therefore, successfully linking implementing agencies with others into mutually supporting networks seems essential to achieving policy goals.

The effectiveness of interorganizational relationships and linkages in carrying out decentralization policies seems to depend on:

(a) the clarity and consistency of policy objectives and the degree to which they give implementing agencies clear direction to pursue activities that will lead to their achievement;

(b) the appropriate allocation of functions among agencies, based on their capacities and resources;

(c) the degree to which planning, budgeting, and implementation procedures are standardized and thereby minimize conflicting intepretations that make programs and policies difficult to coordinate;

(d) the accuracy, consistency, and quality of interorganizational communications that enable organizations involved in policy implementation to understand their roles and tasks and to complement the activities of others; and

(e) the effectiveness of linkags among decentralized administrative units that ensure interaction among organizations and allow coordination of activities.

In Chapter 9, David Leonard reviews the types of organizational linkages that affect rural development projects, and the impact of other coordinative factors is touched on in the discussions of Asian experience by Mathur in Chapter 3 and of the Latin American experience by Harris in Chapter 6. Montgomery contends, in his analysis of factors influencing the implementation of decentralized integrated rural development in Chapter 8, that the interaction among actors at different levels and in different positions of government is crucial to designing effective projects.

**Resources for Policy and
Program Implementation**

A conducive environment and effective organization relationships are necessary but not sufficient conditions for successfully implementing decentralization policies. The extent to which agencies receive sufficient financial, administrative, and technical support also determines the outcome and effects of decentralization programs. The degree to which implementing agencies have control over funds, the adequacy of budgetary allocations to perform decentralized functions, the timely availability of those resources to the implementing agencies, and the adequacy or revenue-raising and expenditure authority at the local level affect policy implementation as well. In order for regional and local organizations to carry out decentralization programs they must also have the support of national political leaders, local officials, and elites, and they must receive administrative and technical support from the central bureaucracy. Local governments and subnational administrative units in most developing countries lack both the resources and the authority to raise sufficient revenues to carry out the tasks transferred from the center. Rondinelli's study of decentralization in East Africa and Nellis's analysis of North African experience, like Mathur's review of Asian decentralization programs, underline the importance of financial resources, administrative capacity, and technical support to successful development planning and management at the regional and local levels.

Characteristics of Implementing Agencies

The internal organizational characteristics of implementing agencies form another significant set of factors that determine the success of policy execution. These include the technical, managerial, and political skills of the agency's staff; its capacity to coordinate, control, and integrate the decisions of its subunits; and the strength of its political support from national political leaders, administrators in other organizations, and clientele groups. Moreover, the nature and quality of internal communications, the agency's relationships with its clients and supporters, and the effectiveness of its linkages with private or voluntary organizations are also important, as are the quality of leadership within the agency, the acceptance of and commitment to policy objectives among its staff, and, often, the location of the agency within the bureaucratic hierarchy. All of the authors of the following chapters, to one degree or another, observe the influence of these internal characteristics of implementing agencies on carrying out decentralized development planning and management functions.

Performance and Impact

The results of decentralization policies thus depend on four sets of related variables: environmental conditions, interorganizational relations, resources for program and policy execution, and characteristics of the implementing agencies. The performance and impact of decentralized policies and programs could be measured on the basis of the achievement of the policy's stated goals; effects on the capacity of local units of government and institutions for planning, resource mobilization, and implementation; and effects on productivity, income, popular participation, and access to government facilities.

CONCLUSIONS

In the chapters that follow, three dimensions of decentralization and development are analyzed: national policies, regional and local administration, and project design and implementation. In Chapter 2, Harry Friedman further explores and extends the concept of decentralization and reviews the alternative approaches that have been taken at the local level in Asia. Kuldeep Mathur, in Chapter 3, describes national decentralization policies in South and Southeast Asia, assesses their impact, and discusses the factors that seem to have been most important in affecting implementation. The experience with decentralization policies in East Africa — especially in the Sudan, Tanzania, and Kenya — is reviewed by Dennis Rondinelli in Chapter 4; and John Nellis, in Chapter 5, traces the history of and experience with different forms of governance and administration in Algeria, Libya, Tunisisa, and Morocco. In Chapter 6, Richard Harris examines the variety of indirect administrative structures that have been used to decentralize planning in Latin America and analyzes the prospects for implementing decentralization policies in South American governments.

In Chapter 7, G. Shabbir Cheema describes the role of voluntary, nongovernment organizations in carryinng out decentralized planning and administrative functions in rural areas of Asia and suggests a number of ways these organizations can be srengthened to perform their tasks more effectively. John Montgomery, in Chapter 8, focuses on issues affecting the implementation of integrated rural development projects and analyzes the complementarities and conflicts among actors in national planning and international assistance agencies, central management support agencies, and field agencies in controlling resources, establishing linkages, defining project goals, and establishing suppport and guidance procedures. In Chapter 9, David Leonard emphasizes the importance of interorganizational linkages for decentralized rural development, especially in areas with weak administrative capacity, and identifies the kinds of linkages that might be established and how they can be used in implementing development programs and projects.

Finally, in the last chapter, Cheema and Rondinelli cull from the various studies conclusions about the most critical factors affecting policy implementation, outline directions for improving the administration of decentralized programs and projects, suggest a framework for further research, and identify ways the implementation of policies might be made more effective in those countries that are committed to greater decentralization of development planning and administration.

NOTES

1. Gunnar Myrdal, *An Approach to the Asian Drama: Methodogical and Theoretical* (New York: Vintage, 1970), p. 175.

2. Conventional theories of economic development are reviewed in various papers collected in A. N. Agarwala and S. P. Singh, eds., *The Economics of Underdevelopment* (London: Oxford University Press, 1970) and D. E. Novack and R. Lekachman, eds., *Development and Society* (New York: St. Martin's Press, 1964).

3. See World Bank, *Rural Development Sector Policy Paper* (Washington, DC: World Bank, 1975), especially annexes 1-5.

4. The problems in Asia are summarized in Dennis A. Rondinelli, "National Investment Planning and Equity Policy in Developing Countries: The Challenge of Decentralized Administration," *Policy Sciences,* vol. 10, no. 1 (1978): 45-74; and in Asia and other developing regions in Albert Waterston, *Development Planning: Lessons of Experience* (Baltimore: Johns Hopkins Press, 1965).

5. Keith Griffin, "Economic Development in a Changing World," *World Development,* vol. 9, no. 3 (1981): 221-226; quote on p. 225.

6. See Dennis A. Rondinelli, "Government Decentralization in Comparative Perspective: Theory and Practice in Developing Countries," *International Review of Administrative Sciences,* vol. XLVII, no. 2 (1981): 133-145, from which this section draws heavily.

7. See Rondinelli, "National Investment Planning," and Dennis A. Rondinelli, "Administration of Integrated Rural Development: The Politics of Agrarian Reform in Developing Countries," *World Politics,* vol. XXI, no. 3 (April 1979): 389-416.

8. Some of these problems in East Africa are discussed by Christopher Trapman, *Changes in Administrative Structure: A Case Study of Kenyan Agricultural Development* (London: Overseas Development Institute, 1974).

9. The concept of political penetration is described in L. Cliffe, J. S. Coleman, and M. R. Doornbos, eds., *Government and Rural Development in East Africa* (The Hague: Martinus Nijhoff, 1977).

10. This argument has been made in many countries, but especially in those such as the Sudan, which is religiously and ethnically heterogeneous. See Dennis A. Rondinelli, "Administrative Decentralization and Economic Development: The Sudan's Experiment with Devolution," *Journal of Modern African Studies*, vol. 19, no. 4 (1981).

11. See U.S. Agency for International Development, *Managing Decentralization* (Washington, DC: USAID, 1979), especially pp. 20-30.

12. The advantages of a regional base for planning are outlined by John Friedmann, *Urbanization, Planning and National Development* (Beverly Hills, CA: Sage, 1973), and various experiences with regional and rural development planning in developing nations are explored in Walter Stohr and D. R. F. Taylor, eds., *Development From Above or Below?* (London: John Wiley, 1981).

13. The roles of participation in development are reviewed in John M. Cohen and Norman T. Uphoff, "Participation's Place in Rural Development: Seeking Clarity Through Specificity," *World Development*, vol. 8 (1980): 213-235.

14. See Uma Lele, *The Design of Rural Development: Lessons From Africa* (Baltimore: Johns Hopkins University Press, 1975).

15. This assertion is made in USAID, *op.cit., passim.*

16. See Dennis A. Rondinelli and Marcus D. Ingle, "Improving the Implementation of Development Programmes: Beyond Administrative Reform," in *Institutional Dimensions of Regional Development*, ed. G. Shabbir Cheema (Singapore: Maruzen Asia, 1981).

17. Griffin, "Economic Development," p. 225.

18. This section draws heavily on Rondinelli, "Government Decentralization," pp. 137-139.

19. James W. Fesler, "Centralization and Decentralization," in *International Encyclopedia of the Social Sciences*, ed. Davis L. Sills (New York: Macmillan 1968), p. 373.

20. United Nations Technical Assistance Program (UNTAP), *Decentralization for National and Local Development*, Report ST/TAD/M/19 (New York: United Nations, 1962), p. 7.

21. Edward S. Mason and Robert E. Asher, *The World Bank Since Bretton Woods* (Washington: Brookings Institution), 1973.

22. M. J. Boodhoo, "The Organization and Management of Development Agencies: A Comparative Perspective," *International Review of Administrative Sciences*, vol. 42 (1976): 221-236; quote on p. 222.

23. Some theorists have defined decentralization and devolution to be separate phenomena. See Frank P. Sherwood, "Devolution as a Problem of Organization Strategy," in R. T. Daland, ed., *Comparative Urban Research* (Beverly Hills, CA: Sage, 1969), pp. 60-87.

24. *Ibid.*

25. UNTAP, *Decentralization*, p. 26.

26. *Ibid.*, p. 27.

27. Norman Uphoff and Milton J. Esman, *Local Organization for Rural Development in Asia* (Ithaca: Cornell University Center for International Studies, 1974), p. xii.

28. See S. Cohen, J. W. Dyckman, E. Schoenberger, and C. Downs, *Decentralization: A Framework for Policy Analysis,* Project on Managing Decentralization, mimeographed. (Berkeley: Institute of International Studies, University of California, 1981).

29. See Rondinelli, "Administrative Decentralization and Economic Development," for the kinds of problems that arose in the Sudan.

30. Jeffrey L. Pressman and Aaron Wildavsky, *Implementation* (Berkeley: University of California Press, 1973), p. 8.

31. Marcus D. Ingle, "Implementing Development Programs: A State-of-the-Art Review: Final Report," mimeographed. (Washington, DC: U.S. Agency for International Development, 1979).

32. W. E. Smith, F. J. Lethem, and B. A. Thoolen, "The Design of Organizations for Rural Development Projects: A Progress Report," World Bank Staff Working Paper no. 375 (Washington, DC: World Bank, 1980).

CHAPTER 2

DECENTRALIZED DEVELOPMENT IN ASIA
Local Political Alternatives

Harry J. Friedman

Consideration of local government as an instrument of decentralized development is a study of continuing tensions between alternative conceptions, ideas, and definitions, because these are determined by alternative images in the mind of the observer. These tensions, and subsequent confusions, underlie concepts of decentralized development, but they are also important in understanding local government.

It is fairly obvious, but not always made explicit, that local government encompasses a wide variety of structures, roles, and behaviors, a factor that takes on more significance when it is linked with the concept of decentralization. By decentralizing, a "superior" government — one encompassing a larger jurisdiction — assigns responsibility, authority, or functions to a "lower" governmental unit — one encompassing a smaller jurisdiction — that is assumed to have some degree of autonomy. "Local government," however, includes a range of elements, from administrators who are really agents of a higher authority and leave practically no formal autonomy to elected local bodies, which vary considerably in their formal independence. To assume that decentralization is taking place when governments assign a variety of functions to many organizations lumped together under the heading of "local government" can be somewhat misleading.

To overcome some of this confusion, the term "decentralization" is refined and referred to here as deconcentration, delegation, devolution, or the assignment of functions to nongovernmental bodies. Nevertheless, the recurring image of local government as a partially autonomous, somewhat integrated level continues to nag. There seems to be almost a permanent urge to resolve the anomalies. In some countries, however, the confusion is compounded by the tradition of referring to local self-government even when appointed civil servants are the major power.

REVIEW OF DOMINANT TRENDS

Nowhere in Asia has the conflict over treating local governments as an extension of the center while claiming that they should be autonomous been more prominent than in India. During its colonial period, the emphasis was on administration of local areas by centrally recruited and trained personnel, a form that eventually displaced traditional village governance, particularly councils of elders. But the ruling British governments repeatedly tried to reorganize locally elected councils. Since independence, the Indian government has relied heavily on central administration to govern local areas, but it has also made repeated attempts to revitalize locally elected systems. It seems that local government exists as a form of bureaucracy, but the constant revival of the *concept* of local elections reflects either a form of collective conscience that reminds leaders of the positive values in self-government, or a pragmatic approach that recognizes the value of local participation for achieving central goals.

Local administration in India — a system duplicated to a large extent in British colonies throughout the world — centered on the district as a unit and the district officer, variously known as a collector, magistrate, or deputy commissioner, as the key official.[1] Reports on the nature and significance of this omnipresent and sometimes almost legendary figure show that he supervised and was responsible for most governing activities in his jurisdiction, including those of the representatives of the various government departments operating at that level. This form of local government — a centrally directed local administration of revenue collecting, adjudicating, and maintaining law and order — was and is the starting point of the system.

Gradually, modifications and additions were introduced to encourage limited self-government in local affairs, although most of the emphasis seemed to be on deconcentration of central administrative functions rather than on democratization. The first steps were to establish a few municipal corporations. Over the course of two hundred years, periodic commission reports and constitutional revisions concerning the governance of India either recommended or actually introduced such local bodies as village *panchayats* and district boards.

Observers generally agree that shortcomings among such local bodies were widespread and carried over into independent India after 1947. During the 1950s a renewed emphasis on local government grew out of Community Development,[2] a comprehensive program for motivating village dwellers and channeling assistance to them. When such efforts flagged, the Planning Commission appointed the Balwantray Mehta Team to recommend changes. As a result, a nationwide system of local councils was established that was geared to the twin principles of direct and indirect elections, and an interlocking three-tiered government was set up, although implementation was purposely allowed to vary among the states.

Since then, what has been referred to as local government has been the *panchayati raj* system. The formal structure in most states consisted of elected village panchayats with indirectly elected *panchayat samiti* at the block level (encompassing approximately 60,000 residents) and an indirectly chosen *zilla parishad* at the district level. With the assistance of administrative personnel assigned by and to executive departments of the state governments, these councils were expected to deal with such development functions as agriculture, animal husbandry, rural infrastructure, and rural social services.

Since their establishment, the panchayati raj have failed to carry out many of their decentralized functions, although a few states have had some success with this form of local government. In 1978, the Ashok Mehta Committee recommended ways of improving the system, but, as is case generally in Asia, central government leaders have been unable to resolve the conflict between treating local institutions as an extension of the center and referring to them as autonomous units.

In Pakistan, because of the common heritage with India and the circumstances of its creation, some local government characteristics are similar, but there has been an even sharper turn away from earlier notions. Pakistan, too, established local councils in an interlocking system in the 1950s, one that the government of Ayub Khan called Basic Democracies. Also three-tiered, the system was assigned functions similar to those in India's panchayati raj.[3]

Elections to the Basic Democracies councils were held at the lowest tier, called Union Councils, but at that time martial law extended over the country and elected representatives were usually people who were not active in national political affairs and who, because they owed their very existence to the national government, supported the martial-law regime in a plebiscite.

Despite this rather contrived form of decentralization, the Union Councils and their next highest level, the Tehsil or Thana Councils, were able to perform a few limited functions.[4] While these "local governments" possessed little authority, almost no funding, and even less power to influence major economic decisions, in West Pakistan they were able to perform an adjudicating function among villagers, a time-honored need in a society with extremely scarce resources. In what was then East Pakistan, later Bangladesh, some Thana Councils and their supporting Union Councils were able to play a role in rural infrastructure development and establishment of rural cooperatives, but that was largely in the area influenced by the experimentally inclined Academy for Rural Development in Comilla.

Today the Basic Democracies policy, while never officially wiped off the books, has fallen into relative neglect. For now the dilemma noted in India of how far to go to in permitting an autonomous system has been resolved in favor of the central bureaucracy; local government is essentially seen as an arm of the central ministries.

In three other countries the perception of local government as an extension of central bureaucracy is also dominant. In Thailand, for example, district administration is the bedrock of "local" government. Over the years there have been attempts to integrate villages into the structure of governance, but these have always been "administered" in a top-down fashion.[5]

During the short-lived Kukrit government, national rural development projects were aimed at assisting the *tambol,* a form of rural government. These projects added to the number of governing institutions in society. Some of them — community development centers, farmers' marketing organizations, rural banks, and agricultural cooperatives — continue to exist.

Local government in Thailand remains, however, a series of centrally administered projects, directed by officials who are centrally oriented. Malaysia, in partial contrast, intended to move toward a system of local autonomy, although subsequent events altered original plans.[6] Constitutionally, local government in Malaysia is the responsibility of state governments, as in India. What is defined as local government consists of town councils, town boards, and local councils (rural). In a familiar pattern, these were added to the existing district administration, and, once again, perhaps the most realistic view is to regard district administration as truly governing "locally."

During the 1960s, elections to town and local councils were marked by high turnouts of voters, but in the 1970s elections were banned when the country experienced serious problems with communal divisions. Under the original legislation, Malaysia actually distinguished among town boards and the other two kinds of councils by the provision of financial autonomy. In practice, financial resources were severely restricted; in fact, council functions are limited to providing relatively routine services. The district officer continues to play a significant role in local government and in relations with councils.

Ironically, before the 1970s brought a general shift in the nature of governance in Malaysia, the traditional district administration had been heavily criticized in a Royal Commission Report that recommended a buildup of a more autonomously functioning local government system. The current practice of relying heavily on central projects for local needs, however, indicates the likelihood of continued dependence on the central government.

Some contrasts may be seen in the Philippines, but not in the widespread phenomenon of tight central control. Rather, the differences spring from the Philippines' colonial heritage and reflect formal, structural alternatives, rather than new conceptions of government. The influence of the United States on Philippine institutions, for example, is most apparent in the lack of district administration.

Before martial law, the Philippines had constitutionally differentiated provincial governments and a variety of elected, governing bodies and officials, primarily at the municipal and barrio levels, covering both urban and rural sectors of society. While the financial resources needed to govern were always lacking, a complicated and politically influenced system of grants made the local government system in the Philippines more autonomous than in other Asian countries. The "system" generated its own leadership, its own needs, and its own problems, not always with positive effects for the population, of course, but with the potential for continued political development not discernible everywhere.

Under the present regime, numerous and frequent changes in local government have been accompanied by the rhetoric of increasing self-government but appear to be a tightening of central control through technocratic bureaucratization.[7] For example, the 1973 constitution guarantees the "autonomy of local government units." A series of presidential decrees renamed citizen assemblies as *barangays* (citizens' assemblies) to help identify them with traditional Filipino institutions, offered guarantees of financial assistance, expanded membership in voting to 15-year-olds, and combined barangays into federations to enhance their power in legislative matters. Comparable institutions for urban areas, *sangguniang bayan* (consultative councils) and their counterparts at other levels, replaced previous boards. Rather elaborate systems of representation from functional and sectoral areas of society are intended to be incorporated into these structures.

Local-level institutions with economic and social functions, but which are also governing institutions, have also been established as precursors to cooperatives. Called *samahang nayon,* these precooperatives do not engage in business activities, but rather provide "learning opportunities" for barrio residents.

In practice, the early use of barangays to ratify martial-law institutions and the continued reorganization of local structures by decrees from above illustrate attempts to control local activities from the center.

Obviously, these examples do not describe local government throughout Asia, but the intent here is to describe a sufficient number of organizational characteristics to document a basic thesis: Local government is a consequence of the interpretation applied to the uses and functions of local institutions by more powerful governing authorities in society. In every case, the perceived "needs" of the central government have determined the appropriate description of local government.

More consequential than the interpretive view of local government, however, is the effect of different models and images on the concept of decentralized development. The dominant assumption on the part of policymakers is that the sole legitimate conception of development is formulated at the central, national level and is in the best interests of the total population. Furthermore, it is assumed that the conception of development requires some sort of decentralization primarily to achieve its effective implementation, not to reformulate its basic assumptions.

While it is true that a case may be made for supporting the value of centrally determined goals, nevertheless there are alternative interests in any society, sometimes sharply different in their conception of legitimate goals. The expression of such differences in local governments is not unusual, and the very conception of decentralization depends on how development is conceived. Setting aside the admittedly important content of development policy, the significance of the model alone helps to determine how local government is described in decentralization policies.

ALTERNATIVE IMAGES

When decentralization of development is regarded as implementation of national policies and programs, it is not simply a "given," based on unanimous agreement. It comes face to face with an alternative, what may be regarded as some form of social and political development, the local determination of local needs, and at least a contribution to the solution of local problems. The tension between the two is not necessarily resolved by having one conquer the other. The most frequent outcome, however, is the attempt by national governments to implement their own development programs with only rhetorical attention to, or ingeniously disguised structural changes for, the quieting of local expressions.

Whether decentralization is "working" or should take one form or another depends on definitions of the process — implementation or sociopolitical development. In each case, description and analysis will come out differently, depending on which definition is being used.

Implementation is likely to be bureaucratic and efficient. It relies on hierarchy as a principle of organization and a source of authority. Implementation means that there is an assumption that virtually everybody agrees on the meaning of implementation: the carrying out of national policies and programs. As such, it may be termed a success or failure.

A rapidly growing body of literature, not yet cross-cultural, is attempting to go beyond the study of individual cases and begin the process of developing conceptual frameworks for analyzing implementation. Some of this will be discussed later, but with a cautionary note. Because of the nature of implementation as a concept, some analyses still deal with it in terms of organizational considerations. There are new attempts, however, to deal with implementation in a broader context: its consequences for communities and societies.

In much of Asia, local governments are frequently perceived as bureaucratic instruments of implementation. Viewing them as *subjects* of political development, rather than *objects* of decentralization, may offer a choice of models for practitioners and analysts alike. As distinguished from implementation, then, political development is likely to be community-oriented. It relies on shared aims and communicative interactions as principles of organization and sources of authority. It assumes that there is never unanimity on the meaning of development and that the criteria of success or failure are still evolving. The concept, again distinguished from implementation, resembles what Norton Long has called an ecology of games.[8] Policymakers would perceive appropriate strategies as experimental and a premium would be placed on entrepreneurship.

In the perception of local leaders with interests different from those of national policymakers, policies and programs are either handed down to them or enforced on them. The evolving of ideas, structures, and roles is thereby denied to them and their suspicions are aroused. Some analysts have theorized that those suspicions and the resulting resistance become exaggerated when the national policies being implemented are tied closely to the interests of forces external to society, that is, global and international forces of both a public and private nature.[9]

The use of alternative terms, such as implementation and political development, is not the key issue. What is contended here is that decentralized development, as a policy, can be perceived in at least these two ways and that the description and analysis of it will vary according to which perceptual lens is used.

Governments in Asia have used contradictory language in policy statements over the years that have been used to propound two different types of policies, even when the language is similar in both cases. That may be one reason (although admittedly not the only one) for the changing emphases in decentralization policies over the past two to three decades. For example, to cite three changes common to many countries, community development programs, local councils, and administrative reorganization have all been termed forms of decentralization at one time or another (and, incidentally, usually for the purpose of improving the implementation of national plans), even though their practical consequences, as well as their forms and processes, have varied considerably.

National policymakers have been known, too, to rely heavily on the use of "participation" as a rhetorical device, implying that many changes in the restructuring of intergovernmental relations in the direction of decentralization are proposed for the purpose of attaining greater popular participation in decision making. (Sometimes, the goal of participation is made more specific, such as "development planning," instead of all types of decision making). Not infrequently, however, these same changes include a heavier reliance on a process of bureaucratization — strengthening of the hierarchy, assignment of specific roles, more, not less, centralized decision making, and external goal setting — or, in short, the antithesis of participation.[10]

Local governments that are seen essentially as administrative arms of central bureaucracies are not without advantages, of course.

On the contrary, they have been the dominant force primarily because they fill their assigned roles so well. Local councils that share power with, or are dominated by, civil servants, for example, can serve as mobilizing institutions without using their mobilizing powers to undermine development policies. To decentralize by assigning limited planning and allocation authority to them has been regarded by some as gaining cooperation from local constituents without risking the displacement of (central) development goals by local political aims. This advantage is not gained automatically, however, by the existence of such a structure. Apparently, the trick is to strike an appropriate balance between limited participation and central control in order to achieve efficient implementation. Council members who represent local political interests and are confined by the limited formal roles within such structures can bring considerable pressure to bear on individual bureaucrats within their jurisdiction. If the balance is tipped in the opposite direction, however, administrators can so dominate local planning and administrative processes that whatever degree of participation is sought may be easily lost.

CONTROLLED DECENTRALIZATION

Susan G. Hadden has described this successful balancing act, although the unit of local government does not quite match the local councils that are familiar in such systems as India's panchayati raj and Pakistan's Basic Democracies. In this case the unit of decentralization is a district agricultural production committee (DAPD),[11] consisting of local politicians, administrators, and technicians.

A rural electrification program in the north Indian state of Rajasthan was planned and initiated in a centralized fashion by higher-level administrators, but a particular and significant function was decentralized to the DAPD. An autonomous State Electricity Board established the economic criteria for allocation of electrification to rural areas. But Hadden points out that, in the near-desert environment of Rajasthan, every village presumably wants and needs electricity "to be used for irrigation, for lifting drinking water, for lighting." Thus, she notes that the "selection of villages to receive electricity becomes a focal point for the pressures and counterpressures." Consequently, political criteria must be added to economic criteria for selecting beneficiaries and the political criteria were determined by local governing bodies.

The combination of economic and political criteria can best be applied, Hadden points out, by using "controlled decentralization," a technique for recognizing and accepting centralized bureaucratic power, but attempting to use that power for limited objectives and in a tutelary fashion by encouraging partial local participation.

Hadden confines the definition of success in the program to efficiency, which, in turn, is defined as the extent to which the economic criteria (laid down by the "superior" government) are met. A narrow construction of success, therefore, may be useful only for those specific programs that have well-defined goals. When used that way, however, she concludes that the approach has the following advantages:

> Controlled decentralization thus may retain the best features of centralization and decentralization. It employs the long-range perspective of higher level bodies that set the technical criteria, while incorporating the short-range perspective of local officials who set additional political criteria. It may also make officials more accessible, thereby increasing participation, responsibility, and responsiveness. And whereas ordinary decentralization procedures have tended *not* to increase efficiency, controlled decentralization in this instance appears to have increased both economic and political efficiency by using the same resources to accomplish economic and political ends more effectively. . . . Finally, controlled decentralization may lower the cost to higher levels of government of control over lower levels by making the granting of funds routinely contingent upon the fulfillment of certain conditions.[12]

While the technique of controlled decentralization is interesting in itself as one form of government, the more general point here is that the image of implementation continues to be one of enforcing economic plans and criteria which are devised by central bureaucracies. Such a model can be advantageous when goals are limited and specific, but it may add more advantages by increasing participation to achieve a wider variety of ends.

CO-OPTING LOCAL LEADERS

The limitations on the autonomy of local political institutions are likely to be deliberate policies in most places. In order to assure the continued functioning of the bureaucratization process at local levels, it sometimes is necessary to find means of co-opting local political leaders into the centralized framework. This can be accomplished even when controlling institutions do not outwardly appear to be bureaucracies. Such a system has been well described by Stephen Chee in his studies of rural local government in Malaysia.[13]

While "the major responsibility for the implementation of rural strategy was assigned to the civil bureaucracy," he points out, traditional leaders assist the formal administrators at the lower levels of the system. Although these linkages are "an ingenious manipulation of tradition for rural modernization," Chee notes, "it is nevertheless a generalist structure attempting not quite successfully to perform the dual functions of local custodial government and development administration."

Apparently, the Malaysian form of local governance is not modeled after even the limited form of autonomy seen as "controlled decentralization." Instead the emphasis is on political mobilization, conducted by the far-ranging United Malay National Organization. In Chee's description:

> Although the central political leadership has carefully avoided allowing the local political branches a direct function as parallel bureaucracies in rural development goal-setting, planning or resource mobilization, local political leaders are important articulators and aggregators of constituency interests. Local elected political representatives have been coopted into the administrative structure of rural development committees. As a branch of the ruling party, the village UMNO leader has direct access to district, state and national political authority. . . . But this image of great local power is not matched by political control over rural development decision-making. . . . Consequently, though peasants seem to be highly mobilized, their participation in the rural development program is not politically institutionalized.[14]

From this description, it would seem that the government's avowed aim of enhancing the status of Malaysia's rural people beyond economic improvements may be limited by the single-minded picture that emerges from the implementation of centralized programs. Even the addition of such other organizations as cooperatives, farmers' associations, and youth groups is confined to restricted roles. To explore all the ramifications of decentralization to local government, therefore, it may be necessary to see such a policy as a spectrum that stretches to a very considerable degree of autonomy at one end.

What is being called devolution or "the legal transfer of decision-making power" to local governments may have positive value greater than deconcentration — the administrative shifting of workloads to field offices — for implementing a variety of development goals, but applying a model of political development, rather than implementation alone, may require more complex innovations. It could involve a pattern of relations akin to a combination of delegation, devolution, and debureaucratization. For example, some attention could be paid to the political values inherent in some institutions normally considered to be nonpolitical.

LOCAL POLITICIZATION

The more extreme of such an approach, such as factories in the People's Republic of China, may not be appropriate everywhere, but they serve to illustrate the point. In some localities in China, factories are also political divisions governed by their collective owners, who make decisions about the allocation of benefits, uses of profits, and external relations.[15]

During the current stage of transition, some changes are taking place at the local level, and one trend may be an increase in bureaucratic controls from the center, combined with a clearer role for traditional party functionaries. Until recently, however, revolutionary committees served as the permanent administrative body at the commune and brigade levels between sessions of elected representative assemblies. But even the avowed attempts in China to build a society based on the eventual creation of a common consciousness were subject to a need to build governing bridges between the central state and local governing bodies. For instance, a main function of the smallest governing unit, the production team and its "leading group," was to draw up production plans based on targets set by the state. During that period, however, under Mao's leadership, China was regularly engaged in efforts to circumvent what some leaders saw as the shackles of bureaucratic control from the center and to maintain alternative structures, stressing political consciousness, at the local level.

Two illustrations from the Philippines may serve as clearer guides to the governing possibilities in otherwise nonpolitical bodies. Carlos D. Isles has reported on the promising use of indigenous organizations in rural areas to promote participation in the decisions of irrigation associations.[16] A pilot project of the National Irrigation Administration seemed to be more successful, according to Isles, than the typical government-sponsored rural organization. He attributes the failure of most such organizations to elicit widespread participation to "a very limited understanding" of what participation means.

Isles describes a government project for an irrigation system in which engineers conduct a survey, draw up a design, present it at a meeting with prospective water users, and then politely, but firmly, reject farmers' suggestions for change. As a consequence, he states, results have sometimes been catastrophic, including washed-out dams, inaccurate water measures, and floods. Local users apparently were more aware of topographical quirks than were outside engineers. Furthermore, he adds, when schedules are drawn for repayment of irrigation fees, water distribution, and quota allocations, the same rejection of significant participation eventually ends with the farmers exhibiting indifference to the entire scheme.

Isles notes that government development projects have eliminated many indigenous organizations and substituted artificial organizations, sometimes based on foreign models. The pilot project leaders insist on the use of existing social organizations as a first step. Where such groups are lacking, skilled community organizers help create them. The approach is to involve as many general members as possible, rather than a few leaders only, and the intent is to avoid creating still more bureaucracies. Isles believes that there is more general communication among farmers as equals in determining local policies. From the point of view taken here, participatory irrigation associations are also local governments, although in an admittedly limited sense, for the purpose of one aspect of decentralized development.

All four forms of decentralization — deconcentration, delegation, devolution, and debureaucratization — are indirectly compared in a study of five rural health delivery mechanisms by Ledivina V. Carino and her associates for the purposes of comparison. In fact, two of them are creations of private institutions. However, they provide additional clues to the value of using alternative perceptual models, not merely alternative techniques within one framework.

The health delivery services were carried out in five different locations by the following organizations: (1) the Rural Health Unit (RHU), the municipal-level office of the Ministry of Health; (2) the Comprehensive Community Health Program (CCHP), originally sponsored by the College of Medicine at the University of the Philippines and later joined by other units at the university; (3) Project Compassion (ProCom), a product of four foundations established for different purposes by Imelda Marcos, the President's wife, who holds several government offices; (4) Makapawa, an acronym for a title of a community-based health program, one of several Catholic social action programs; and (5) Sudtonggan Human Development Program (ICA/SHDP), sponsored by the Institute of Cultural Affairs, a Protestant church-supported organization.

The Rural Health Unit is characterized as a traditional government structure, and, despite some shifting from a strictly passive clinic to limited active extension work, it retains its character as part of the national bureaucracy. Provincial and regional health officers supervise the RHU under regulations issued by Manila offices. The CCHP serves partly to provide rural internships for medical students but also partly duplicates RHU services and structures. ProCom is financed by its own four foundations, assisted by UNICEF. Local governments that accept its services become the sponsors and chief financiers. ProCom attempts to integrate local government offices with the private sector for family-focused services, using family associations and some nonmedical college graduates.

Makapawa operates at the diocesan level with a coordinator, community organizers, an office secretary, and a mobile health team, while at the parish level a priest works with community organizations and two trained persons, plus multipurpose volunteers and leading church members. Funds come from international church organizations. The commitments of the participants extend beyond services. The program seeks involvement by the people in its aims. Among other things, it tries to deemphasize Western health practices and attempts to reorient health care away from professionals, clinics, and cures toward preventive, self-reliant methods. As a Catholic social action program, it is concerned with total human development, including political conscientization and religious recommitment.

SHDP uses Western medicine techniques with a team of seven Americans and one Filipino on its staff, but it aims at making residents of the community more self-reliant, which is the reason that the program extends beyond health care to include provision for schooling, small industry and business assistance, and village administration. To achieve these goals, it makes use, too, of "celebrations," aimed at galvanizing a community spirit, and of programs to build confidence in individuals by special counseling and teaching. This particular project was, in fact, turned over to the residents of Sudtonggan in 1980, thereby achieving its ultimate goal of community self-reliance.

The study of these five systems is a complex one, the details of which are too lengthy to be repeated here. It is worth noting that, after the weighing of a variety of factors, both citizen participation and program effectiveness were two variables that correlated highly. Perhaps even more relevant for consideration of decentralization, however, was the finding that the two nonbureaucratic programs ranked highest in both participation and effectiveness. ProCom, which made an effort to adopt a nonbureaucratic style by combining public and private auspices, ranked lowest in effectiveness but actually could not count as an alternative style, because it quickly shrank in scope when few local jurisdictions continued to accept a place in the program. The two government programs unabashedly bureaucratic, were effective in some aspects, but not overall.

This type of study should not be considered a conclusive one, by any means. What is significant again, however, is that students of implementation can find examples of decentralization that local governments can consider worth evaluating and possibly emulating and, in this case, a form of decentralization — debureaucratization — frequently overlooked.

In the Philippines, there has been a rather extensive revamping of some aspects of local government in recent years, much of it accompanied by a rhetoric of decentralization, participation, even "democratization."[18] The intent here is not to single out the Philippines for analysis, but rather to illustrate a process common to several Asian countries. In this case what is often said to be devolution turns out to be deconcentration at best, or even increased centralization. Apparently, the notion of decentralization has such a positive image in a number of places that when new bodies are constructed, an effort is made to emphasize their representative nature even when they are deliberately designed to be centrally controlled. Such has been the case in the Philippines with the creation of the barangays sangguniang bayan and regional development councils, all of which are less representative in function than they are administrative — that is, instruments subject to direction by the combination of bureaucrats and technocrats currently responsible for implementing centrally directed plans and goals.[19]

TWO COMPARATIVE APPROACHES

The meaning of decentralization becomes a little clearer when alternative images are used to probe more thoroughly into local governments after new functions have been assigned to them. The well-documented panchayati raj system of India is one of the more obvious examples.

Throughout a long history of colonial administration and well into the period of independence, political leaders in India made clear their beliefs that increased popular involvement in the local governing process would improve administration and, presumably, thereby improve the lot of the vast majority of people living in rural areas.

In recent years, however, significant theoretical questions have arisen as to whether (a) popular participation would improve administration and (b) improved administration would better the people's living conditions. Once again, because the difference strikes at the heart of local government's role in decentralized development, it is worth comparing alternative models of analysis rather than attempting here a detailed study of the system.

One way of analyzing the institutions is to draw a comparison of the degree and types of decentralization within the system. B.S. Khanna and S. Bhatnagar, after a useful, brief summary of the history and status of local government and administration in India, describe the now-familiar three-tiered structure of panchayati raj: village panchayats, block-level panchayat samiti, and the district *zilla parishad*. The structures of these councils, consisting of both elected leaders and administrative personnel, vary somewhat from state to state in India's federal system and therefore are subject to useful comparisons.[20]

Khanna and Bhatnagar point out the difference between those having three tiers and those having two, but the more significant differences, from their point of view, lie in the degree and type of decentralization. Three factors are relevant:

(1) Maharashtra and Gujerat provide "very substantial" decentralization, Rajasthan and Andhra a middle range, and the rest are scattered along a decreasing continuum.

(2) Some states went so far as to withdraw decentralization, disillusioned over its failures, although some withdrawals resulted from political conflicts.

(3) Distribution of powers among the tiers of the system varies. In Maharasthra, the zilla parishad is the most powerful; in Gujerat, powers are shared, but the zilla parishad has the most; in Rajasthan, the panchayat samiti has been assigned the central role.

Maharashtra and Gujerat had the most success by far not only in the efficiency of their operations, but also in the achievement of political, economic, and social goals. Overall, however, Khanna and Bhatnagar conclude that panchayati raj has had mixed success politically and socially; the economic impact has been significant.

Finally, they recommend a series of measures designed to strengthen local government, to make it more respectable, "rational," and "modern." Despite their assertion that local government should be regarded as a partner of the states instead of a subordinate, their essential approach is to reveal panchayati raj as an instrument of other levels of government. This image inevitably leads to the kind of analysis and recommendations that leave the structure of relevant forces — those that have produced the existing local government system — untouched.

In contrast, it is possible to devise a comparison that would call for fundamental changes if the implications were to be taken seriously. This alternative, being used in studies by D. and J. Sankaran, emphasizes the potential for local government to perform functions other than that of being an extension of the central bureaucracy.[21]

The mere legal existence of panchayati raj does not assure decentralization, it is true, but what becomes important in this approach is how it is used. There is an attempt to link local government with alternative development strategies. The study by D. Sankaran is particularly appropriate for India, where, as has been shown, the federal system encourages comparisons, but it is undoubtedly relevant for other countries.

Three rural development strategies, designated technocratic, radical, and reformist, are related to the uses, or lack of use, of the panchayati raj system in three Indian states. The emphasis of the technocratic strategy is on increased productivity by technological modernization and managerial efficiency. Top-down control of planning with an emphasis on "growth first, redistribution later" came to be questioned as the gap between rich and poor widened and the percentage of people below the poverty line increased, but states, nevertheless, continued to pursue the technocratic strategy. It is usually in those states, such as Bihar, that the use of the representative local councils has declined.

The radical strategy begins by assuming that poverty is not only deprivation but also a combination of deprivation for the many and affluence for the few. Consequently, the strategy is to change the socioeconomic structure. In West Bengal, the dominant Marxist party has been attempting to reorganize the rural political structure, by engaging "in the task of reviving the dormant panchayati raj system of rural development." Whereas the system is heavily bureaucratized in most other states, in West Bengal "sustained mass participation encouraged by this government has . . . helped to prevent increasing bureaucratization. . . . The few research studies on the efficacy of this model of rural development point to its increasing success in inducing equity oriented development."

The reformist strategy is linked to local governments in ways similar to the radical, although the rationale and economic actions are slightly different. In Maharashtra, which seems to stand out in the use of panchayati raj, there is "active participation of the directly elected representatives of the people at various levels. . . . The system was intended to actively promote an integrated programme of rural development." The reason is similar to that found in Bengal: an explicit recognition of the need for redistribution along with growth to overcome "an inequitable distribution of the means of production." The major means of production is land, but in a pioneering study by V. M. Dandekar and N. Rath, it is noted that "there is not enough land to redistribute so that everyone may employ himself on his land and earn a minimum desirable living. It also does not appear to be a solution which can be maintained in the face of economic forces operating in an economy in which the means of production are privately owned."[22]

The recommended alternative, then — the basis for the reformist strategy — was a "scheme of labour intensive rural industries to increase the purchasing power of the rural poor," with the industries geared to the rural and semiurban markets. Panchayati raj was then seen as a necessary component of the strategy to provide for active participation of elected representatives in planning and maintaining the system.

Even before empirical studies that support these comparisons are completed, it is evident that local government in India seems to have more relevant meaning when it is seen in the context of alternative models that reveal different uses and purposes. What is more, it is likely that these uses are applicable generally. They are not, after all, confined to an analysis of local government. Rather, they have relevance for implementation and decentralization generally.

IMPLICATIONS FOR ORGANIZATION THEORY

In recent years there have been conscious attempts in the theoretical literature to tie together organization models and intergovernmental relations in the study of policy implementation. Although most of these works are based on American settings, certain aspects of the literature at least touch on some of the developmental issues discussed earlier.

Luther Gulick does not believe in preconceived categories of policy functions for assignment to a particular level of government. Regarding education, for example, he says:

> I think local institutions have responsibilities in education along with intermediate regional bodies and state and federal administrations. The problems is that of identifying at any given time the nature of the service or function that has to be performed, and then taking aspects of that function and putting some in the hands of local people, other aspects at the regional level, others at the state, and still other aspects at the federal level.[23]

The key, he argues, is to identify "the proper level at which a function shall be discharged and how to pay for it."

Gulick's reference to financial resources is apt inasmuch as the lack of resources often becomes the single biggest obstacle to successful decentralization of functions to local government. In the heyday of Pakistan's Basic Democracies, almost constant demands for taxing powers from local councils were an indication of the limited funds available from the central government. In the Philippines a long-standing advocacy of establishing a national Department of Local Government was a consequence of mayors' and barrio leaders' need for a voice in national policymaking to lobby for more funds. When the department was eventually established, however, it was quickly downgraded, and local governments were reorganized and made more than ever dependent on external sources of funding.

In the United States, too, for that matter, intergovernmental relations are plagued by changing conceptions of resource capability. In their frequently cited article, "The Policy Implementation Process: A Conceptual Framework," van Meter and van Horn report that "the limited supply of federal incentives was a major contributor to the failure" of the "new towns" program. On the other hand, when national government leaders are attempting to secure the implementation of programs by local governments, the single most effective device is to promise increased financial resources. "Research has shown," state van Meter and van Horn, "that the amount of federal influence over aspects of a program increases as the percentage of the federal contribution rises."[24]

The more abstract the model, however, the more applicable it may be to cross-cultural settings. If it is correct to say that organizational models are applicable, at least in part, to intergovernmental relations, then Elmore's four types — systems management, bureaucratic process, organizational development, and conflict and bargaining — provide a fairly complete statement of useful forms of analysis.[25] Perhaps a little more applicable, however, are the so-called implementation linkages between policymakers and implementers described by Nakamura and Smallwood.[26] In this typology, there are five categories:

(1) Classic technocrats — policymakers delimit goals and implementers support them; policymakers delegate technical authority to implementers.

(2) Instructed delegation — policymakers delegate administrative authority.

(3) Bargaining — policymakers bargain with implementers over goals and procedures.

(4) Discretionary experimentation — policymakers support abstract goals and delegate broad discretionary authority to implementers.

(5) Bureaucratic entrepreneurship — policymakers support the goals and means formulated by implementers.

Perhaps the fifth type comes closest to the alternative model of decentralization posited at the beginning of this chapter, an alternative in which the assumption is not that "higher," central decision makers have a monopoly on definitions of development requiring implementation by the "subordinate" local governments, but rather that decentralization can be interpreted in ways that draw out the creative energies of local constituencies.

The application of this type of policy implementation scheme to decentralized systems of local government should not be overstated, because of the danger of misinterpreting the use of organizational models. The goal here would not be to rely solely on bureaucratic innovation, as the typology suggests; rather, the goal would be to treat such entrepreneurship as an analogy for more autonomy for local government leaders.

Just as bureaucratic implementers (presumably at "lower" levels of a bureaucracy) would be encouraged to design goals and means by having "higher" administrators — that is, policymakers — defer to the implementers and support them, so could central governments encourage initiative and creativity in local governments by supporting local goals and means.

To make that feasible, local leadership would have to be genuinely representative, as well as competent — goals for which no foolproof system can be devised to guarantee. Local leaders would have to become spokespersons for "opposition" to the center, generating distrust and threatening the success of decentralization policies.

Throughout Asia, local government leaders are perceived as lower-level bureaucrats — recipients of communications, implementers of policies devised elsewhere, supporters of "higher" authorities. In short, the implementing of policy decisions relies primarily on "classical" technocrats and instructed delegation. Local governments are permitted technical and administrative authority to implement — as in the cases of rural credit, revenue raising, and infrastructure building — but never the political authority to create ideas suited to their local environments, supported by the power of the central government.

That may be one reason that implementation of many rural development projects falls short. It may also help to explain why frequently repeated calls for local self-rule are rarely followed by sustained action. What may be called "local government entrepreneurship" (instead of "bureaucratic entrepreneurship") would constitute an alternative model more useful for both interpretation and implementation.

NOTES

1. The literature on district administration is vast. For this limited purpose, useful summaries appear in S. Bhatnagar, *Rural Local Government in India* (New Delhi: Light & Life Publishers, 1978); B. S. Khanna and S. Bhatnagar, "India," in *International Handbook on Local Government Reorganization: Contemporary Developments,* ed. Donald C. Rowat (Westport, CT: Greenwood Press, 1980), Ch. 36.

2. *Ibid.*

3. This description is referred to in Norman K. Nicholson and Delawar Ali Khan, *Basic Democracies and Rural Development in Pakistan* (Ithaca, NY: Rural Development Committee, Center for International Studies, Cornell University, 1974). In addition to the references cited in note 1, p. 35, one of the earliest descriptions and analyses is found in S. M. Z. Rizvi, *Basic Democracies* (Peshawar: Pakistan Academy for Rural Development, 1960).

4. *Ibid.,* p. 80. Also, see the *Journal of the East Pakistan Academy for Rural Development* in the decade of the 1960s and other publications from that institution.

5. Recent perceptions of rural local government in Thailand are described in Werasit Sittatrai, "Villagers and Government in Two Northern Thai Villages" (Paper presented at the annual conference of Asian Studies on the Pacific Coast, Honolulu, June 25-27, 1981).

6. Material presented here on Malaysia is based on J. H. Beaglehole, *The District* (London: Oxford University Press, 1976), Ch. 3.

7. See Blondie Po, *Rural Organizations and Rural Development in the Philippines: A Documentary Study* (Quezon City: Institute of Philippine Culture, Ateneo de Manila University, 1977).

8. Norton Long, "The Local Community as an Ecology of Games," *American Sociological Review* (1958).

9. Among the leading basic works delineating the nature of relationships among First World and Third World countries are Johan Galtung, "A Structural Theory of Imperialism," *Journal of Peace Research,* Vol. 8, No. 2 (1971); Immanuel Wallerstein, *The Modern World-System,* vol. I (New York: Academic Press, 1976), vol. II (1980); Robert B. Stauffer, "Transnational Corporations and the Political Economy of Development: The Continuing Philippine Debate," Research Monograph no. 11, Transnational Corporations Research Project, University of Sydney, 1980.

10. A discussion of these contrasts may be found in Harry J. Friedman, "Bureaucratic Power and modernization in the Philippines" (Paper delivered at the Second International Philippine Studies Conference, June 27-30, 1981, Honolulu). Examples discussed below of Hadden's "controlled decentralization," Isles's irrigation associations, and Carino's health delivery mechanisms also may be found in the same paper in slightly different form.

11. Susan G. Hadden, "Controlled Decentralization and Policy Implementation: The Case of Rural Electrification in Rajasthan," in Merilee S. Grindle, ed., *Politics and Policy Implementation in the Third World* (Princeton: Princeton University Press, 1980).

12. *Ibid.,* pp. 172-173.

13. Stephen Chee, "Rural Development in the Plural Society of West Malaysia," in Inayatullah, ed., *Approaches to Rural Development: Some Asian Experiences* (Kuala Lumpur: APDAC, 1979).

14. *Ibid.,* p. 43.

15. See Robert E. Bedeski, "People's Republic of China," in Rowat, *International Handbook,* Ch. 37.

16. Carlos D. Isles, "Irrigation Organization and Social Participation: the NIA Experience" (Paper delivered at the National Convention of the Philippine Sociological Society, 1980).

17. Ledivina V. Carino, *Integration, Participation and Effectiveness: An Analysis of Five Rural Health Delivery Mechanisms and Their Effects* (Manila: College of Public Administration, University of the Philippines, August 1980).

18. Ferdinand E. Marcos, *Revolution From the Center* (Hong Kong: Raya Books, 1978).

19. Ma. Aurora Carbonell, "National Developments," *Philippine Journal of Public Administration,* vol. 20, no. 1 (January 1976): 115-118.

20. B. S. Khanna and S. Bhatnagar, "India," in Rowat, *International Handbook,* Ch. 36.

21. D. Sankaran, "Rural Development and Communication: Strategy in Three Indian States," and J. Sankaran, "Social Inequity and Public Policy: "Implementation of Rural Development and Communication Policies in India" (Dissertation proposals, Department of Political Science, University of Hawaii).

22. V. M. Dandekar and N. Rath, "Poverty in India," *Economic and Political Weekly,* vol. 6, nos. 1 and 2 (January 2 and 9, 1971), cited in Sankaran, *ibid.*

23. Stephen K. Blumberg, "A Tribute to Luther Gulick," *Public Administration Review,* vol. 41, no. 2 (March/April 1981): 247.

24. Donald S. van Meter and Carl E. van Horn, "The Policy Implementation Process: A Conceptual Framework," *Administration and Society,* vol. 6, no. 4 (February 1975): 445-487.

25. Richard F. Elmore, "Organizational Models of Social Program Implementation," *Public Policy,* vol. 26, no. 2 (Spring 1978).

26. Robert T. Nakamura and Frank Smallwood, *The Politics of Policy Implementation* (New York: St. Martin's Press, 1980), Ch. 7.

CHAPTER 3

ADMINISTRATIVE DECENTRALIZATION IN ASIA

Kuldeep Mathur

Decentralization has resurfaced as a prominent issue in the literature of public administration. During the years following World War II, debates over the desirability of decentralized administration focused on the acceptability of the Soviet style of centralized planning as a means of mobilizing and using scarce resources optimally in countries that were emerging from colonial rule. The debate concerned freedom and liberty; many who argued against central planning believed that it would lead developing nations down the raod to serfdom. The issues were political and ideological, and those advancing the cause of central planning were usually labeled supporters of a socialist state.

During the last decade, the debate has continued, but the framework for discussion has changed. Despite criticism, central planning was adopted in most Asian countries, not only because of the Soviet Union's apparent success in mobilizing investment resources but also because international lending agencies insisted that grants and loans be made in conformance with coherent plans for national development.[1] Even capitalist economies adopted planning mechanisms that had once been associated with socialist systems. As a result, the debate over centralization and decentralization began to cut across political and ideological lines.

The major criticism of central planning now is its failure to achieve the intended impacts — the inability of centralized planning systems to provide for equitable distribution of the benefits of economic growth among regions and groups within developing countries. The cause of decentralization is now being advanced because it is assumed that a "decentralized mode of policy and program implementation is conducive to more effective coordination and consistency, greater access to governmental activities, increased involvement of people in the development process, more efficient delivery of public services for meeting basic human needs and increased accountability of government agencies."[2]

Whatever other questions may have arisen, attempts to decentralize development planning and implementation in Asia were closely associated with increasing concern for reducing regional disparities in standards of living, which were seen as a threat to national stability. In Thailand, a special fund for regional development was created in the Second Five-Year National Development Plan (1967-1971) after the prime minister discovered from his inspection trips the backwardness of the northeastern region. Communist subversion in the region prompted him to take action.[3] In India, the closing years of the 1960s were marked by widespread rural strife. A report to the government of India in 1969 blamed the increasing tensions on inequitable distribution of the benefits of development. With the Fifth Five-Year Plan on the anvil, regional development schemes as well as programs for various social groups began to take shape. In Malaysia, where ethnic heterogeneity is a crucial social factor in all policies, the outbreak of racial riots in 1969 was an important milestone in national development strategies, which were made more specific and which accelerated government efforts to correct economic imbalances in the country.[4]

Thus, the new debate over decentralization emerged from the failure of centralized planning and implementation to provide for equitable distribution of the benefits of development and from the realization that inequity creates political instability and social strife. The response of most governments in Asia has been to pay greater attention to regional development by decentralizing development administration and planning.

DECENTRALIZATION IN ASIA

Administrative decentralization came about, in part, as a response to the different ways regional development was being pursued and to how governments in each Asian nation perceived regional demands. Decentralization can take various institutional forms, distinguished by the extent of autonomy given to local and provincial administrative units.[5]

Provincial Development Planning in Thailand

In Thailand, the government attempted to make central planning more flexible and more responsive to local needs. Although the Second Plan (1967-1971) emphasized the need for regional development planning explicitly, strategies were delineated only in the Fourth National Development Plan of 1977-1981. These included decentralizing industries and spreading employment opportunities, decentralizing basic economic services to increase rural production, and decentralizing social services to reach the maximum number of people.

Provincial development planning, introduced in 1977, made the province the key unit in subnational development. A Central Committee on Provincial Development was established, with the Minister of Interior, who supervises the provincial government acts, as chairman and the Director of the Division of Regional Planning of the National Economic and Social Development Board (NESDB) as secretary. The NESDB representative provides the link between the national plan and provincial plan. This committee proposes allocation of development funds to the provinces and formulates objectives for provincial social and economic policies. It is also the agency that recommends termination of any project approved by the cabinet on the request of a provincial government.

The Provincial Development Planning Committee, with the governor as chairman and the provincial planning officer as secretary, draws up the five-year social and economic plan of the province, allocates funds for projects to local administration units, and submits reports of performance to the Central Committee on Provincial Development.

The second aspect of decentralization was the decision to distribute 1 percent of the national budget for provincial development. At the national level, the Central Committee on Provincial Development weighs requests according to the population size of the province, level of provincial per capita income, and the amount of land under irrigation. At the provincial level, 80 percent of the funds are allocated to rural projects of the Changwat Administrative Organization, and 20 percent to municipal and sanitary district projects.

A New Village Development Scheme was initiated in 1979 to develop about 5,000 poor villages within two years. People at the village level are allowed to submit projects for employment promotion, construction of minor infrastructure, and promotion of group organization. Funds are allocated by the Central Committee.

The governor and district officer are appointed by the central government in Bangkok. Both are senior officials of the Ministry of Interior and are given the authority to supervise officials of other agencies posted in their areas of jurisdiction. In addition, they are empowered to control local government units. However, the governor and the administrative officer have very limited power to appoint, transfer, punish, or reward provincial or district officers.

All three levels of administration (central, provincial, and local) are responsible for various aspects of development. But under the present system, the central administration plays the pivotal role. The provincial administration makes only minor decisions and local administrators have relatively little funds for development.[6]

The crucial role in integrating development activities in Thailand is played by the staff of the National Economic and Social Development Board. It not only prepares guidelines for national planning but monitors and reviews the efforts of other agencies. Being directly under the Prime Minister's Office, the NESDB is influential, since it is organized to do both macro- and micro-level planning and the law requires that all line agencies and regional governments submit development projects to NESDB for review and appraisal before being sent to the Budget Bureau.

Regionalization in the Philippines

In the Philippines, regional development strategy was established in 1972. The objective of the Reorganization Plan was to decentralize policymaking and implementation to regional levels with line agency activities coordinated by National Economic and Development Authority (NEDA).

Regionalization represented complex shifts in the structure and conduct of government, enabling regional institutions to take decisions more expeditiously.[7] Administrative reorganization was therefore inherent in the regionalization plan, which attempted to provide spatial or area dimensions to national development planning. Regional development plans were to integrate sectoral and areal dimensions to national development planning, and this approach, according to NEDA, underlined the importance of integrating physical development with economic, social, administrative, and financial aspects into a common plan for a given area.

The Reorganization Plan of 1972 provided for the division of the country into eleven regions (later increased to twelve), each with a regional center and a regional development council. The National Economic Development Authority (NEDA) was established at the central level, with the president at its helm, to formulate policies and guidelines for development and prepare the national plan in cooperation with other ministries and agencies and in consultation with the private sector and local governments.

Regional planning is undertaken by regional development councils (RDCs), which are composed of provincial governors, city mayors, and regional directors of national ministries, managers of subregional authorities, and the regional director of NEDA. The RDCs prepare a comprehensive survey of regional resources, specify regional goals and objectives, extend technical assistance and expertise in planning, and coordinate local and regional planning.[8] The RDC keeps track of the development plans of the provinces and cities within its region. Plans are reviewed to ensure that they are relevant to national development objectives. These development plans are funded by the national ministries and local governments in the region. The RDC acts as a consultative and planning body, with the regional officers participating in its deliberations. These officers are supposed to provide the impetus and the technical skills for initiating regional planning and integrating it with the national plan.

Regional development authorities (RDAs), which are special-purpose agencies with corporate powers, were also created to plan and implement development projects in the regions, but their planning functions are now performed by the RDCs. To cut across the lines of various ministries and expedite action, the president appointed his own regional action officers, who monitor and oversee the speedy and effective implementation of high-priority regional projects.

Another aspect of regionalization has been purely administrative. The Integrated Reorganization Plan that created RDCs also provided for decentralization of central government ministries. It suggested that, "as a general pattern, the department will have regional offices organized on a department-wise basis, with staff bureaus advising and assisting the office of the secretary on matters pertaining to their respective areas of specialization including the formulation of relevant plans, programmes and operating standards and methods."[9] But a general pattern was not followed by all ministries. Some followed the departmental model; others accepted the bureau model in creating regional offices.

Decentralized Budgeting in Sri Lanka

In other countries, attempts were made to decentralize the national budget. A decentralized budget system has been in operation in Sri Lanka since 1974, when the food crisis required special funds to be released to local agencies to expedite operations. As the years passed and the food crisis abated, decentralized budget allocations were earmarked for such local facilities as school buildings, roads, rural electrification, and other needs that were determined by members of Parliament. This system is strengthened by the establishment of elected district development councils, to which such funds will be allocated on a multiyear basis.

The decentralized budget system is supported by two other measures. First is the appointment of district ministers, to provide political direction on local development activities and to coordinate the activities of all the government officials in the district. The district minister reports directly to the president and has the rank of deputy minister; the government agent in each district serves as his secretary.

Second is the increasing emphasis placed on regional development planning, with the districts serving as regional planning entities.[10] Five administrative districts were selected for the first round of an exercise in integrated development planning, and external assistance has been sought to finance district development projects.

Province Development Planning in Indonesia

In Indonesia, the history of central-local relationships is characterised by a continuous swing of the pendulum between the central and local governments.[11] World War II and ensuing regional rebellions required the central government to rebuild all infrastructural facilities, which was the focus of the nation's first five-year plan. In the Second Plan, REPELITA II, greater attention was paid to regional development.

During the REPELITA II period, the strategies for rural development took two forms: one embodied in sectoral development strategy provided large-scale projects, such as dams, reservoirs, and road networks, that usually affect economic activities across provinces; the other was embodied in budget allocation strategy through which subsidies were allotted to local governments to implement specific projects. Provincial governments were asked to prepare their own plans within guidelines established by the central government. These plans, together with the regional development strategy formulated in Jakarta, helped determine budgetary allocations for sectoral projects and local government subsidies.

The sectoral budget, therefore, is allotted to departments and other institutions in the provinces according to national and provincial priorities, while subsidies for local projects are granted according to local needs. The latter are known as INPRES projects. Since the Second Plan, nine INPRES programs have been implemented and have included infrastructure, education, health, and market facilities projects.

Several types of planning agencies were established to identify local and regional needs and to monitor regional development, both required by the INPRES program. The National Economic Planning Board (BAPPENAS) divided Indonesia into four regions and designated in each a growth center to act as a catalyst for the development of its surrounding area. In 1974, a presidential decree established a planning board (BAPPEDA) in each province to assist the governor in formulating and implementing regional (provincial) development policies. The BAPPEDA staff is expected to prepare a provincial five-year development plan as a guideline for an annual sectoral program and for coordinating the plans of line agencies working in the province, ensuring that national development will take place in a way that keeps regions and sectors in balance. Further, to integrate their plans with those of the provinces some municipalities have established their own planning organizations (BAPPEMKOs), but due to the shortage of manpower the process has been slow.[12]

The government has also formed a Horizontal Coordinating Committee (RKH) at the national level, to integrate rural development efforts; local development working units (UDKP) in districts;

and village social committees (LSD), later called village people's endurance organizations (LKMD). The UDKP does not have any funds of its own and simply coordinates development activities within its boundaries. The LSD has limited funds, but those of its projects that are funded from higher levels must be approved by the subdistrict and by BAPPEMKOs.

Coordinating Plan Implementation in Malaysia

In Malaysia, decentralization is more concerned with improving policy implementation and with project planning and management than with administrative reorganization.[13] Regional development plans are formulated at the center, and differences among provinces are taken into account during implementation. To make this kind of planning as realistic as possible, the government created an interlocking web of committees ranging from the village to the national level. Thus, the Village Development and Security Committee (JKKK) is responsible for proposing local development projects, which are scrutinized or modified by the District Action Committee and then sent to the State Action Committee, which is directly linked to central agencies that frame the national development plan. Minor projects can be approved and financed by the Implementation Coordination Unit of the prime minister's department, but others have to go to the cabinet for approval.

The primary strategy of regional development, however, is centered on land development and resettlement of the poor in new communities, tasks performed by state or federal development authorities. For projects carried out by federal authorities, the states provide the land and the federal government provides other resources and expertise. The most important organization in charge of land development schemes is the Federal Land Development Authority (FELDA), which was established in 1956. Land resettlement and rehabilitation schemes are also implemented by the Federal Land Consolidation and Rehabilitation Authority (FELCRA), and some state governments, like Pahang and Johar, have established state land development authorities.

Decentralization in India

Some Asian countries are creating entirely new institutions at the local or regional level for planning and managing development. In India, the federal government has established "centrally sponsored schemes," experiments in administrative decentralization begun with the Community Development Program of the early 1950s. A few years later, democratic institutions known as *panchayati raj* were built around the community development institutions, and all development activities were to be channeled through them. An elaborate scheme of financial devolution was prepared, and in addition to central and state government grants, the panchayati raj were also empowered to raise resources on their own.

A number of events, however, conspired to undermine the panchayati raj and to make them ineffective in the late 1960s. The *Report of the Committee on Panchayati Raj Institutions* pointed out in 1978 that the essential idea that all development activities should flow through block-level organizations lost credibility, though the *panchayat samiti* (the elected body) was in most cases coterminus with the block. As this committee pointed out, the government argued that as development activities became more complex, they demanded a greater level of expertise that was not available at the local level, and thus it introduced special schemes that could fulfill the need for technical assistance. But by diverting funds to these agencies, local democratic and decentralized agencies were considerably weakened.

Thus, in the past decade, a remarkable shift of emphasis has occurred. There is now increasing reliance on centrally directed administrative institutions, not on local governments to plan and implement development programs. Interest in decentralization has gradually faded, and attention has turned to creating organizations that can perform specialized development tasks. In most cases these institutions have not been embedded in the normal administrative system but have been given some autonomy and flexibility to make decisions. Agencies like the Drought Prone Area Programme or Command Area Development Agency are area-based; others, such as the Small Farmers and Marginal Farmers Development Agency, focus their attention on special groups. Most are registered societies. In some cases a district collector acts as the chair of the agency, with a full-time project officer taking administrative responsibility; in others, where more than one district is covered, a senior officer or commissioner heads the agency. Statutory units, such as tribal development corporations and dairy development corporations, have also been established at the state level.

Another attempt at decentralization has been in the planning process. A working group was established in 1978 to formulate guidelines for preparing block-level plans, which were similar to those prepared at the district level a decade earlier. While these efforts are taking root, the need for area planning and multilevel planning has been recognized by the government. One of the major recommendations of a government working group is to improve district capability for local-level planning; a team of professionals is needed at the district level to generate and collate data and prepare local plans.

THE NATURE OF DECENTRALIZATION POLICIES

Even though the objectives of decentralization in most Asian countries are closely linked with policies promoting regionalization of planning and development, methods and strategies differ. Most of the policies and institutions are still in a formative stage, because they have given explicit emphasis to regional development only recently.

Central Control Over Decentralized Procedures

One remarkable feature of administrative reorganization in these countries is that decentralization policies have usually emanated from the center. It is the central government that has accepted the necessity of decentralized administration and designed institutions and processes to provide it. The central government chose to transfer some of its own authority and power to agencies at other levels of government, and decentralization was seen primarily as a mechanism to increase the central government's effectiveness. Consequently, the process was accompanied by elaborate supervision and control. Thus, while recognizing the need for decentralization, the central government also emphasized that local agencies needed guidance and a well-defined scope of activity to function well.

Detailed criteria were established for the allocation of funds. The central governments in Indonesia, Thailand, Sri Lanka determined the objectives and methods of spending by local institutions. If functions were decentralized, then the institutions were subjected to constant review. The regional development councils in the Philippines, provincial development committees in Thailand, and BAPPEDAs in Indonesia were linked with central institutions in a way that clearly constrained their discretion. If the decentralized institutions demanded coordination among themselves, it was the central government institutions that provided it. Thus, sometimes in the name of financial propriety and at other times in the name of supervision, guidance, and coordination, the central governments weakened the very processes they initiated. It had been widely observed that in most developing countries there is a gap in decentralization policies between what was proposed and what was implemented. The enthusiasm expressed in the plans for regional development has not been matched by changes in institutions and administrative procedures.

Limited Popular Participation

Another characteristic of decentralization in much of Asia is that the need for popular participation in development planning has not been widely recognized. Undoubtedly, small-scale projects such as minor irrigation facilities, village roads, and bridges are financed through subsidies to villages. Those granted for INPRES projects in Indonesia, Tambon projects in Thailand, and the Food for Work Program in India have been allocated to villages according to priorities formulated by them. But such activities are only a small part of development. Dispersal of power, essentially, has taken place within administrative institutions that are constrained by centrally imposed rules, regulations, and civil service procedures.

Thus, in most Asian countries decentralization has taken two major forms: One has been the deconcentration of responsibility for development functions to field agencies without giving them discretion or autonomy; the other has been delegation of functions to agencies that are outside the regular administrative system. Little sympathy exists for devolution of authority to local governments.

Thus, in Asia, attempts at decentralization have been concerned with changes in the administrative system, and it is to the constraints in transforming the administrative system that we turn in the next section.

ISSUES AND PROBLEMS
IN DECENTRALIZATION

Administrative and Political Support

An important issue that needs to be examined in making policies for administrative decentralization more effective is whether the larger administrative-political system in which the newly created institutions are embedded supports decentralization. Most Asian countries have had highly centralized governments during periods of colonial or monarchical rule. Independence brought with it problems of maintaining national unity. Fissiparous tendencies had to be curbed, and immediate tasks were therefore directed toward nation building, which led to various kinds of social tensions and conflicts.

One response to these problems has been a tendency toward greater centralization and hesitation to give autonomy to peripheral regions. In some cases, nations have been born in the midst of severe internal strife; India, for instance, with intense communal riots faced tremendous population migration problems. The constitution makers were conscious of this social conflict. Even though they envisioned a federal government, they inserted in the constitution provisions that made the states in some respects dependent on the center.

The central government has enjoyed wide powers for formulating economic and social development policies and for development of individual sectors of the economy. Even though agriculture and rural development are state responsibilities, the center has created many programs that promote central objectives. In cases where state government interests are weak, the center seeks to strengthen them through financial grants, which means that, more often than not, the involvement of the states is determined by the amount of funds they receive. Use of financial grants in this way not only helps control the "decentralized" agencies but also determines their scope for independent action.

Similar circumstances are found in other Asian countries, especially in Thailand, the Philippines, and Sri Lanka. Local officials and beneficiary groups look to the center for funds and authority that help forge a dependency relationship. The INPRES projects in Indonesia are strictly supervised. In fact, all development planning, funding, and management activities transferred to the regions remain the responsibility of the central government.[14] In the Philippines, it has been argued that the reorganization plan has decentralized responsibilities to regions without severing their dependence on central authorities.[15] Even the delegation of power for planning and implementation was accompanied by rigorous supervision procedures. Thus, local administrations lack confidence in pursuing new programs or ideas and even where they have competence to do so hesitate to take initiative. Within such an environment, therefore, a new institution or an innovative procedure is either quickly routinized or rejected by the central government.

The constitutional restraints are further strengthened by a centralized civil service system. In at least the nations born of the British colonial tradition, an elitist, generalist cadre forms the backbone of the civil service. Members of this cadre hold crucial positions both in the field and at headquarters. Despite many changes, this cadre continues to hold its preeminent position and, remarkably, has developed strong intragroup loyalties that often play an important role in maintaining the dominance of central government decision making. The most skilled professionals in government are concentrated within this central cadre. District or field jobs are held only to qualify for better posts in the central bureaucracy.

Wanashinghe has analyzed the impact of such a system on decentralization in Sri Lanka.[16] He argues that the success of giving greater authority for coordination and expenditure to government agents in the district was dependent on the political backing of the prime minister and on the posting of senior administrators in the districts to assure leadership for coordinative arrangements. But because these administrators always attempted to return to the capital after a year or two in the districts, the original thrust of decentralization lost its momentum and the innovative procedures were quickly routinized.

**Attitudes and Behavior of
Central Government Officials**

What is significant is that such a constitutional and civil service structure gives rise to attitudes that tend to blunt the spirit of decentralization. A centrist ideology is built up to justify the belief that initiatives and control should come from the center. A corollary of this view is the belief that field staff are incompetent and lazy, one that inhibits the transfer of discretion and responsibility from the center and initiative on the part of field agents.[17] There are few incentives for officials to take up field jobs that are physically demanding and in which living conditions are poor.

The Constraints of Administrative Procedures

In this environment certain characteristics of the administrative system also have an important bearing on the way decentralization policies are implemented. One is departmentalization. Most of the new decentralized institutions that have been created are concerned with either specific geographical areas or particular social groups. The rationale for such organizations is that they would look at development in an integrated fashion and not view it segmentally, as do functional departments. But the difficulty has been that departmental loyalties stand in the way and create competition rather than cooperation.

In the case of Sri Lanka, the departments work in isolation, each pursuing its own activities and schedules and responding to directions from departmental headquarters. Their commitment is to the development activities of their own departments.[18] In the Drought Prone Areas Program Agency in India, the district collector is the chair, while other officials from development departments are deputed to work within the agency. Officials are expected to prepare areawide projects, but departmental loyalties overtake them and sectoral schemes are often planned and implemented. Assessments of administrative performance in Thailand's rural development program indicate that the present structure of administration at local levels creates obstacles to integrating development efforts toward common goals.[19]

Thus, the high degree of departmental centralization tends to weaken the decentralized organizations. Autonomy is diluted and local officials look to their own headquarters for direction. The essential point is that administrative decentralization is difficult if the organizational structure in which it is to take place has not undergone change. It is not enough to make administrative reforms in individual institutions.

Need for Administrative Capacity

Another condition for decentralization is the creation of substantially higher levels of administrative capacity than now exist in most Asian countries. In most governments, the staff needed to support decentralized agencies is usually inadequate. The challenge is to generate increased managerial capability for project planning and implementation at the local level. As noted earlier, centralist ideology tends to attract talented and capable persons away from the local level and toward the center. Those who are at the center are not inclined to return to the field after having completed the necessary stint for advancement. The result is that at the local level one finds either unwilling workers who are seeking opportunities to leave or those who have tried unsuccessfully to leave. Expertise is often scarce where it is most needed. To make a decentralized system of administration work effectively, capability at the local level is a necessity, and indeed, at least in the initial stages, high-level staff must be placed in the field and given greater responsibility.[20]

Two actions were taken in the course of an applied research project to improve planning and implementation capability of the DPAP staff in six districts of India. One was to assign a professional to work with a project staff member to help him prepare and formulate better project plans. Another was to organize seminars or discussion groups around specific management techniques that would be used to improve performance. However, in some cases, when local officials were convinced of the need for changes in procedure, higher authorities were hesitant to issue appropriate regulations. In other cases, project managers intending to spend only a brief time in rural areas before trying to get transferred were in a hurry to spend their budgets with little or no planning. In many districts, there were six or seven changes in the post of project officer in the short span of three years.

Thus, administrative reforms require commitment at the local level. Frequent transfers, a centralized civil service, and intense departmental loyalties do not create support for decentralization. Decentralized institutions become alien in an otherwise centralized administrative system and are perceived as "data feeding units." A fundamental reorientation in planning and implementation processes is needed, and this requires stronger political support than has been demonstrated in recent years.

Political Factors in Decentralization

As already noted, the history of an administrative system has an important bearing on the degree of decentralization that is possible. Colonial administration by its very nature is highly centralized, and the peaceful transition to independence has essentially meant that the old institutions and procedures have continued to flourish. Leaders of new nations have hesitated to touch those very colonial institutions that were the object of criticism earlier. In the process, such institutions have become stronger, and new reasons have been found to sustain them. A centralized civil service in India, for example, has been seen as a unifying and integrating force for the country.

Successful administrative decentralization can mean an increase in the power not only of local bureaucrats but also of local vested interests. The greater the scope of decision making by local officials, the greater will be the pressure on them to design activities to help particular groups. In Sri Lanka, members of Parliament wielded considerable influence over projects financed by the decentralized budget. In India, decentralization led to increased local politicking, and the strength of organized pressure groups or vested interests determined the extent to which administration could be decentralized.

This issue presents a major dilemma. In societies where there are great economic disparities among regions, decentralization may exacerbate inequalities. Central planning and administration may be better instruments for balancing the use of national resources and underplaying the role of local pressures.

CONCLUSION

What needs to be stressed is that while there is ample concern being shown for decentralizing administration to respond to the needs of different regions and to reduce social and economic imbalances within Asian countries, attempts at reforming the total administrative system to support such efforts is halting and hesitant. Sometimes innovative organizations are established, but little thought is given to their linkages with the existing system. At other times, financial and personnel flexibility is not provided, but efforts are made to push decisions down to lower levels of government. What really happens in both cases is the creation of greater local dependency.

This, however, does not mean that decentralization policies cannot be adopted unless the total political and administrative system is transformed. What it does mean is that decentralization has to be more carefully thought out. Its linkages with regional development policies have to be clearly defined. The implications of these linkages have to be taken into account in the financial and institutional changes proposed to make decentralized institutions and processes work more effectively.

NOTES

1. Dennis A. Rondinelli, "National Investment Planning and Equity Policy in Developing Countries: The Challenge of Decentralized Administration." *Policy Sciences,* vol. 10 (1978): 46.

2. G. Shabbir Cheema and Dennis A. Rondinelli, "Implementing Decentralization Policies and Programmes: A Project Description" (Paper delivered at the Consultative Workshop on Implementing Decentralization Policies and Programs, UNCRD, Nagoya, 1981), p. 4.

3. Chakrit Noranitipadungkarn, "Decentralization, Coordination and Development in Thailand," in G. S. Cheema, ed. *Institutional Dimensions of Regional Development,* ed. G. Shabbir Cheema (Singapore: Maruzen Asia, 1981), p. 118.

4. Johari Mat, "Coordination, Institutional Capability and Development Performance in Malaysia," in Cheema, *Institutional Dimensions,* p. 91.

5. Rondinelli and Cheema make a distinction between deconcentration, devolution, and debureaucratization in Chapter 1 of this book. If specified functions are made the responsibility of lower units of government while maintaining advisory and basic supervisory control over the performance of these functions, the process is known as devolution. In contrast, deconcentration implies only a transfer or shifting of workload without transfer of actual authority to make decisions concerning planning and management. Debureaucratization is devolution to nonbureaucratic organizations like voluntary agencies and community organizations. For our purposes, it is important to emphasize the distinction between deconcentration and devolution. Deconcentration is concerned with dispersal of power within the same hierarchical structure and the same command system. Devolution implies autonomy, freedom to behave outside the constraint of direct control. Thus, what we have is deconcentration describing the intraorganizational pattern of power relationships and devolution describing the interorganizational pattern of power relationships. This distinction needs to be kept in mind in understanding the genesis and content of decentralization policies in Asian countries and in evaluating the performance of such policies.

6. Chakrit Noranitipadungkarn, "Decentralization," p. 129.

7. Raul P. de Guzman, et. al., "The Political/Administrative Aspects of Regionalization and Development in the Philippines: Issues, Problems and Prospects (Paper delivered at the National Conference on Public Administration, Manila, 1977), pp. 1-2.

8. Raul P. de Guzman, "Administrative Reforms for Decentralized Development: Philippines," in *Administrative Reforms for Decentralized Development,* ed. A. P. Saxena (Kuala Lumpur: Asian and Pacific Development Administration, 1980), p. 148.

9. Republic of the Philippines, Presidential Commission on Reorganization, *Integrated Reorganization Plan* (Manila: Commission on Reorganization, 1972), p. 150.

10. H. S. Wanashinghe, "Administrative Reform for Decentralized Development: Sri Lanka," in Saxena, *Administrative Reforms,* p. 201.

11. Moeljarto Tjokrownoto, "Implementing Decentralization Policies and Programmes in Indonesia" (Paper delivered at the Consultative Workshop on Implementing Decentralization Policies and Programs, UNCRD, Nagoya, 1981), p. 9.

12. R. Kamaluddin, "Regional Development in Indonesia," in Institute of Developing Economies, *Regional Development in South East Asian Countries,* p. 63.

13. M. A. Nor Ghani, "Decentralization Policies in Malaysia: The Malaysian Experience" (Paper presented at Consultative Workshop on Implementing Decentralization Policies and Programmes, UNCRD, Nagoya, 1981), p. 4.

14. Atar Sibero, "Institutional Capability for Regional Development in Indonesia: Focus on Coordination" (Paper presented at Senior Level Seminar, UNCRD, Nagoya, 1980), p. 10.

15. Gabriel U. Iglesias, "Political and Administrative Issues in Regional Planning and Development," *Philippine Journal of Public Administration,* vol. 21, nos. 3/4 (1977): 324-334.

16. Wanasinghe, "Administrative Reform," p. 192.

17. Robert Chambers, *Managing Rural Development: Ideas and Experience from East Africa* (Uppsala: Scandinavian Institute of African Studies, 1974), p. 30.

18. Wanasinghe, "Administrative Reform," p. 189.

19. S. Mekapaiboon, "Administrative Reforms for Decentralized Development: Thailand" in Saxena, *Administrative Reforms,* p. 220.

20. Chambers, *Managing Rural Development,* p. 31.

CHAPTER 4

DECENTRALIZATION OF DEVELOPMENT ADMINISTRATION IN EAST AFRICA

Dennis A. Rondinelli

Decentralization became an important policy objective during the 1970s and 1980s as governments in developing countries sought to create more socially equitable patterns of economic growth and to meet the basic needs of the poor. Some policy analysts contend that decentralization is necessary to accelerate economic growth and to spread its benefits to those groups traditionally bypassed by economic progress.[1] Former World Bank president Robert S. McNamara noted, for example, that if governments are serious about distributing the benefits of development more equitably, then "experience shows that there is a greater chance of success if institutions provide for popular participation, local leadership and decentralization of authority."[2] This conclusion was confirmed in a study of more than 200 rural development projects sponsored by the United Nations Development Program (UNDP). It found that the ability of rural communities to influence the priorities of public agencies and to obtain efficient service delivery depended on effective local organization.[3] Overcentralization of authority has been a serious problem in administering local development projects in many developing countries.

For these and other reasons, decentralization policies were promulgated widely in East Africa during the 1970s. Among the most notable experiments were those in Kenya, Tanzania, and the Sudan.

In 1972, the government of Tanzania abolished traditional local governments, absorbed local officers into the national civil service, decentralized national ministries, and attempted to consolidate the rural population into villages that could be provided with services and facilities efficiently. In Kenya, provincial and district development advisory committees were established to "coordinate and stimulate development at the local level by involving in the planning process not only Government officials but also the people through their representatives."[5] District development committees were created to provide technical assistance to local planning organizations. But the most extensive program of decentralization was undertaken in 1971 in the Sudan, where the Local Government Act expanded the duties of Province Commissioners and created province executive councils to coordinate the work of local officials and central ministry representatives in the provinces. Plans were also made to grant administrative autonomy to regional governments and to devolve nearly all domestic administrative responsibilities to regions and provinces.[6]

In practice, however, these countries have faced severe problems in implementing decentralization policies. Picard concluded that in Tanzania, although decentralization "has brought about a modicum of deconcentration of power to the regions and districts, the administrative structure has not been able to establish the mechanisms that will ensure increased participation at the district and subdistrict level."[7] Freyhold described the disillusionment resulting from ineffective implementation:

> For the majority of the peasants the decade after the Arusha Declaration was not so much a period during which Ujamaa had failed but simply a period where they had been subjected to many government directives and orders without witnessing much economic development. If they had ever believed in promises of a better future at independence or during the Ujamaa campaign, they were no longer inclined to do so.[8]

Similar conclusions can be drawn from the experience in Kenya, where development planning and administration remain highly centralized despite reforms and reorganizations. The Sudan has seen more than a decade of political conflict over the devolution of development planning and management, with little apparent improvement in the living conditions of the majority of the poor.[9]

Any attempt to bring about social change quickly meets political and bureaucratic obstacles but, because of its profound consequences, decentralization requires special preconditions and supporting policies that many governments have not always been willing or able to provide. Essential changes in attitudes and behavior have been especially difficult to achieve. Ironically, many of the weaknesses in central government that decentralization policies were designed to overcome have been the strongest obstacles to their implementation.

Thus, it is necessary to reassess the experience with decentralization in East Africa. This chapter describes the policies that emerged during the 1970s and the forms of decentralization that were enacted. It identifies the social, economic, physical, and political factors that influenced implementation and, with the benefit of hindsight, suggests how implementation can be improved.

FORM AND STRUCTURE OF DECENTRALIZATION

Governments in East Africa have encouraged three forms of decentralization: deconcentration, delegation, and devolution. In the three countries examined in this study, attempts were made to deconcentrate authority by creating field agencies of central ministries or by reassigning officials to province or district levels. Although some functions were delegated to district and provincial planning committees in Kenya, decentralization policies there rarely went far beyond deconcentration. Political leaders in the Sudan initially delegated some functions to provinces and later devolved more to regional, provincial and local administrative units. Tanzania delegated some central functions to regional and district planning organizations and tried a limited form of devolution by creating *ujamaa* villages.

Deconcentration and Delegation in Kenya

The government of Kenya began to deconcentrate responsibilities for development planning and administration to provinces and districts in 1970. Reforms were prompted by dissatisfaction with national planning and with the lack of participation by local authorities and field administrators in the identification and execution of development projects. The government was quite frank in its evaluation of previous experience, noting in the National Plan for 1970-1974 that the bureaucracy was more concerned with "passive administration" than with development. It pointed out that national planning was difficult to implement because of the government's inability to identify and prepare projects, the shortage of professionals and technicians needed to carry out development programs, and the weak coordination among national ministries. Those who drafted Kenya's development plan in 1970 were critical of the national ministries' lack of commitment to previous plans and of the resistance within the central bureaucracy to innovative ideas.[10] World Bank evaluators praised the planners' technical skill but found consistent weaknesses in follow-up and execution of projects, a lack of central government support for projects identified by field administrators, and inadequate sectoral planning capacity within ministries.

The government also recognized the weaknesses in local government's capacity to deliver services effectively and the financial constraints on initiating new programs. It was not satisfied with the performance of municipalities and county councils or with the growing disparities in economic development among districts.

Creation of Province Development Committees

In 1970, the government embarked on an extensive reorganization that would place provinces and districts at the center of rural development planning. Those who designed the reforms believed that decentralization was essential for achieving Kenya's rural development goals and for increasing the productivity of small-scale farms and industries. Officially, decentralization was described as an essential component of the government's plans "to give new meaning to the phrase 'rural development' so that the principles of African socialism involving the equitable distribution of the benefits of prosperity can be given greater reality."[11] Responsibility for rural development planning was initially delegated to the provinces. Provincial development committees (DPCs) were established to review district project proposals, coordinate provincial plans, and monitor their implementation. The PDCs were chaired by the province commissioner and included all ministry department heads working in the province. A planning officer (PO) served as executive secretary and did most of the technical work.

But evaluations of the system a few years later found that the PDCs' effectiveness varied widely and that many of the committees actually did little to promote rural development. Most had no influence on national decisions; ministries in Nairobi largely ignored their recommendations. Their functions were never clearly defined. Most were short of staff and financial resources and few received adequate guidance from Nairobi. Only where the provincial commissioners made a deliberate effort to include the committees in development planning were they more than *pro forma* organizations.[12]

An investigation of field administration in 1971 by the Ndegwa commission found severe limitations on the ability of province committees to participate in "bottom-up" development. The commission reported an urgent need for more trained personnel within provinces and districts, better integration of the central ministries' field activities, and deconcentration of authority to plan and administer development programs to the districts. Some of the recommendations were accepted and, in 1974, districts were given greater responsibility for rural development planning. District development officers (DDOs) and district planning officers (DPOs) were assigned to assist district development committees (DDCs), which had been expanded to give representation to government officials, members of parliament, and local organizations. Expatriate advisers were recruited to assist the PPOs, and district planning officers were trained to provide the DDCs with assistance in industrial, natural resource, infrastructure, and human resources development.

Delegation to District Development Committees

The District Development Committees were given three major planning functions. First, they were to review the early drafts of national development plans, identify the implications for their districts, and determine how "gaps" in the plan could be filled through self-help and local development projects. These "gap-filling" responsibilities would help to adapt national programs to local conditions and supplement national plans with projects financed and carried out locally. Second, the committees were to identify projects and programs for meeting specific needs and opportunities within the district, using hitherto untapped or underutilized resources. They could also recommend to the central ministries new activities that were consistent with national development objectives. Third, the committees were to help the district commissioner and other local officials to create and apply a development management system that could narrow the gap between planning and implementation by coordinating local and sectoral programs, and help ministries and local officials to implement district projects.

In 1974, the DDCs were also given responsibility to formulate district plans and to identify local projects in such fields as agricultural production, cottage and small-scale industries, cooperatives, community development, extension, primary education, health, sanitation, family planning, housing, and small road construction. Central ministries would continue to formulate their own plans and provide funds for some district projects, but DDCs could obtain funds for planning studies and for high-priority local projects not covered in the operating budgets of central ministries from district development grants. The PDCs would provide districts with technical assistance and assign priorities to and coordinate the implementation of projects involving more than one district.[13]

Decentralization of rural development planning was seen not only as a way of obtaining better information about local development needs and priorities but as a mechanism for satisfying political demands for more participation by local officials and private organizations. Thus, the 1974-1978 National Plan urged that "every district should participate in the development program, in order to (i) seek willing and active participation of local communities in the planning and implementation of development programs and (ii) train local leaders and officials with a view to making them planning-conscious and to providing them a wider understanding of the development process."[14]

The District Planning Process

Formally, district planning was to operate as follows. First, the Ministry of Finance and Planning would issue guidelines to provincial planning officers, and other ministries would provide sectoral guidelines to their field officers and to provincial and district departmental heads, outlining major objectives, policies, and strategies for the next national plan. The provincial planning officer would then meet with province development committees and district development officers to explain national policies and objectives and to discuss strategies for achieving them. The province planning officer would assist the district planners to identify local objectives and strategies. Those that were consistent with national goals would be reviewed by the district development committee. The province planning officer would then reconcile district objectives to make them consistent with province strategies, which in turn would be reviewed by the provincial representatives of the central ministries. After local objectives were approved in principle, district planners would work with ministry field administrators to identify potential projects that could be included in the district plan. The district plan would be sent to the province development committee for reconciliation with other plans, and they would then be sent to the Ministry of Finance and Planning and to operating ministries in Nairobi for review and amendment.[15]

The district committees were not only to identify projects, but also to allocate services and facilities among rural communities and to mobilize resources for local projects. The DDOs would provide technical expertise, act as coordinators, disseminate information on national policies, and prepare the initial drafts of the district plan, as well as coordinate activities to implement it.

Although the process was quite elaborate, the principles of decentralization and participation described in the 1974-1978 development plan were not fully supported by the Ministry of Finance and Planning or by other ministries in Nairobi. MOFP officials made it clear in their guidance to the provinces and districts, for example, that the development committees were only to perform review and approval functions and not to take an active part in day-to-day planning. The directives sought to minimize political conflicts within the DDCs and dampen local political pressures on the national government. For a number of reasons that will be discussed later, rural development planning and administration in Kenya remain centralized, and province and district development committees continue to play relatively weak roles. The central ministries retain control over sectoral plans and budgets, and recommendations from the districts rarely influence national policy.

Delegation and Limited Devolution in Tanzania

Attempts to decentralize planning and administration in Tanzania cannot be fully understood without an appreciation of their political and ideological background. Tanzania's philosophy of development was strongly influenced by President Julius K. Nyerere's conviction that his country's progress depended on achieving self-reliance, meeting basic human needs, and distributing the benefits of economic growth equitably. Thus, the government attempted during the 1970s to attain these objectives by abolishing private enterprise, nationalizing agricultural estates, promoting communal agricultural production, channeling investment through parastatal organizations, and reducing the nation's dependence on foreign assistance and private investors. A limited amount of private investment was allowed in a few industries that were not controlled by the government. A national income distribution policy sought to narrow the disparities in income and wealth between urban and rural areas and among various social classes.[16]

In 1967, the Arusha Declaration emphasized the importance of agriculture to Tanzania's goals of self-reliant and socially equitable development and called for national programs to transform subsistence agriculture into a more productive system, mainly by promoting communal farming in ujamaa villages. Decentralization of decision making and widespread participation in development planning were considered essential to attaining these goals.

As in Kenya and the Sudan, organizational reforms in Tanzania emerged in response to both external criticism and internal dissatisfactions. In the years prior to 1972, the ministries in Dar-es-Salaam controlled nearly all development activities, even the creation of new settlements in rural areas. Although regional commissioners exercised substantial power within their jurisdictions, the central bureaucracy controlled administrative and technical personnel, services, and the flow of funds. Planning, budgeting, and project identification were done by central ministries without much knowledge of local conditions or needs. Rural development planning was fragmented among ministries and agencies in which administrators had little motivation or ability to coordinate and integrate their activities. As a result, peasants were sometimes forced to move to villages that had unsuitable soils, climate, and agricultural conditions. Thus, people responded apathetically to national programs; conflicts arose between ministry officials who were promoting productive investments and local councillors who wanted social services and facilities, and TANU leaders were frustrated in their attempts to implement government policies through district councils.[17]

Delegation of Development Planning

The first steps toward decentralization were taken in the mid-1960s, when economic secretaries were appointed to help regional commissioners with development planning and analysis. But in 1968 evaluations revealed that regional planning was largely ineffective because of the shortage of trained professionals, the inability of regional planners to identify feasible projects, and the continued interference by central ministries in local affairs. Many projects were included in regional plans because of pressures brought by local political factions or the regional commissioners. One evaluation found that most of the projects were selected by commissioners and that funds were "quickly appropriated to implement the programs, often with only a modicum of debate, and other projects [were] abandoned or postponed regardless of their comparative merits."[18] Despite the elaborate arrangements for bottom-up planning and widespread participation announced in the Arusha Declaration, even the Ministry of Economic Affairs and Development Planning admitted that "in practice the preparation [of the national plan] was highly centralized" and that "an enthusiastic local official received little guidance from the plan in organizing local effort, and the plan provided no immediate and specific targets."[19] None of the nation's development plans during the 1960s and early 1970s emphasized regional planning, and most local projects were still identified and implemented by central ministries.

Creation of a System of Local Administration

To make administrative structure more consistent with the philosophy of participation and self-reliance, the government created a centrally guided system of decentralized, bottom-up planning. The Decentralization of Government Act of 1972 abolished local governments but transferred many of the functions previously performed by national ministries to regions and districts where former local officials and technical officers continued to serve as members of the national civil service. The central ministries retained responsibility for national planning and development activities and for managing large-scale projects. Thus, conceptually, Tanzania's decentralization policy fell somewhere between deconcentration and delegation, but clearly it was more a system of local administration than of local government.

The reorganization was based on principles that rural development be locally managed, with widespread popular participation, but coordinated from the center. A four-tiered, hierarchical structure was created in which the president and central ministries presided over international affairs and the national economy, and in which three levels of local administration were responsible for planning and implementing regional and community development. Regional and district administrations were headed by commissioners, and wards and villages were headed by party secretaries. Ujamaa villages had their own governing structures and could deal directly with district administrators.

The reorganization also increased the influence of the Tanganyika African Union (TANU), the nation's only political party, over development at all levels. The party structure paralleled the new administrative structure, and technical officers who previously worked for the ministries were brought under the control of regional commissioners, who also headed TANU regional organizations. The TANU executive committees could review and approve developments plans at each administrative level.[20]

Regional and area commissioners were given cabinet rank and reported to the Prime Minister's Office, which became the main channel of communications between central and local administrations. Development directors were appointed to assist regional and district commissioners with administration, supervise and coordinate technical officers, and promote ujamaa villages. They, together with technical officers, assisted regional and district development committees to formulate local plans, implement projects, and elicit public participation.[21]

The administrative structure also provided the framework for bottom-up planning. Short-range planning was tied closely to annual and development budgeting, and longer-range regional and district plans were to influence the national five-year plan. The bottom-up planning procedure began with village development committees — a group of not more than twenty-five villagers, chaired by the local TANU secretary — submitting ideas for local projects. These suggestions were passed to the ward development committee — consisting of leaders of the TANU ten-house cell groups, technical officers working in the ward, and selected members of the ward council — for consideration and approval. The approved projects were then sent to the district development committee, which assessed preliminary costs and placed high-priority projects in the preliminary district plan. The plan then had to be reviewed and approved by the TANU district executive committee. The district development proposal was sent to the regional development committee and the regional executive committee of TANU, which combined district plans into a regional plan and submitted it to the Prime Minister's Office. The approved plan was then to be implemented by regional and district development directors.[22] Small-scale village projects that were not included in the regional plans could be financed through the Regional Development Fund, which the central government allocated to regions on the basis of their population size.

Limited Devolution Through the Ujamaa Program

In 1973, TANU leaders called for acceleration of the ujamaa village program.[23] The communal structure to be established in ujamaa villages would allow peasants to work together toward common objectives and to participate in local government and development planning in an organized and democratic way.[24] Through ujamaa, which means "familyhood," the Tanzanian economy would become a network of cooperatives through which rural people would work to increase agricultural production for their own benefit and contribute to the well-being of the community by improving commonly owned assets.[25]

Ujamaa villages were to be settlements with clearly delineated boundaries and populations of at least 250 families. The program was supposed to be voluntary, but the government and TANU frequently used pressure and coerced families to move into the new settlements. Government assisted with site preparation and provided transportation, food, water, and construction materials. The members of the new villages would work together to clear land, draw a constitution, organize an assembly, and establish credit with the Tanzanian Rural Development Bank.

Each new village was to form an assembly consisting of all residents over the age of 18 that would elect a village council from among the members over the age of 21. A settlement could be registered officially as a ujamaa village when residents demonstrated that they could work cooperatively and that the settlement was economically viable, had strong leadership, and was organized along lines prescribed by ujamaa principles.[26] Actually, many villages were registered without meeting all of the criteria; and the difficulty that villages experienced in meeting official standards was symptomatic of the problems that plagued the ujamaa program throughout its history.[27]

Devolution of Planning and Administration in the Sudan

Administrative decentralization and widespread participation in public decision making were basic principles in the socialist philosophy of leaders who staged the 1969 May Revolution in the Sudan. The coup was justified by the military as the only means of changing the old political order, in which "the people were denied their basic and legitimate rights as makers of the political life of the country." The system of native administration, inherited from British colonial rule, had given religious and ethnic leaders and elites from influential families substantial control over local politics. Narrowly based political factions and bureaucratic elites maintained a near stranglehold on national politics. Powers of provincial and local governments were undermined by central ministries and public corporations. A bureaucracy primarily concerned with regulation rather than with development or with providing services to the people controlled the technical and administrative agencies in Khartoum and ran many of the nation's industries. Many provincial governments were controlled by local political factions that pressed their own special interests. The boundaries of many provinces and local units were drawn to encompass a single tribe or to allow village or district sheikhs *(omdas)* or paramount sheikhs *(nazirs)* to dominate the areas, or local religious leaders *(imams)* to exercise influence, thus rendering provincial commissioners and executive officers powerless to carry out their functions without interference. The inability of local administrators to solve local problems and the fragmentation of political power within provinces and districts inevitably pushed those problems, and with them increasing power, toward central ministries in Khartoum. Delegations from the provinces regularly traveled to the capital to ask central authorities to settle local disputes. Both central and local governments were viewed as corrupt, inefficient, and ineffective. Moreover, the inability of the central government to resolve the civil war between the Islamic northern provinces and the black southern region added to the difficulties of maintaining political order and pursuing economic development. In 1969, the military claimed that neither the central government nor local political factions were responsible to the Sudanese people and that both had become remote from and unresponsive to local needs.[28] The revolutionary leaders promised a "new democracy based upon the principle of enabling the people to exercise all their will on all levels — political, social, and administrative — in a sober and responsible way."[29]

Creating a System of Local Administration

The revolutionary government's commitment to decentralization was most clearly reflected in the People's Local Government Act, promulgated by President Gaafar Mohammed Nimeiry after the government was transformed from a military command to a republic in 1971. The major thrust of decentralization was to strengthen the authority and decision-making powers of the provinces and to expand participation in local planning and administration. Chapter III of the act established a provincial administration consisting of a "people's province executive council" and a provincial commissioner. By strict definition, however, the title of the act was a misnomer, for the law did not so much create a system of local government as one of local administration. The commissioner of each province was less a "governor" than a prefect; he was a representative of central government appointed by the president and expected to be the political agent of the ruling party, the Sudan Socialist Union (SSU). The 1971 act stipulated that each commissioner would be a person of administrative ability "and of political consciousness and an ardent supporter of the aims of the May Revolution."[30] Commissioners were not expected to represent a local constituency, but rather to organize local residents to be "responsive to the general policy of the government."[31] The commissioner was to supervise, coordinate, and control all government officials working in the province, to maintain order and security, and, together with the provincial executive council, to prepare annual operating and development budgets.

The duties of the councils, as described in the Local Government Act, also pointed to a system of local administration rather than of local government. They were established by warrant from the Council of Ministers and could be amended by it at any time. The province commissioners were *ex officio* the chairmen of the councils and were granted veto power over decisions that they judged to be "contrary to public interest or the general policy of the state or [that] threatens the security or prejudices the rights of citizens or the principles of equality."[32] The executive councils were to be made up of members of functional organizations — women's groups, youth organizations, political party members, and representatives from district, village, and town development committees — as well as officials from various ministries working in the provinces.

The duties of the executive councils combined political mobilization with general administration. Broadly, the Local Government Act of 1971 charged them with responsibility for "political enlightenment, people's mobilization, economic and social development and consolidation of national unity" and with the promotion of socialist ideology as defined by the SSU. The political overtones were strong — the councils were expected not only to help the central government to eliminate traditional political influences that dominated local and national affairs prior to the 1969 revolution, but also to help mobilize political support within the provinces by organizing village development committees and "May legions" for men, women, and youth.

The administrative duties of each council included a broad range of local activities, excluding only five reserved functions: national security, posts and communications, foreign affairs, banking, and the judiciary.[33] Undoubtedly, the councils' most important function was to prepare annual budgets. They were charged with estimating annual revenue and expenditure needs, calculating tax levies, and determining the amounts required from central government ministries. The sectoral requests were to be prepared in cooperation with the ministries, and the final budget recommendations would be approved by the Council of Ministers.[34]

The provincial councils could employ staff, but most of the technical posts were filled by civil servants seconded from the central government. An average 15 to 20 staff members were assigned to the executive council, working under the supervision of the deputy commissioner for administration. The major institutional channel for extending services to, and eliciting participation from, localities was through "people's local councils." Under the provisions of the Local Government Act of 1971, the province councils could establish local councils for districts, towns, rural areas, and villages, as well as for nomadic groups.

The 1971 act required council seats to be filled by election and that one-fourth of the members be women. A local government inspector headed the district administration that had responsibility for primary and secondary education, public health, cooperatives, clerical and accounting activities, and public works. The district councils generally had few direct administrative duties; they acted primarily as links between the province executive councils and local councils to coordinate local budgets.[35] As a result of the 1971 act, all former local government units were abolished and only provinces were given corporate status. But the creation of councils drastically increased the number of local administrative units within the provinces from 86 to more than 5,000.

From Deconcentration to Devolution

Implementation of the Local Government Act greatly increased the administrative responsibilities of the provinces but also created serious problems for the provincial and local councils, notably because of inadequate finance. Although the president had transferred many functions previously performed by central ministries to provincial executive councils, adequate financing to perform the tasks was not provided. Instead, a dual budgeting system emerged in which provinces earmarked some funds for local activities and worked with the ministries in budgeting for projects that the ministries would undertake in the provinces. About 12 percent of the provinces' budgets could be devoted to local development projects. Although the executive councils were required to specify the sources of revenue for budgeted expenditures, their limited tax base meant that their main source of funding would continue to be the central government through deficit financing — a form of "revenue sharing" that provided the difference between provincial incomes and expenditures. In addition, central ministries also placed line items in their own budgets for capital construction and equipment purchases, which then became part of the province budget. Maintenance costs and staff salaries for all projects undertaken by the central ministries were passed to the provinces after the projects were completed, and became recurring local expenditures. This increased the financial burdens on the provinces and the amounts that were needed each year from the central government through deficit financing.

As a result, the provinces lacked adequate facilities, equipment, supplies, and trained personnel to perform their newly assigned duties. Although the central ministries were required to assign field staff to the provinces, many commissioners complained that the central ministries did not second staff in sufficient numbers or quality. High rates of turnover, resentment on the part of some employees who were involuntarily transferred from Khartoum, and frequent changes in assignment made administration in the provinces unstable.

Because of these and other weaknesses, many local councils remained "paper organizations"; they existed legally but performed few important functions. Thus, administrative reform, in the first few years after the Local Government Act, had little influence on changing the structure of informal leadership in villages and rural areas. The traditional leaders merely took on new roles within the local councils. "The picture that emerges is of an informal leadership group at the village level based on respected familiar loyalties," Howell notes. "This group is likely to fill any of the institutional roles that are required by visiting government or party officials."[36]

In 1976, the National Assembly's Select Committee for the Study and Revision of the People's Local Government Act concluded that the 1971 law did not really devolve power. It deconcentrated it from some central ministries and reconsolidated it in others and in the provincial commissioners' offices. The Select Committee noted that "power thus becomes centered in the headquarters of the province and thus the administrative shade expands at the same time it was meant to be contracted by the establishment of such a tremendous number of people's local councils."[37]

To overcome some of these problems, President Nimeiry and the leaders of the Sudan Socialist Union announced new administrative reforms in 1977. Nimeiry reorganized some central ministries and abolished others, transferring their functions to the office of the president or to the provinces. He also gave province commissioners greater executive and coordinative authority and changed the way the national budget would be formulated. Beginning in the next fiscal year, provincial rather than ministry expenditures would become the basis for national budgeting, and residual funds from the consolidated province budgets would be allocated for central operations and development.[38]

President Nimeiry followed up his initial changes with others in 1978. Because of the reluctance of many national ministries to support decentralization, he greatly curtailed their powers. The Ministry of Local Government, to which the province commissioners had previously reported, was abolished, and the commissioners were elevated to cabinet rank. The Ministry of Planning was ordered to establish offices in each of the provinces to assist the executive councils with short-range development planning, and the Ministry of Finance was told to provide technical assistance to every province for budget preparation and fiscal programming. The provincial planning teams would collect the socioeconomic data needed to prepare province and district development plans and would assist the councils and commissioners in integrating local projects into provincial plans and in coordinating provincial with national planning. In 1979, Nimeiry abolished seven national ministries and curtailed the functions of, or reorganized, four others. He terminated the Ministries of Education, Interior, Religious Affairs, Social Affairs, Youth and Sports, Cooperation, and Commerce and Supply. Operational responsibilities for many functions previously performed by these ministries had already been transferred to the provinces, and the residual national functions were consolidated and transferred to other central government offices. Two new ministries — Education and Orientation, and Cooperation, Commerce, and Supply — were established. The president also ordered other ministries — Transport, Finance, Energy, and Culture and Information — to begin preparing to decentralize some of their functions. Moreover, all remaining central ministries were given new special assignments to assist the provinces to perform more effectively responsibilities transferred from the central government.[39]

Toward Regional Government in the Sudan

At the same time, other forms of decentralization were planned to move the Sudan toward a federal system with semi-autonomous regional governments created to direct public activities and coordinate them between the central government and the provinces. In 1981, President Nimeiry proposed that the Northern Sudan be given three regional governments with semi-autonomous powers similar to those granted to the Southern Sudan in 1972. As there, the regional institutions in the North would have responsibility for supervising administration, maintaining order and security, and planning for and implementing regional economic development. Unlike the South, however, where the president of the High Executive Council is elected and can be removed only by the Regional Assembly, the governors of the proposed new regions would be appointed by the president of the republic. Nimeiry offered the proposal as a "realistic administrative pattern that reflects national unity, attains efficiency, promotes production, and ensures proper growth of national resources and a fair distribution of wealth."[40] The arrangement would provide a governmental structure that would promote equity in regional development and guard against social imbalance. It would create a political system in which national resources would be more equitably distributed and in which national development activities could be coordinated and implemented more effectively. The proposals were endorsed by the SSU, and a special commission was created to work out financial, administrative, and structural details.

Although regionalization in the Sudan is only in its initial stages, it is clear that Nimeiry sees its successful implementation as a political necessity for maintaining national unity as well as a practical means of achieving more responsive and efficient administration. He has told the nation that "regionalization proposals constitute radical solutions for our supply, economic, and political problems," that they were an essential alternative to temporary solutions, and that they "open new horizons for national action and constitute a progressive step and an additional experience to the systems of administration, government, and democracy." He claims decentralization to be a "genuine response to the aspirations of the masses" that could "help forestall tendencies of discord and conflict."[41]

But in the Sudan, belief in decentralization and widespread participation is still an article of faith. The tangible benefits have not yet appeared. Achievement of these goals will depend in part on the central government's ability to control serious economic problems, to maintain political stability, and to obtain the cooperation and support of the national bureaucracy, local officials and elites, and ethnic and religious leaders. Moreover, Nimeiry must be able to institutionalize decentralization policies that have been created largely as the result of his own political leadership and persuasion. Finally, he must find the substantial financial resources and skilled manpower needed to give life to what remain essentially "paper plans."

PROBLEMS OF IMPLEMENTING DECENTRALIZATION POLICY IN EAST AFRICA

More than a decade of experience in East Africa suggests that Tanzania, Kenya, and the Sudan have had mixed results with decentralization, which was introduced in each country in different ways and for different purposes. Many of the difficulties encountered by governments in the three countries, however, are similar. A review of the problems not only reveals the constraints under which the policies must be carried out but also suggests conditions that must be established to make them more effective. Among the most important problems have been weaknesses in political commitment and support for decentralization, administrative difficulties in translating policies and programs into action, behavioral problems that undermined the intent of decentralization policies, shortages of critical resources needed to carry out the policies effectively, and physical and organizational problems that made policy objectives difficult to attain.

Political Constraints

Among the most critical problems in all three countries were the weaknesses in political commitment and support among national leaders, the resistance of central bureaucracies to transferring functions from their control, and passive support or outright opposition to decentralization by some local leaders and elites.

Weaknesses in Political Support Among National Leaders

Political commitment to decentralization appears to have been weak, not only among national leaders but also among bureaucrats, local leaders, and citizens, in all three countries. In both Tanzania and the Sudan, decentralization and participation were promulgated by strong-willed presidents. Nyerere had the general support of important political leaders in Tanzania but received little cooperation from the bureaucracy. Nimeiry acted in the Sudan with the backing of only a small group of associates within the Sudan Socialist Union. In Kenya, decentralization was advocated primarily by expatriate advisers and a small group of leaders in the central government, with some support by tribal or regional leaders who saw decentralization as a way of strengthening their positions in the competition for national resources. But little evidence suggests that there was widespread political support for decentralized decision making. In all three countries, strong leadership was required over a long period of time to make the concept — even in the limited forms recognized in East Africa — politically palatable. The difficulties of building commitment to decentralization among political leaders delayed and sometimes obstructed progress in all three countries.

Advocates of decentralization had to exert a good deal of influence to convince political leaders of the merits of bottom-up planning and decisionmaking. Nimeiry had to reiterate the theme almost constantly for a decade, and even then support for devolution remained shallow among military leaders and many politicians outside Nimeiry's faction of the Sudan Socialist Union. Some central government officials felt that devolution would fragment the country and allow regional leaders to build semi-autonomous fiefdoms within the Sudan. Others argued that shifting functions to the provinces would weaken the central government's control over development and would maintain the provincialism that for so long prevented the Sudan from achieving national unity. Thus, only a few of the reforms initiated by the Local Government Act of 1971 were institutionalized.

Similarly, observers of Tanzania's political history note that it took nearly a decade for Nyerere's concepts of ujamaa, formulated in the late 1950s and early 1960s, to be incorporated into national policy, and yet another decade to implement the policy.[42] Throughout that period, intense political pressure had to be applied by Nyerere, who "pushed, prodded, cajoled, persuaded, and led the people" toward socialism and decentralization.[43] Both leaders had to resort to coercion — Nimeiry by constantly manipulating his cabinet and abolishing those ministries that opposed decentralization and Nyerere by imposing the control of a single political party, TANU, over both the bureaucracy and local units of administration.

The weaknesses in political commitment to decentralization should not be surprising, given East Africa's tradition of highly centralized and authoritarian government. Under both colonial regimes and independence movements, national and local political leaders benefited from centrism and paternalism.[44] Thus, the commitment of even those political leaders who ostensibly supported decentralization was often shallow and limited to deconcentration, which allowed them to maintain their influence over local activities. Decentralization was supported only if it allowed national policies to penetrate the periphery or elicited greater support in rural areas for central government programs. But commitment to popular participation in development planning and decision making was severely constrained. As one observer noted, in Kenya, little enthusiasm could be mustered among political leaders for policies that might change the "leadership or the character of the system, and the goals — including the conception of development — to which the system is already committed to pursuing."[45] And although greater popular control over local affairs was sought in Tanzania, there is little evidence that Tanzanians achieved much more influence than Kenyans over the direction of development policy.

Resistance of Central Government Bureaucracies
to the Transfer of
Development Responsibilities

Another obstacle to implementing decentralized planning and administration in East Africa was the continuing resistance of central government officials to "decision making from below." In Kenya and Tanzania the central bureaucracies successfully maintained control over regional, provincial, and district development planning; when they were not able to obstruct the transfer of functions, they attempted to extend their control to lower levels of administration. In the Sudan, the only effective force for making decentralization work was within the office of the provincial commissioner, but bureaucrats within the commissioners' offices were often ministry technicians and neither they nor provincial executive councils were willing to extend authority for decision making to local councils.

In Kenya and the Sudan national bureaucracies supported decentralization policies only reluctantly, and in Tanzania the bureaucracy backed decentralization policies halfheartedly even after coming under the control of TANU. National ministry officials in the Sudan resented the transfer of their functions to the provinces and attempted to maintain control over them, directly or indirectly, for as long as possible. Only the abolition of some central ministries removed the most intransigent bureaucratic obstacles — at least temporarily — and served warning to other ministries that their cooperation was mandatory. Less drastic measures in Tanzania and Kenya left the central ministries in control of lower levels of administration or allowed them to reconsolidate power and authority within regional or province administrations.

The central ministries and agencies amassed sufficient resources to protect their growing influence over rural development planning in Kenya. The power of Nairobi's central bureaucracy and "its overall complex of institutions, specialists, and services for rural development has reached the threshold of self-sustaining interaction," Moris observed. "Nairobi can very nearly generate its own solutions to Kenya's internal technological needs." But as Moris argued, the attention of central government officials was "becoming involuted because of the sheer complexity of the many different agencies and interests caught up in this interaction. . . . It is not stretching the point to say that most rural development initiatives in Kenya are launched from Nairobi; many never leave Nairobi."[46] The central ministries did not often support innovations or experiments originating outside of their own organizations. Experience with Kenya's Special Rural Development Program showed quite clearly the power of the national bureaucracy to delay implementation and prevent projects that they opposed from receiving financial and administrative support.[47]

The ability of the central bureaucracy to penetrate local administrative units or reconsolidate power was evident in all three countries. Devolution in the Sudan simply reconcentrated power at the provincial level by reducing the decision-making authority and resources of the central ministries and local governments. Although province executive councils had authority to devolve functions to lower-level councils, none but Khartoum's did so. An evaluation of the decentralization program in Southern Darfur Province concluded that "this has in effect meant the loss of identity by the lower councils, which are entirely dependent upon the province councils for staff, equipment, and authority to spend even the smallest amounts of money."[48] In Kenya, the power of many province and district officials increased with decentralization, as it did at the regional and district levels in Tanzania. Cliffe pointed out that "the general pattern emerging in Tanzania is that the intentions of the leadership have not been realized." In reality, he claimed, the ujamaa program became a "bureaucratic exercise in relocation; villagization has led to more local projects but power has passed to the more numerous officials in the regions, not to the people."[49]

Passive Support for or Opposition to
Decentralization by Many
Local Leaders and Traditional Elites

One objective of decentralization in East Africa was to reduce traditional political influence by establishing administrative procedures that would weaken the influence of traditional elites by bringing younger leaders into community decision making or by strengthening the role of centrally appointed officials at the local level. As noted earlier, participative arrangements were seen by central government officials primarily as a means of mobilizing local support for national development policies. But in the rural areas, especially in the Sudan, the ethnic, tribal, religious, linguistic, and nomadic groups had no common heritage or sense of nationalism. As in many parts of rural Kenya and Tanzania, obligations, responsibilities, and loyalties rarely extended far beyond family, tribe, or village. Under these conditions the concept of nationalism was virtually meaningless, and traditional leaders and elites easily opposed or undermined decentralization policies and maintained control over local decision making.

In Tanzania, local leaders and elites often joined with small landowners in obstructing or neutralizing programs that expanded participation in development planning or that reallocated resources for development to the poor. Members of Parliament, fearing the loss of their seats, passively supported or resisted the ujamaa program in districts where it was unpopular. One MP asked a district development director in Shinyanga, for instance, "How do you expect me to do something that threatens the continuance of my monthly parliamentary salary?" Former chiefs and subchiefs often disassociated themselves entirely from ujamaa, referring to government officials as "these people who have come to move you."[50] The kulaks — richer farmers, landowners, and shopkeepers — resisted communal production schemes until the government forced rural families to move into villages. Then they pressured officials to have their villages designated as ujamaa communities so that they would make larger profits or gain political influence. The support usually remained halfhearted, however, and as Freyhold points out, "communal activities meant to these kulaks nothing but a gesture to please the administration. They did not believe any progress would or should come from communalisation and were careful to limit its scope to activities which did not interfere with their own."[51]

Local elites and large landowners in Kenya often formed alliances with central ministry officials or members of Parliament to protect the current pattern of resource allocation or to resist changes proposed by district development committees and development officers. As Cliffe observed, "the position of both political leaders and of senior government officials depends on a patronage pattern which provides a link between their ambitions, and in turn their ability to deflect resources 'back home,' and the aspirations of the local notables on whose organized support they partially depend."[52]

The persistent influence of local elites in all three countries is partially explained by the widespread acceptance of paternalistic leadership. In much of East Africa the interaction between traditional leaders and peasants was hierarchical. Leaders protected their authority by discouraging others from making decisions without their consent or consultation. Thus, rural people were often reluctant to challenge local elites who opposed decentralization, and subordinate officials were hesitant to take action that would upset their superiors. The strong dependence of rural people on traditional leaders was difficult to break simply by creating new organizations or planning procedures. The rural peasantry in Tanzania, for instance, continued to look to progressive farmers for leadership. In many villages, the rural poor elected kulaks to village development committees and local TANU posts, and as Sherwin has observed, the richer farmers did "their utmost to block collectivization and reinforce their position by lobbying for improved social benefits for their constituencies."[53] Thus, the local elites could undermine central government programs not only by opposing the expansion of ujamaa directly but also by pressuring for social investments with high recurrent costs.

Early experiences with decentralization in the Sudan were similar to those in Tanzania. In many Sudanese villages traditional leaders emerged as local councillors, and their demands were for social rather than productive investments. "The most powerful councillors are either traders or party leaders from the small market towns, which are the effective face of government activity," Howell observed. "Demands for 'development' centre upon the provision of schools and clinics in particular, with questions of increased agricultural productivity not figuring in the infrequent council deliberations."[54]

Administrative and Operational Problems

In addition to political opposition, decentralization was hampered by ambiguities in the laws and by the inability of central ministries and agencies to provide technical and managerial assistance to local administrative units.

Ambiguity in the Design of Decentralization Policies

In all three countries, decentralization laws were quite ambiguous about the extent and purpose of the reforms, the procedures for participation, and the roles of officials at various levels of administration. Public pronouncements often implied that decentralization would create local government. Indeed, the language of the decentralization laws — and even their titles — used the term "local government." But leaders in all three countries really intended only to establish local administration, which would be guided, controlled, and influenced from the center. Moreover, much of the political rhetoric accompanying decentralization implied that government was seeking to promote widespread participation; but the policies only created new arrangements for bureaucracies to control local development.

Some of the ambiguities in Tanzania's decentralization policies arose from the way procedures were designed. Ironically, in a country whose president was loudly extolling the virtues of socialism and self-reliance, the government had contracted with an American management firm, the McKinsey Corporation, to design the decentralization program. The consultants apparently did so without knowing much about Tanzanian culture or decision-making practices and even without a real understanding of the political situation. As a result, one analyst points out that "much of what they proposed was absolutely contrary to the mode by which policies were made in Tanzania under the principle of party supremacy."[55] Senior civil servants accepted the procedures believing that they would enhance the bureaucracy's power, but as Goran Hyden has pointed out, "many of the principal features of the system introduced by the McKinsey consultants have subsequently been ignored."[56]

Uncertainty about how to implement decentralization was pervasive in both the Sudan and Tanzania. Province executive councils in the Sudan received little technical assistance from the center, and the Tanzanian government issued so few guidelines on implementing ujamaa that, as one district development director later pointed out, "the implementation strategy was virtually left to each region and to each district to formulate. Most districts throughout the country were, of course, perplexed as to how they could go about implementing the program."[81] In the absence of guidance or technical assistance, many local programs were established with little foresight or planning. Decisions were often made arbitrarily. In moving people to ujamaa villages, for instance, little attention was given to the needs of old people without families or of single women. Site selection was often haphazard and detrimental to production goals. Essential services were not provided before families were moved, and sites were often chosen that benefited kulaks and rich farmers rather than the peasants.

Moreover, in all three countries, the multiple levels of review and approval through which local plans had to pass created delays that discouraged enthusiastic participation, reinforced the power of the bureaucracy to veto or modify proposals, and created greater uncertainty and perplexity among rural people.[58] Ironically, the formal structure of decentralization adversely affected some self-help and rural participation programs in Kenya and Tanzania. With decentralization came greater bureaucratic interference in the operation of rural development funds in both countries and in the selection of ujamaa projects in Tanzania.[59]

*Weaknesses in the Capacity of
Central Administrative Agencies to
Support and Assist Decentralized Units*

Even if the central ministries were committed to more extensive decentralization, they had little capacity to support and facilitate local planning and administration in any of the three countries. The success of decentralization depends, at least in the early stages, on the strength and competence of the central administration to support field agencies and to help create greater administrative capacity at lower levels of government. However, in all three East African countries, the administrative capacity of central ministries and agencies was weak. Most central ministries were overstaffed, but technical and managerial skills were not well developed in lower levels of administration. Bureaucracies in each country were inefficient and ineffective in performing national development functions and unwilling or unable to provide the technical, financial, personnel, and other resources needed by lower levels to carry out development activities. Weaknesses in administrative capacity at the center weakened the entire administrative structure and redounded throughout the system.

Although problems were similar in all three countries, the weaknesses of public administration were most pronounced in the Sudan, where operating agencies and public corporations could not coordinate and manage development activities at any level. An analysis by the Sudan Management Development and Productivity Center found that planning procedures were confusing and the plans of various agencies and ministries were often conflicting, coordination was weak, and in most agencies planning was merely a "paper exercise." Public organizations had long chains of command, managers had large spans of control, and distinctions were not made between activities and results. Thus, there was usually little relationship between an organization's activities and its formal objectives.[60] Similar conditions existed in Kenya and Tanzania, where administration was highly political and administrative control was maintained through patronage alliances between senior and junior staff. "Whom one knows and not what one does is regarded as the key to personal betterment," Moris pointed out. "Distrust of associates is common and many senior officials employ protective strategies vis-à-vis the younger generation of officials as a matter of routine."[61]

But the interminable delays and inefficiencies that undermined decentralization in East Africa cannot be attributed entirely to inadequate administrative procedures or discretion to make decisions at lower levels. Many complaints about bureaucratic behavior in East Africa arose from two seemingly inconsistent conditions: slavish conformity to complex, detailed, and ponderous procedures to accomplish even the simplest and most routine tasks, and ignorance of or deviation from established procedure in dealing with the public. Nellis noted that in both situations ineffectiveness was due primarily to the overwhelming fear by lower- and middle-level administrators of making mistakes and to the pervasive practice of passing problems on to others in order to lighten workloads. He argued that although "the bureaucracy is over-bureaucratized and over-routinized, it is at the same time under-bureaucratized; meaning that officials use routine to reduce rather than to expedite work."[62] Problems were passed on from one organization to another, because "cases and events that are out of the ordinary contain numerous possibilities for making mistakes; even minor errors are avoided at all costs, and the result is a strict, indeed constricting interpretation of the rules."[63] However, arbitrariness, preferential treatment, failure to follow established procedures, ignorance of the rules, and other behavior allowed bureaucrats to cut through red tape when it suited their purposes. In the Sudan, the inevitable long queues in any government office could be circumvented if the client was a relative or member of the same village or tribe as the government official in charge, or was recognized as an "important person." The ubiquitous bribe, of course, could bring preferential treatment in any East African country.

The inability or unwillingness of most ministries and agencies to coordinate their own field offices also undermined decentralization policy. Trapman noted that in Kenya coordination led to ambiguous decisions in Nairobi and to confusion in the provinces and districts. Often, he observed, "decisions have been made in isolation by heads of technical divisions and circulated as directives to the provincial offices without consultation either of the planners or of the field staff themselves." Standard directives were often irrelevant. "Coupled with the attitudes of field staff, who tend to implement directives unquestioningly, this has led to some strange combinations of agricultural policy at the field level," he pointed out.[64] Field staff attempted to apply directives about cropping priorities, for instance, even in districts where the crops were difficult or impossible to raise. Inappropriate priorities and targets were often incorporated into district plans without question.

Ineffective administration in East Africa can be attributed in part to the legacy of colonial domination and to cultural traditions. Under Egyptian and British rule, the Sudanese civil servants were neither well trained nor allowed to assume positions of responsibility. When Sudan achieved independence in 1954, the government filled nearly all positions with Sudanese officials within fifteen months. Poorly trained and inexperienced Sudanese were promoted, and lower-level positions were filled with those who had little education or training. As one analyst observed, "the vision and intellectual horizon of, and the standards set by, those promoted to the top grades in 1954-55 have had a continuing influence."[65] A quarter of a century later, the bureaucracy remained overstaffed but was desperately short of skilled professionals, a problem that was aggravated in the 1960s by the government's policy of guaranteeing jobs to all college graduates who could not find other employment. Since virtually none of the civil servants could be dismissed or disciplined, the central bureaucracy remained large but ineffective. The strong tradition of face-to-face communications heavily burdened middle- and high-level administrators, who spent enormous amounts of time in personal meetings with others, rather than dispatching work through indirect or written communications. The Moslem concept of *shura* required mutual consultation to solve problems, and anyone who took individual initiative was condemned. Communications systems were inefficient outside Khartoum, and a large majority of the population was illiterate, making problem solving a slow, time-consuming, and uncertain process.[66]

Serious shortages of trained personnel within central ministries were aggravated by frequent post transfers. Personal relationships within Sudanese organizations encouraged frequent changes, and indeed, many civil servants associated transfer with promotion. When a superior was transferred, he often took his closest subordinates with him. Moreover, instability and inefficiency were exacerbated by the high rates of absenteeism at all levels of the bureaucracy. Both religious practices and the demands of large, extended families combined to justify long periods of paid annual leave given to Sudanese employees — at least forty days a year were allowed and often more were taken at full or partial pay. Also, middle- and higher-level officials considered educational leave, especially overseas training, to be a prerequisite of their jobs. Thus, key employees were often absent, and their work was passed from one employee to another or not performed at all.

Moreover, the inability of administrators to dismiss or even severely reprimand incompetent public employees accounted for the lack of discipline and widespread corruption within the civil service. One regional minister, who had formerly been a provincial commissioner, described the case of a clerk who continually filed originals of letters, failed to tell his superiors about serious problems, and performed his duties lackadaisically. "He should be dismissed," the minister contended. "But he has three wives and nine children and if I take disciplinary steps I will become the object of scorn; a *kawaja* (white man) they will call me."[67] Even if charges against incompetent public employees were filed, social pressures would inhibit members of the disciplinary committee from recommending serious punishment. The traditional Sudanese concept of *malesh* required wrongdoers to be forgiven and inhibited punishment. Thus Sudanese bureaucrats were generally apathetic about performing their duties or serving clients; there was little concern for meeting schedules; work was done at a slow pace, and when tasks were not completed on time or according to fixed standards, the general attitude of all was that "it is God's will."

Psychological and Behavioral Problems

The low levels of capacity within central administrative agencies to support decentralization were reinforced by the behavioral characteristics of central administrators, who dealt with lower-level officials and rural people in a paternalistic and authoritarian manner, and by the deep and pervasive distrust of government officials by the rural population in all three countries.

Authoritarian and Paternalistic Behavior of Central Government Officials in Dealing with Rural People

Administrative decentralization and regional planning in East Africa were weakened by the paternalistic attitudes of many government officials and by their scorn for peasants. In the Sudan, local officials attempted to work around members of district and village councils rather than with them. "Distrust of the ability and probity of local councillors is ingrained and instructions on grass roots democracy are cynically administered," Howell concluded.[68] Technical officers controlled local planning and budgeting, and when they consulted the councils it was usually only to ratify decisions.

In Tanzania, government officials in the regions and districts also took primary responsibility for development planning and administration, and TANU leaders could veto their proposals. Many of the problems with implementing ujamaa arose from the fact that, as Ergas has pointed out in a recent evaluation,

> the bureaucrats in general are allergic to dialogue with the peasants, both by training and by class interest. They regard them as ignorant, conservative, and irrational, and propose that their 'resistance to change' be broken by energetic, authoritarian action. . . . This being the situation, it is easy to understand why every time the central government in Tanzania attempted to give decision-making powers to the rural periphery, a number of bureaucrats exploited the opportunity to reinforce their own authority — and indeed, any real challenge was ruthlessly crushed.[69]

The government's pronouncements were often belied by the attitudes and behavior of field staff. Thoden Van Velzen's study of the behavior of government staff in Rungwe District in Tanzania vividly illustrated the disparities between the rhetoric of decentralization and participation, and the attitudes of district officials, who maintained an air of superiority in dealing with rural people.[70] They rarely participated in time-honored village activities and rituals; they dressed differently, expected and demanded deference, and attempted to obtain cooperation from peasants through threats and coercion.

The way staff addressed and dealt with rural people made it clear that they did not expect their participation in development planning. Van Velzen recalled one government extension agent telling members of a village development committee in Rungwe District: "Remember, you farmers are the chickens and we are the mother hens. If you follow our example you will survive, but if you are not attentive you will perish."[71] The remarks were particularly ironic because most junior extension agents were poorly trained and knew little about local agricultural conditions. This paternalism may simply have been amusing to some farmers, but it proved to others that government officials could not be trusted. Local staff not only threatened but also insulted villagers. "I know you are truly blind," Van Velzen quoted one community development officer telling villagers, "otherwise you would have appreciated more the program that staff have brought to Bulambia. Now we are going to make you rise from a long sleep. I have strong medicine for this job, we will give it to all lazy people."[72] This arrogance created resentment or hostility and added to the uncertainty about the government's intentions and motivations.

Often the attitudes and behavior of local administrators toward rural people were similar to those of senior officials toward local staff. In Kenya, field staff were often controlled by senior officers who considered them lazy and unreliable and who were reluctant to delegate responsibility to them for even routine activities. As a result, nearly all of the attention of field officers went to implementing higher-level directives, and little went to discovering the needs of the people or to finding innovative ways of meeting them. Even when field officers attempted to comply, their initiatives were often ignored. "The poor experience with plan preparation at the field level," Trapman concluded from his study of agricultural development administration in Kenya, may be explained in part by "a lack of support in the past for proposals which field staff have taken the trouble to prepare. This has created a disillusioned attitude toward further efforts in this direction. The same applies to the preparation of estimates annually by district and provincial staff, which are rarely given consideration in annual estimates discussions."[73] Despite the rhetoric in Kenya's national plans about the importance of bottom-up rural development planning and the need to involve rural people in decision making, the district development committees were designed primarily to be coordinating mechanisms through which technical officers, local administrators, and members of Parliament might reconcile their differences over resource allocations. The committees were created to approve the technical decisions of district and province officials rather than to participate actively in development planning. The district planning manual issued by the Ministry of Finance and Planning clearly instructed district development officers and technical staff to take control of the planning process and warned that the DDOs should "not begin to see the DDC (because of the new emphasis on district planning) as the real arena where actual planning will take place."[74] Distrust of rural people and leaders was implicit in many of the directions given to the DDOs; both the competence and the political motivations of rural people were continually called into question.

Fear and Distrust of Government
Officials by Rural People

Implementation of decentralization in East Africa was also hampered by the rural population's distrust of government officials and their unwillingness to believe the government's promises. This mutual distrust often led local staff to identify and select projects without consulting rural people and encouraged local residents to sabotage or undermine development projects they did not want or understand or that they felt were not in their interests. Rural people refused to participate in family planning clinics in some areas of Kenya because they thought the programs were established to castrate men before drafting them into the armed forces. They did not allow land to be used for agricultural demonstrations in other places, fearing that government would later take over the improved property. Rural road construction was disrupted by some rural villagers who thought that the new roads would allow government patrols to catch stock raiders more easily.[75] Because they did not always understand the rationale for programs chosen by regional or district officials, villagers in Tanzania often refused to participate in local development activities and limited their involvement to those projects providing immediate social benefits — such as schools, clinics, and water supply facilities — for which the central government paid recurrent costs. But local contributions were more difficult to obtain for other projects, and participation came only through pressures and threats by local officials.[76] The threats created resentment and led rural people to question further the motivation and intent of government officials.

Resource Scarcities

Decentralization programs in East Africa were also obstructed by the scarcity of resources, especially money and skilled professionals, needed to carry them out.

Shortages of Skilled Personnel
at the Local Level

In each of the three East African countries, problems with implementing administrative decentralization and area development planning resulted from serious shortages of trained manpower to perform local functions. Shortages of trained personnel plagued every level of government in these countries, but those skilled technicians and managers who were available were quickly claimed by national ministries and public corporations, leaving local administrative units chronically short of talent. Local posts were usually seen as "hardship duty," temporary jobs to be held until a promotion — a post in the national capital — was received. The unwillingness of many trained officials, especially those who obtained their education abroad, to serve in local posts weakened the ability of local units to participate effectively in development planning and administration.

A World Bank evaluation of the ujamaa program in Tanzania noted that decentralization has dispersed skilled personnel to regions and districts, further weakening the administrative capacity of central government ministries. "Weak leadership and management have proved, and will continue to prove [to be] very serious problems. The field staff assigned to the ujamaa villages — agricultural field agents and cooperative and ujamaa village field assistants — cannot provide much help. They are ill-equipped to provide assistance of a technical much less organizational nature," the evaluators concluded. "In addition to being very young and inexperienced, the vast majority of them have weak technical training." The pressure on the small number of skilled technical and managerial personnel in Tanzania had become so great as a result of decentralization by the mid-1970s that the World Bank team predicted that "it will be a long time before the various key positions can be filled by professionals."[77] Because of the shortages of trained personnel, government was able to provide only limited technical assistance to farmers.

In Kenya the vast majority of skilled technicians and managers were concentrated in Nairobi. But as USAID evaluators pointed out, "the numbers of adequately trained personnel are sufficient to meet only the principal needs for the top levels of the public and private sectors." Even top-level administrators had only technical training and little or no managerial experience. The USAID analysts concluded that "management capability at this and the middle level is woefully lacking and is having an increasingly negative impact on implementation of development programs." Demand for agricultural technicians to implement existing development programs was expected to outpace the capacity or training institutions to provide them.

The Sudan had the most severe shortages of skilled personnel, even within central ministries. Devolution, and the brain drain of technically skilled Sudanese to high-paying jobs in Saudi Arabia and other oil-producing countries, exacerbated the problem. Personnel shortages seriously impeded decentralization in the Sudan and limited the ability of provincial administrators to provide even basic services.

Staffing problems were especially severe in the Southern Region, where a long civil war had depleted the ranks of younger administrators. In 1976 nearly half of all administrative, professional, and technical positions in the Southern Regional Government were still unfilled, and nearly one-third of the clerical and 15 percent of the unclassified positions were vacant. Widespread disruption of primary and secondary education and destruction of schools left the majority of southern people illiterate, making it nearly impossible to find adequate numbers of qualified candidates for technical training and education. The 3 million people of the Southern Sudan were served by only 54 medical doctors, 18 nursing sisters, and 285 health paraprofessionals in 1979. A year earlier, only two of the provinces had assistant commissioners for health, and the shortage of health officers made the supervision of paraprofessionals difficult.[79] An evaluation of decentralization in Southern Darfur Province summarized the effects of these conditions concisely: "If staff are not moved to the provinces and the corresponding resource allocations are not made to allow them to work and live there satisfactorily, then the success of the whole policy of decentralization will be jeopardized."

Financial Constraints and Limited
Revenue-Raising Capacity at the
Local Level

The greatest ambiguity in decentralization policy was the insistence of national leaders on transferring planning and administrative functions without providing localities with sufficient financial resources or adequate legal powers to collect and allocate revenues. These financial limitations were aggravated by national economic problems. From the mid-1970s, all three countries faced serious balance-of-payments problems, high rates of inflation, rising costs of fuel, and rapid increases in recurrent expenditures. All became increasingly dependent on scarce foreign capital. Even Kenya, which had the most stable financial situation, required at least $400 million a year in foreign financing to undertake planned development activities through the early 1980s.[81] The costs of social services demanded by

ujamaa villages in Tanzania increased recurrent expenditures there
beyond the government's ability to pay. National financial problems
in Tanzania slowed progress on decentralization. The Prime Minister's Office, which coordinated regional planning, had been given
only about 10 percent of the total development budget. In 1977 the
government asked foreign assistance donors to increase their aid, a
request that recognized Tanzania's inability to finance local and regional development activities.[82]

In the Sudan, domestic savings were inadequate to finance new
investments without extensive foreign aid and domestic bank borrowing. From 1970 to 1977 the central government's deficits rose from a
little more than 3 percent to over 10 percent of gross domestic product.
The increasing deficits were temporarily controlled in 1978 by imposing tight constraints on current expenditures, but they adversely
affected completion and maintenance of projects already under way.
In 1979, the government again faced sharply rising deficits. The
inflation rate fluctuated between 20 and 30 percent a year in the late
1970s, balance-of-payments deficits were about a half-billion dollars,
and foreign debt service was one billion dollars in arrears.[83] Financial
problems forced the government to revise the National Plan for
1977-1983 only a year after it was published.[84] These severe financial
constraints were exacerbated by the inability of many central ministries to spend the available funds. In the years between 1971 and 1978,
for example, the Ministry of Health had been able to spend only 30 to
66 percent of its appropriated funds, except for one in which it slightly
overspent, because of administrative inefficiency within the ministry
and the inability of the Ministry of Public Works to construct health
facilities.[85]

The shortage of operating and development funds in the Sudan
cast serious doubts on the feasibility or wisdom of devolution. The
People's Assembly Committee that evaluated the results of the Local
Government Act in 1976 was blunt in its conclusions: "It became
apparent that the insufficiency of funds was the basic cause . . . of
weaknesses . . . in the institutions of the People's Local Government
and of turning them into empty skeletons," the committee reported.
"It also . . . killed any ambitions or hope for developing current
services, let alone for presenting new services to the people."[86]

A detailed study of decentralization in Southern Darfur Province
of the Sudan during 1976 revealed that the financial resources transferred to the province through the budget were far below amounts
needed to implement functions transferred from the central minis-

tries. The Ministry of Finance cut the budget requested by the province executive council by 50 percent, and the province was never reimbursed for minor public works expenditures. Moreover, the central government increased the amounts of local taxes that the province would have to collect, resulting in a severe shortfall in revenues that constrained the executive council's ability to provide services or undertake development projects.[87]

In much of the Sudan the revenue base was simply too small to provide adequate tax resources. Those that could be imposed on subsistence economies, such as personal property taxes, were difficult to assess and collect, as were nonproductive personal property levies, on which most provinces depended.

"Environmental" Constraints

Finally, the implementation of decentralization in East Africa was inhibited by a set of adverse "environmental" conditions.

Inadequate Physical Infrastructure, Transport, and Communications Linkages

The ability of localities in all three countries to carry out development responsibilities was limited by adverse physical conditions and inadequate physical infrastructure, transportation facilities, communications networks, and roads. Physical conditions in the countryside limited the interaction among local and central government administrators and the ability of local officials to mobilize resources, supervise field personnel, distribute services, and disseminate information.

In the Sudan only a few surfaced highways connected Khartoum to eastern and central provinces; large parts of the north, west, and south were inaccessible. Some river transport allowed travel to the south, but equipment was old and inadequate. The national railway system that connected Port Sudan and Khartoum was decrepit; tracks were poorly maintained and much of rolling stock was in disrepair. Sudan Airways provided only limited service to some of the larger towns in the interior. Whatever coordination took place depended on infrequent personal communications. Many provinces lacked cable, wireless, or telex communications equipment. and local officials often could not communicate with either the national capital or with many towns and villages within their jurisdictions. The inadequacy of physical infrastructure and transport, combined with serious financial problems and administrative inefficiency, severely limited local administrative activities and created physical obstacles to widespread participation in local decision making.[88]

Similar problems were found in Tanzania and Kenya. In Tanzania, there were less than 34,000 kilometers of roads in 1979; only about 10 percent of them were of all-weather construction, and those were not well maintained. Villages not directly connected to a paved road were isolated much of the time. The USAID Mission in Tanzania estimated that only a small percentage of all farm families in Tanzania lived within a day's walking distance of an access road, making it difficult or impossible to distribute government services or information to them.[89] Trapman observes that in many parts of Kenya, "accessibility is one of the major problems of providing an extension service to a mass of small-scale farmers, with only a limited number of extension staff, who lack proper transportation facilities and supplies."[90] Inadequately surfaced roads and unreliable transportation forced conscientious agricultural extension workers to spend up to five hours a day traveling to and from locations where farmers lived.

*Unintegrated and Unarticulated
Settlement Systems*

The lack of sufficient physical infrastructure, transportation, and communications were symptomatic of a more serious problem that inhibited decentralized planning and management in East African countries. These nations have spatial systems that are not conducive to equitable development, the integration of urban and rural areas, or interaction among communities. Services and facilities are highly concentrated in one or a few large metropolitan centers, and the vast majority of the population is dispersed in villages that are too small to support productive functions or services, or scattered on physically isolated and inaccessible farmsteads. Market towns and middle-sized cities that might effectively link larger towns with rural areas are few in number and unevenly distributed. Settlements of all sizes are only weakly linked to each other or to larger places, constraining interaction among them.

Most of the Sudan's 16 million people were dispersed over a nation the size of Western Europe, and had little or no access to regional or local markets, agricultural inputs, or other basic resources. Physicians and health care facilities were concentrated in urban centers around Khartoum and Gezira provinces, where each public health care unit served from 3,000 to 4,000 people, compared to up to 15,000 people in other provinces.[90] Rural settlements had few basic services or facilities and were largely inaccessible for marketing or trade. Moreover, the costs of providing services and facilities to these small, scattered settlements were extremely high, and existing facilities were not used efficiently.[91] "Without access to markets, inputs, education, health and other services," the USAID Mission in the Sudan pointed out, "development of the traditional market sector cannot occur."[92] Physical isolation, lack of widely dispersed market centers, inadequate numbers of middle-sized cities, and weak linkages among them constrained production and trade in much of the Sudan and inhibited interaction, especially in peripheral rural regions such as the Southern Sudan.[93]

In Kenya, larger urban centers, favored by concentrated investment in infrastructure, services, and productive facilities, grew, while many rural districts were bypassed by economic progress. Disparities in income and wealth between major metropolitan centers such as Nairobi and Mombasa and rural areas without extensive urban settlements increased during the 1970s.[94] Studies of distribution of services and facilities among districts in Kenya reveal "the sparcity of at least some of the essential services and interregional linkages in major parts or all of the well populated districts of Lamu, Meru, Kisii, Siaya, Elgeo Marakwet, Baringo, Narok and Kajiado, as well as the more sparsely populated districts in northern and northeastern Kenya."[95] The inadequacy of market towns and middle-sized cities left many rural districts without services and facilities that only larger settlements could support, and isolated them from larger economic and administrative centers. The lack of even bus, telephone, or mail service in these areas restricted participation in development planning and management.

Most important, perhaps, the peripheral settlements were politically isolated. Political linkages are crucial for decentralization. "Without well-developed linkages — which we define as valued and stable networks of communications and exchange of resources — between government and members of society, public policy cannot be formulated to respond to the needs of the population," Barkan insists.[96] The patterns of political linkage in Tanzania, Kenya, and the

Sudan were clearly influenced and constrained by the spatial development pattern. Barkan correctly observes that "as in many other
Third World societies, the linkages that exist between the center and
the periphery in Kenya and Tanzania are not spatially extensive, or
intensive, in terms of the volume of communications and resources
they transmit. Most political linkages in Kenya and Tanzania parallel
those of the economy, and are therefore most developed between
urban areas and those rural areas that are centers of production of
cash crops for export."[97]

Weaknesses in Local Organizational
Infrastructure and Linkages

Finally, the disappointing results of decentralization in East Africa
can be explained by the absence of or weaknesses in supporting
institutions — both public and private — needed to complement and
bolster the managerial capacity of local governments, and by the
weaknesses in linkages and interaction between central and local
administrations. Experience with decentralization and rural development in other parts of the Third World have found that a wide
variety of local institutions must contribute to agricultural production
and rural development and that they must be complementary and
integrated. Services and technologies supporting rural development
must mutually reinforce each other. Credit delivered without technical assistance, higher-yielding seed varieties, fertilizers, irrigation,
and improved marketing, for instance, has little impact on production
and income in rural areas. Institutions must be linked both vertically
and horizontally to provide a hierarchy of services and to increase the
quality and reliability of service delivery. In their studies of local
organization in Asia, Uphoff and Esman "found no case where only
one institution was carrying the full responsibility for rural development and where *complementarities* among institutions were not as
important as what the institutions themselves did."[98]

David Leonard also concluded from his study of the organization
of agricultural development in Kenya that "the key concept in rural
administration is *linkages*. The days of autonomous agricultural development are ended. The development of the small farm sector is
critically dependent on government support. The state develops new
agricultural technologies, promotes and finances their acceptance
and determines the dynamism of their growth through price and other

controls."[99] At the same time, central government alone cannot stimulate and sustain agricultural production and rural development. Ultimately, progress depends on the initiative of individual farmers and on the local "organizational environment" to provide support for all aspects of agricultural production, marketing, and distribution and to supplement those services and facilities provided by local administrative units or governments that make living in rural areas tolerable. "There are too many unique local opportunities that are profitable to exploit and location-specific problems that need urgent solution for rural development to be commanded completely by central agricultural planners," Leonard argues. "Where the efforts of the small farmer and the national authorities are closely and effectively linked by a network of local organizations, rural development does occur more rapidly."[100]

But in all three countries, the systems of supporting institutions at the local level — and especially those concerned with agricultural production — were weak. Where linkages existed they tended to be predominantly top-down control mechanisms rather than systems of mutually beneficial, cooperative, and reciprocal interaction. A World Bank survey of the agricultural sector in the Sudan noted that in 1978, only about 200 crop extension and a few range management, land use, and forestry agents were available to serve farmers. Those agents deployed to the provinces usually remained in the capitals and were inaccessible to most farmers. But evaluators reported that rapid expansion of agricultural extension would have little immediate impact on decision making or production because few provinces had applied agricultural research institutions.[101] Moreover, there were few well-organized public or private institutions to supply productive farmers or rural entrepreneurs with materials and equipment. A potentially profitable poultry industry remains underdeveloped because there were no rural enterprises to supply mixed feeds, breeding equipment, or vaccines. Small-scale farmers cannot easily obtain credit, seeds, irrigation equipment, or pump servicing.[102]

The functions usually performed by private enterprises in nonsocialist countries were the responsibilities of parastatal organizations in the Sudan, and with a few exceptions they were poorly organized and managed. Most public corporations made claims on the government budget instead of contributing to it. With the exception of some of the heavily financed organizations in the Gezira scheme, moreover, cooperatives in most provinces were inefficiently managed, usually by nonprofessional local leaders who were frequently replaced. The resulting "confusion and inconsistency of leadership leaves the cooperatives in a dysfunctional state, incapable of weighing alternatives or making sound decisions," USAID analysts concluded.[103] Agricultural cooperatives in the Sudan were chronically short of operating capital and credit; most lacked mechanisms for generating savings, and even those that could mobilize meager surpluses had nowhere to invest them. Rural cooperatives and extension services, moreover, were not supported by national ministries. "Backup support from the Ministry [of Cooperation] is weak in such areas as training, materials, promotion, general supervision and planning because of communications, transport and funding constraints," a USAID technical assistance team discovered. "Headquarters people rarely get to the field," and the staff of the Ministry of Cooperation is "spread so thin that its impact at the village level is negligible in terms of meaningful support and extension services."[104]

The lack of agricultural research and extension services in Tanzania contributed to low agricultural productivity and the paucity of trained village leaders to implement ujamaa programs. The ability of villagers to participate in development planning and management was seriously constrained by inadequate technical assistance from supporting institutions.[105]

IMPLICATIONS FOR IMPROVING
THE IMPLEMENTATION OF
DECENTRALIZATION POLICIES

The experience with decentralization in East Africa suggests that programs could have been more successful if they had been more carefully planned, closely supervised, and strongly supported. A more incremental and sequential approach — tailored to the capacities of local communities to carry out new development functions and to the availability of essential resources — would have been more appropriate than the rapid and comprehensive reforms proposed in these three countries.[106] Crucial political, economic, and social preconditions must be established before decentralization becomes feasible on a large scale, and other conditions must be encouraged as decentralization occurs. The experience in East Africa also suggests that successful implementation involves far more than simply declaring a policy of bottom-up decision making, reorganizing the administrative structure, and creating new local or district planning procedures.[107] Both central government and local communities must be committed to the philosophy of decentralization and to popular participation in decision making. Widespread political support must be generated among national political leaders for transferring planning, decision-making, and managerial authority to field agencies or to lower levels of administration. Until a solid base of political support for decentralization is established, there can be little real change in the way decisions are made and carried out, regardless of administrative and procedural reforms.

This support must also extend to the line agencies of the central bureaucracy, and it is likely that they will be willing to transfer or delegate functions only if they see that decentralization offers them new opportunities. Thus, provisions must be made to strengthen the administrative and technical capacity of central government agencies to perform supporting functions at the same time that planning and managerial functions are delegated or devolved to localities. Sustained political support requires effective channels of political participation or representation through which rural people can express their needs and press their claims.

All of this, in turn, requires changes in attitudes and behavior. Centrist, control-oriented, and paternalistic attitudes are incompatible with the philosophy of decentralization. Training programs must emphasize the facilitative roles that the civil service can perform in a decentralized system. Attention must be given to overcoming the resistance — and to attaining the cooperation — of local elites and traditional leaders. Ultimately, the successful implementation of decentralization requires trust and respect between citizens and public officials and recognition or the important roles that each can perform in the development process. In planning decentralization programs, therefore, provisions must be made for strengthening leadership and administrative capacity within rural communities and for mobilizing the leadership, knowledge, and skills that already exist.

The functions transferred or assigned to local administrative units must be suited to their current or potential managerial capacities and to available resources. Functions should be allocated to local units incrementally, as they meet performance criteria. More complex functions should be transferred only after local units increase their administrative capacities and resources. Decentralization laws must be written concisely, and regulations and directives should describe clearly the relationships among and obligations of officials and citizens, the allocation of functions among units, and the roles and duties of leaders at each level. The procedures for local participation in development planning and administration must be kept relatively simple and not require special technical skills or resources that would exclude all but the elite. They should be kept flexible and adaptable. Communications systems should facilitate mutual interaction, exchange of information, cooperation, and conflict resolution, rather than simply disseminating instructions from the central government.

The East African experience shows clearly that the success of decentralization depends on finding ways of increasing local resources through intergovernmental transfers or by assisting localities to raise the revenues needed to carry out their new responsibilities.

Finally, the East African cases illustrate the importance of creating environmental conditions conducive to decentralized governance. Local administrative and government units need a network of institutions to support them in carrying out development activities. Physical infrastructure, transport, and communications linkages are needed in areas where decentralization is to be promoted. Services and facilities must be distributed in a way that encourages the growth of a well-articulated and integrated settlement system through which people can participate effectively in development planning and administration.

NOTES

1. U.S. Agency for International Development, Office of Rural Development, "Managing Decentralization," Project Paper, mimeographed (Washington, DC: U.S. International Development Cooperation Agency, 1979), p. 24.

2. World Bank, *The Assault on World Poverty* (Baltimore: Johns Hopkins University Press, 1975), pp. 90-98.

3. United Nations Development Program (UNDP), *Rural Development: Issues and Approaches for Technical Cooperation*, Evaluation Study no. 2 (New York: UNDP, 1979), p. 104.

4. For a detailed discussion see Dennis A. Rondinelli, *Administrative Decentralization and Area Development Planning in East Africa: Implications for United States Aid Policy*, Occasional Paper no. 1 (Madison, WI: Regional Planning and Area Development Project, University of Wisconsin, 1980), especially pp. 21-54.

5. Republic of Kenya, *Development Plan 1970-1974* (Nairobi: The Government Printer, 1969), p. 4.

6. A review of early experience can be found in *Local Government and Politics in the Sudan,* ed. John Howell (Khartoum: Khartoum University Press, 1974).

7. Louis Picard, "Socialism and the Field Administrator: Decentralization in Tanzania," *Comparative Politics,* vol. 12, no. 4 (July 1980): 439-457; quote on p. 450.

8. Michaela von Freyhold, *Ujamaa Villages in Tanzania: Analysis of a Social Experiment* (London: Heinemann, 1979), p. 191.

9. See Musa Mahgoub Hamad El-Nil, "The New System of Local Government," *The People's Local Government Journal,* vol. 4, no. 3 (December 1975): 1-26.

10. Republic of Kenya, *Development Plan 1970-1974,* p. 14. The deficiencies in national planning generally are outlined in Dennis A. Rondinelli, "National Investment Planning and Equity Policy in Developing Countries: The Challenge of Decentralized Administration," *Policy Sciences,* vol. 10, no. 1 (August 1978): 45-74; and Dennis A. Rondinelli, "Administration of Integrated Rural Development: The Politics of Agrarian Reform in Developing Countries," *World Politics,* vol. XXI, no. 3 (April 1979): 389-416. Some of these problems in East Africa are discussed in Christopher Trapman, *Changes in Administrative Structure: A Case Study of Kenyan Agricultural Development* (London: Overseas Development Institute, 1974); and John Burrows, *Kenya: Into the Second Decade* (Baltimore: Johns Hopkins University Press, 1975).

11. Republic of Kenya, *Development Plan 1970-1974,* p. 2.

12. A more detailed discussion can be found in World Bank, *Agricultural Sector Survey, Kenya,* vol. II (Washington, DC: World Bank, 1974), annex 8.

13. Republic of Kenya, *Development Plan 1974-1978,* Part I (Nairobi: The Government Printer, 1974), pp. 23-24.

14. *Ibid.,* p. 111.

15. University of Nairobi, Institute of Development Studies, *A Manual for Rural Planning* (Nairobi: Ministry of Finance and Planning, 1974), appendix A.

16. See G. K. Helleiner, "Socialism and Economic Development in Tanzania," *Journal of Development Studies,* vol. 8, no. 2 (1972): 183-204, for a detailed description of Tanzania's development policies.

17. R. P. Lawrence, P. L. Raikes, G. G. Saylor, and D. Warner, "Regional Planning in Tanzania: Some Institutional Problems," *Eastern Africa Journal of Rural Development,* vol. V, nos. 1-2 (1974): 10-45.

18. *Ibid.,* pp. 15-16.

19. Opening speech of Minister of Economic Affairs and Development Planning, Conference on Regional Economic Secretaries, 1970; quoted *ibid.,* p. 17.

20. See P. Abraham and F. Robinson, *Rural Development in Tanzania: A Review of Ujamaa,* Studies in Employment and Rural Development no. 14, mimeographed (Washington, DC: World Bank, 1974), pp. 8-13.

21. The organizational structure of the Tanzanian development system is described in Diana Conyers, "Organization for Development: The Tanzanian Experience," *Journal of Administration Overseas,* vol. 13, no. 3 (July 1974): 438-448; U.S. Agency for International Development, *Tanzania: Arusha Planning and Village Development Project,* Project Paper no. 621-0143 (Washington, DC: USAID, 1978); and Walter J. Sherwin, *Decentralization for Development: The Concept and Its Implications in Ghana and Tanzania* Development Studies Program Occasional Paper no. 2 (Washington, DC: USAID, 1977).

22. Sherwin, *Decentralization for Development,* pp. 12-13.

23. See John Markie, "Ujamaa Villages in Tanzania: A Possible Solution to the Problems of the Rural Poor," *Land Reform, Land Settlement and Cooperatives,* no. 1 (1976): 54-76.

24. The background of the *ujamaa* program is discussed in detail in Helge Kjekshus, "The Tanzanian Villagization Policy: Implementation Lessons and Ecological Dimensions," *Canadian Journal of African Studies,* vol. XI, no. 2 (1977): 269-282; see also Michaela von Freyhold, "The Problems of Rural Development and the Politics of Ujamaa Viijini in Handeni," *The African Review,* vol. 6, no. 2 (1976): 36-64.

25. Lionell Cliffe, "Planning Rural Development," *Development and Change,* vol. 3, no. 3 (1972): 77-98; quote on p. 84.

26. See Abraham and Robinson, *Rural Development in Tanzania,* pp. 24-32.

27. Michael Lofchie, "Agrarian Socialism in the Third World: The Tanzanian Case," *Comparative Politics,* vol. 8, no.3 (April 1976): 479-499; quote on p. 486.

28. See Musa Mahgoub Hamad El-Nil, "The New System," pp. 1-26.

29. Sudan Socialist Union, *Charter for National Action,* p. 13; quoted *ibid.,* p. 22.

30. Democratic Republic of the Sudan, *The People's Local Government Act, 1971,* Chapter III, Section 6 (1).

31. *Ibid.,* Chapter III, Section 6 (6).

32. *Idem.*

33. Typically, the provincial council warrant included all of the following duties, as outlined in the Local Government Act of 1971: (a) to issue orders establishing and regulating the imposition of local taxes and fees; (b) to establish regulations and laws concerning public order and security; (c) to create temporary taxes on recreational activities or commodities in order to finance any public project in the province; (d) to prepare annual budget proposals for the province and approve expenditures appropriated to local councils in the province; (e) to recommend proposals for projects and schemes for development to appropriate central government ministries; (f) to suggest improvements in the operation and administration of institutions within the province to appropriate ministries; (g) to establish, administer, or participate in any commercial or development projects that are self-sustaining and consistent with the national development plan; and (h) to oversee the work of ministries and government departments performing functions in the province and carry out any other duties specified in the warrant for the council.

34. Democratic Republic of the Sudan, *The People's Local Government Act,* Chapter V, Sections 19-26.

35. See K. M. Zein, "The Practice of Public Administration in the Sudan: A Study of a District Center" (Ph.D. diss., Erasmus University, Rotterdam, 1978), Ch. 7.

36. John Howell, "Administration and Rural Development Planning: A Sudanese Case," *Agricultural Administration,* vol. 4 (1977): 99-120.

37. Quoted in Democratic Republic of the Sudan, The People's Assembly, *Final Report of the Selected Committee for Study and Revision of People's Local Government,* translation, mimeographed (Khartoum: The People's Assembly, 1976), p. 24. Referred to hereafter as *Final Report.*

38. Sudan News Agency, *Daily Bulletin,* issue no. 2513 (December 12, 1977), p. 9.

39. Sudan News Agency, *Daily Bulletin,* issue no. 3058 (June 17, 1979), pp. 9-19; quote on p. 14.

40. Sudan News Agency, *Daily Bulletin,* issue no. 2922, (February 2, 1979), pp. 4-6.

41. Quoted in Abdel Moniem Awad El Rayah, "SSU Central Committee Meeting: An Uncompromising Speech," *Sudanow,* vol. 4, no. 4 (April 1979), p. 9.

42. Joel D. Barkan, "Comparing Politics and Public Policy in Kenya and Tanzania," in *Politics and Public Policy in Kenya and Tanzania,* ed. J. D. Barkan and J. J. Okumu (New York: Praeger, 1979), pp. 3-40.

43. Richard N. Blue and James H. Weaver, "A Critical Assessment of the Tanzanian Model of Development," *Agricultural Development Council Reprints,* no. 30 (July 1977): 18.

44. Jon R. Moris, "Administrative Authority and the Problem of Effective Agricultural Administration in East Africa," *The African Review,* vol. 2 (1972): 105-146; quote p. 116.

45. Barkan, "Comparing Politics," p. 27.

46. Moris, "Administrative Authority," p. 113.

47. See J. W. Leach, "The Kenya Special Rural Development Programme," *Journal of Administration Overseas,"* vol. 13, no. 2 (April 1974): 358-365.

48. K. J. Davey, G. W. Glentworth, M. O. Khalifa, and M. S. Idris, eds., *Local Government and Development in the Sudan: The Experience in Southern Dafur Province* (Khartoum: Academy of Administration and Professional Sciences, Ministry Peoples Local Government, 1976), p. 4.

49. Lionel Cliffe, "'Penetration' and Rural Development in the East African Context," in L. Cliffe, J. S. Coleman, and M. R. Doornbos, eds., *Government and Rural Development in East Africa* (The Hague: Martinus Nijhoff, 1977), pp. 19-50; quote at p. 42.

50. Juma Volter Mwapachu, "Operation Planned Villages in Rural Tanzania: A Revolutionary Strategy for Development," *The African Review,* vol. 6, no. 1 (1976): 1-16.

51. Freyhold, "The Problems of Rural Development," p. 55.

52. Barkan, "Comparing Politics and Public Policy," p. 29.

53. Sherwin, *Decentralization for Development,* p. 19.

54. John Howell, "Administration of Rural Development Planning: A Sudanese Case," *Agricultural Administration,* vol. 4 (1977): 99-120; quote on p. 109.

55. Goran Hayden, "Administration and Public Policy," in Barkan and Okumu, *Politics and Public Policy,* pp. 93-113; quote on pp. 102-103.

56. *Idem.*

57. Mwapachu, "Operation Planned Villages," p. 5.

58. For a more detailed discussion of this point, see Frank Holmquist, "Class Structure, Peasant Participation and Rural Self-Help," in Barkan and Okumu, *Politics and Public Policy,* pp. 129-153.

59. See Holmquist, *ibid.,* pp. 144-145.

60. Cited in J. L. Weaver, "Factors Bearing Upon the Performance of the Sudanese Administrative System" mimeographed (Khartoum: USAID Mission Sudan, 1979), pp. 3-4.

61. John R. Moris, "The Transferability of Western Management Concepts and Programs: An East African Perspective," in *Education and Training for Public Sector Management in Developing Countries,* ed. L. D. Stifel, J. S. Coleman, and J. E. Black (New York: Rockefeller Foundation, 1976), pp. 73-84.

62. J. R. Nellis, "Three Aspects of the Kenyan Administrative System," *Cultures et Developpment,* vol. 5 (1973): 541-570.

63. *Ibid.,* p. 548.

64. Trapman, *Changes in Administrative Structure,* p. 34.

65. Oluwadare Aguda, "The Sudan Civil Service 1964-1971," *Quarterly Journal of Administration,* vol. 6 (April 1972): 333-347, quote on p. 33; see also Al-Agab A. Al

124   East Africa

Terafi, "Localization of Policies and Programming in the Sudan, 1945-1970," *Journal of Administration Overseas*, vol. 12 (April 1973): 125-135; and M. El Bashir, "Bureaucracy and Development: General Impressions from the Sudanese Experience," *African Administrative Studies*, no. 16 (1976): 21-25.

66. See Zein, "The Practice of Public Administration," pp. 39-47.

67. Quoted in Jakob J. Akol, "Old Attitudes Die Hard: Five Ministerial Views," *Sudanow*, vol. 2, no. 12 (December 1977): 15.

68. Howell, "Administration and Rural Development Planning," p. 109.

69. Zaki Ergas, "Why Did the Ujamaa Village Policy Fail? Towards a Global Analysis," *Journal of Modern African Studies*, vol. 18, no. 3 (1980): 387-410; quote on p. 389.

70. H.U.E. Thoden Von Velzen, "Staff, Kulaks and Peasants: A Study of a Political Field," in Cliffe, Coleman and Doornbos, *op. cit.*, pp. 221-250.

71. *Ibid.*, p. 228.

72. *Ibid.*, p. 231.

73. Christopher Trapman, *Changes in Administrative Structure*, p. 39. See also David K. Leonard, *Reaching the Peasant Farmer: Organization Theory and Practice in Kenya* (Chicago: University of Chicago Press, 1977).

74. University of Nairobi, *A Manual for Rural Planning*, p. 40.

75. Philip Mbithi and Carolyn Barnes, *A Conceptual Analysis of Approaches to Rural Development*, Discussion Paper no. 204, mimeographed (Nairobi: Institute of Development Studies, University of Nairobi, 1975), p. 5.

76. Sherwin, *Decentralization of Development*, p. 17.

77. Abraham and Robinson, *Rural Development in Tanzania*, p. 63. See also Paul Collins, "The Working of Tanzania's Rural Development Fund: A Problem in Decentralization," *East African Journal of Rural Development*, vol. 5 (1972): 144-162.

78. U.S. Agency for International Development, *Country Development Strategy Statement, Kenya 1980-1984* (Washington, DC: USAID, 1979), p. 5. Referred to hereafter as *CDSS, Kenya*.

79. The estimates are made in Democratic Republic of the Sudan, Southern Regional Ministry of Finance and Economic Planning, *Southern Regional Six Year Plan of Economic and Social Development, 1977/78-1982/83* (Juba: Directorate of Planning, 1977), pp. 27-28.

80. Davey et al., *op. cit.*, p. 19.

81. USAID, *CDSS, Kenya*, pp. 14-16.

82. USAID, *CDSS, Tanzania*, p. 35.

83. U.S. Agency for International Development, *Country Development Strategy Statement, FY 1981 Sudan*, (Washington: USAID, 1979), p. 18. Referred to hereafter as *CDSS, Sudan*.

84. International Monetary Fund, *Sudan: Recent Economic Developments*, (Washington: IMF, 1979), pp. 18-23.

85. The figures are cited in U.S. Agency for International Development, *Project Identification Document: Health Sector Support* (Khartoum: USAID Mission/Sudan, 1979), p. 22.

86. *Final Report*, p. 38; See also W. Ouma Oyugi, "Local Government and Development in Kenya," Discussion Paper no. 131 (Sussex: Institute of Development Studies, University of Sussex, 1978), for a discussion of similar problems in Kenya.

87. Davey et al., *op. cit.*, p. 38.

88. *Ibid.*, pp. 23-24.

89. USAID, *CDSS, Tanzania*, p. 31.

90. Trapman, *Changes in Administrative Structure*, p. 91; the argument is made in greater detail in Dennis A. Rondinelli and Kenneth Ruddle, *Urbanization and Rural Development: A Spatial Policy for Equitable Growth* (New York: Praeger, 1978).

91. USAID, *CDSS, Sudan*, p. 3.

92. *Ibid.*, p. 8.

93. *Ibid.*, p. 29.

94. See D.R.F. Taylor, "Spatial Aspects of the Development Process," in *The Spatial Structure of Development: A Study of Kenya*, ed. R. A. Obudho and D.R.F. Taylor (Boulder, CO: Westview Press, 1979), pp. 1-27.

95. Wayne McKim, "Patterns of Spatial Interaction," *ibid.*, pp. 176-200; quote on p. 195.

96. Joel D. Barkan, "Legislators, Elections and Political Linkage," in Barkan and Okumu, *Politics and Public Policy*, pp. 64-92; quote on p. 66.

97. *Idem.*

98. Norman Uphoff and Milton Esman, *Local Organization for Rural Development: Analysis of Asian Experience* (Ithaca: Cornell University Center for International Studies, 1974), pp. xi-xii.

99. Leonard, *Reaching the Peasant Farmer*, p. 210.

100. *Ibid.*, pp. 209-210.

101. World Bank, *Sudan Agricultural Sector Survey*, annex 9, p. 2.

102. *Ibid.*, p. 16.

103. U.S. Agency for International Development, *Blue Nile Rural Development Project Paper* (Khartoum: USAID/Sudan, 1978), p. 83.

104. *Ibid.*, p. 86.

105. Leonard, *Reaching the Peasant Farmer*, p. 213.

106. A more detailed set of suggestions for improving the implementation of decentralization policies was outlined in Dennis A. Rondinelli and Marcus D. Ingle, "Improving the Implementation of Development Programs: Beyond Administrative Reform," in *Institutional Capability for Regional Development*, ed. G. Shabbir Cheema (Singapore: Maruzen Asia, 1981).

107. The complexities are described in D. A. Rondinelli and K. Ruddle, "Political Commitment and Administrative Support: Preconditions for Growth-with-Equity Policy," *Journal of Administration Overseas*, vol. XVII, no. 1 (January 1978): 43-60; Dennis A. Rondinelli, "Administration of Integrated Rural Development: The Politics of Agrarian Reform in Developing Countries," *World Politics*, vol. XXXI, no. 3 (April 1979): 389-416; Uphoff and Esman, *Local Organization;* and various studies in Asian Center for Development Administration, *Approaches to Rural Development in Asia: The South Asian Experience* (Kuala Lumpur: ACDA, 1975), *passim.*

CHAPTER 5

DECENTRALIZATION IN NORTH AFRICA
Problems of Policy Implementation

John R. Nellis

The four North African states of the Maghreb region appear to be particularly unsuitable locales for decentralization in any form: political, economic, or administrative. A variety of powerful factors — history, culture and religion, the colonial experience, the constraints of underdevelopment, the ideologies and self-interest of the region's dominant elites — appear to have impelled the postcolonial regimes of Morocco, Algeria, Tunisia, and Libya to rely on centralist and centralizing development strategies and modes of governance. Nevertheless, the governments of all four of these countries now claim to have embarked on a process of putting power and responsibility into the hands of "the people" in their states. Throughout the region, the claim is that democratically elected, representative local institutions have been given — or are in the process of being given — jurisdiction over issues and areas formerly controlled solely by central-level decision makers. To back up the claim, all four governments point to various tasks, the power of regulation of which has been transferred from national bureaucrats to local councils, or at least to local officials. (In the formerly French-controlled parts of the Maghreb, a distinction is made between these processes. " Deconcentration" is used to refer to delegating responsibilities and capabilities to local-level officials of the central government; "decentralization" means the transfer of authority for certain fields of activity to locally elected councils.)

In Morocco, Algeria, and Tunisia these claims are buttressed by the assignment of cadres to supporting civil service positions in the local government system and by efforts to create training schools and special services for local government administrators (who will, however, continue to be central government employees). Libya has gone further; the entirety of its civil service has been disaggregated and devolved to locally based popular committees. These, supposedly, are directly and fully supervised by locally constituted basic popular congresses.

In all four of these situations one can uncover very little information on the key issue of local public finance, but what data are available indicate that performance has, of yet, nowhere matched stated intentions and that financial authority remains well entrenched in the center. On nonfinancial fronts, as well, the implementation of decentralization policies appears to be going rather slowly, partly due to extreme shortages of skilled personnel and equally to ingrained habits of deference to established central authority on the part of local officials, representatives, and the people. Libyan events may offer an exception to this conclusion; a journalist's report from Tripoli in September 1981 noted:

> The Libyan people, or at least those that a westerner is able to meet, seem to believe that their unique structure of peoples' congresses allow them all to have a say, and even a veto, over the foreign policy of their country. They are accustomed now to deciding for themselves on the building and operation of schools and health centres and industrial projects. In a country of only three million people, it is not impossible to make this kind of direct democracy function — after a fashion.[1]

Of course, one cannot assess Libyan system performance on the basis of a glimpse, no matter how intriguing. For the other three countries in the region, one does not even have many positive impressions to fall back on; the scholarly and journalistic assessments of decentralization efforts in Algeria, Tunisia, and Morocco have been essentially negative.

Still, decentralizing pressures and trends have begun to emerge in the Maghreb states. In this chapter I will try to show that these pressures are yielding concrete results that, while limited, are significant. Admittedly, any analysis of the issue must begin with a clear admission and thorough discussion of the strength of the factors that have contributed to centralization.

HISTORY

Foremost among these factors is a prevalent interpretation of regional history that explains both post-1500 North African "decadence" and the imposition of colonial rule in the nineteenth and twentieth centuries as stemming from the lack of a stable, coherent, powerful, and well-structured — in a word, centralized — state, which could compete effectively with the first emerging and then triumphant nation-states of Europe. Lucette Valensi, for example, writes of precolonial North Africa that "the limited nature of the state sometimes caused its citizens to lose sight of its necessity." She notes that in the region, especially Morocco, "there was almost no administrative apparatus — no salaried functionaries and no centralized administration whose employees were named by the government."[2] Another historian, Andrew Hess, describes North Africa in 1500 as "a large number of cohesive kin groups with no political center" and asserts the "chronic instability of a society made up of small units, each of which derived its inner cohesion from opposition to a changing exterior threat."[3] This malaise was of such force as to affect the Turkish rulers of much of the area: "Political decentralization became the main manifestation of Ottoman decline in North Africa."[4] Robert Montagne put the issue most succinctly: The "feebleness of the Arab states" in the whole of North Africa was "the result of the impotence of a central government."[5]

The most abundant and persuasive evidence to support the case for chronic, excessive decentralization comes from studies of the Moroccan situation, but historians and analysts, from Ibn Khaldoun onward, have reached the same conclusion concerning other parts of the region. L. Carl Brown attributes both the long-standing acquiescence of the rural peasantry to the Turkish Bey in Tunis and the inability of the precolonial system to maintain itself in the face of European pressures to the limited nature of the state.[6] Raphael Danziger's study of Abd al-Qadir portrays pre-1830 Algeria as a weak system, able to maintain internal equilibrium among its divided though interacting components, but neither sufficiently united nor sufficiently advanced technologically to resist European invasion.[7]

Historians attribute the deep divisions of Maghrebian precolonial societies to the area's geography, cultural systems, the eleventh-century invasions of the nomadic and supposedly civilization-destroying Beni Hilal, to Islam in general, to Ottoman divide and rule tactics, and to the area's quasi-feudal modes of production, "which had in common the absence of antagonistic classes and a relative inertia."[8]

All these factors meshed to create a balanced but severely fragmented and segmented precapitalist system, possessing cyclical and not forward movement. Despite its position on the very fringe of a Europe in ferment, despite its commercial and military interaction with the increasingly centralized and frequently threatening European powers, the Maghreb polity continued to function with

> a perfect coherence between the spiritual, economic and social aspects of its culture. That culture was, however, different from Europe's, particularly in that nothing arose within it to stimulate the society as a whole. Its population growth was too late and too abrupt; there was not enough vitality in urban crafts or foreign commerce; and there was no intellectual renewal. The Maghrib lived at a slower pace, and this no doubt was one of the reasons for its colonization yesterday and its underdevelopment today.[9]

In sum, the historian's picture of precolonial North Africa is that of a system caught in a permanent, and thus nondevelopmental, conflict between "forces of cohesion and forces of disintegration."[10]

The question is by no means settled as to which of the factors mentioned is most responsible for the failure to produce centralized state structures. Many modern Western observers favor the cultural and religious factors as the prime explanations. Neo-Marxist and indigenous scholars view the mode of production issue and the actions of the European powers as the major determinants. Few observers, even the most materialist in orientation, reject totally the cultural issue.

The point here is that a study of Maghrebian history from any methodological or ideological point of view supports the conclusion that lack of centralization was the prime cause for the region's "colonization yesterday and its underdevelopment today." Since that lack is widely viewed as responsible for the region's past and present difficulties, it is natural that postcolonial regimes have tended to stress the need for the unification of the society, usually by means of a strong and thoroughly centralized state apparatus.

CULTURE AND RELIGION

Most historians mention only in passing the decentralizing effects of the area's precolonial cultural systems. Anthropologists, not surprisingly, tend to view the effects of culture as of more than historical significance. That is, there is considerable agreement among anthropological students of the region that many decentralizing cultural traits either survived the colonial intrusion or were actually strengthened by the European presence. The continued existence of these traits helps to explain and justify the postcolonial centralist policies, the latter being viewed as necessary to overcome the powerful centrifugal forces embedded in Maghrebian culture.

What was or is this "culture"? From Cyrenaica to Morocco, and particularly in those rural areas peopled by Berbers or groups basing their sociopolitical systems on Berber models, one found until recently (and perhaps still finds) societies described as "segmented." The term refers to a complex cluster of behavior, organizational patterns, and attitudes. Ernest Gellner has summarized the core concept: " Divide that you not be ruled."[11] Segmented societies were entirely based on divisions that were *not* cross-cutting or overlapping, but rather that divided society into opposing and balancing sections. At every level in the social system there was an opposing "them" to the core "us." Segmentation was a system of permanent flux, of shifting allegiances and alliances in which each individual found himself or herself "at the centre of a series of concentric, 'nested' circles, a series of larger and larger groups to which he belongs, whose boundaries never cut across each other."[12] In such structural circumstances the difficulties of constructing a central state, and maintaining it once it was built, were enormous. And lest one think that the notion of segmentation simply describes some sort of normal, nonunified functioning of precapitalist societies, Gellner adds: "What defines a segmentary society is not that this [absence of cross-cutting ties] occurs, but that this is very nearly all that occurs."[13]

Once again, the strongest evidence to support the notion of a cultural tradition inhibiting state formation — a cultural tradition against which precolonial rulers struggled and the effects of which modern rulers still must deal with — comes from studies of rural

Morocco. Moreover, the notion of segmentation applies formally only to rural dwellers of Berber tradition. What of the large section of population living in cities, either far removed from or never touched by Berber cultural patterns, in and out of Morocco?

L. Carl Brown's superb study of precolonial Tunis portrays an urban Arab culture substantially different from that of the Berber tribes of the Atlas, but a culture that nonetheless was a hindrance to the formation of a central state. Urban Arab culture was conservative, hierarchical, and above all aloof: "The head of family preferred to bar himself from either the emulation or the envy of the outside world."[14] It was a culture that, according to Brown, "sought only to order . . . life in conformity with the existing patterns,"[15] in which one consciously avoided distinction and notions such as the belief that "men, working together, using their heads, would manage to make things better. They would probably make things worse."[16] A culture that saw the human being as neither "the measure of all things nor the master of his fate"[17] provided little support to the efforts at defensive modernization undertaken by a few of the more farsighted rulers. The customary balancing of numerous small groupings suited the Tunisian's sense of order, argues Brown — but it was a custom that eased the French takeover of 1881.

Thus, both history and culture are factors that contributed and continue to contribute to centralizing policies in the Maghreb, because of the negative examples they provide to modern leaders concerning the effects of excessive decentralization. The other factors to be considered are positive, in the sense that they contribute directly to centralizing trends.

One important positive factor is, supposedly, the Muslim religion. It was reformist Islamic religious figures and their followers who historically came closest to overcoming the decentralizing pressures and imposing a central state structure on the region as a whole. The Almoravids and the Almohads effectively disappeared at the end of the medieval era; their example is today remote — though it is important to note, in light of the recent resurgence of Islam, that religion was the mechanism that most effectively, for a time, welded the segmented Berbers into a united front.

In the modern, postcolonial period it has been observers of Algeria who have most frequently called attention to the centralizing inlfuence of religion. Bruno Etienne, a leading interpreter of Algerian affairs, has coined the unwieldy term "unanimitarism" to typify the prime policy of the independent Algerian regimes, which "consists of nationalizing all political action and in particular the entire socialization process."[18] This policy stems from a "unifying doctrine . . . in part socially radical," which asserts that strict central control is necessary "to impose from the top economic and social modernization."[19] Of course, many Third World regimes cloak rigid control in the guise of developmental need; what is unusual in Algeria's case is that observers such as Etienne attribute the roots of this policy to the country's religion, "which favors a type of unanimous consensus."[20] Etienne describes Algeria as a society so divided, indeed shattered, by colonialism that it was thrust back on the one factor that remained secure through the 130-year French period — the Muslim religion. When Algerians began openly to struggle against the French, their rallying cry was not *"Vive l'Algérie libre,"* but rather *"Vive l'Algérie musulmane."*[21] Etienne and others view Islam's stress on the unity of the community of believers as contributing directly to the political belief that all classes, groups, interests, and regions must be thoroughly integrated into an organic whole. The idea seems to be that just as Muslim theology tolerates no intermediaries between God and man, so too the ideal social order is one that places a morally proper leadership in a clear, direct, and unencumbered relationship with the citizenry. Etienne (and others) implies that separation of powers, checks and balances, and countervailing institutions appear alien to Islamic philosophical tradition and theological common sense. Obviously, this is debatable.

Nonetheless, the result in Algeria is what two other scholars, Jean Leca and Jean-Claude Vatin, view as "an obsession with organic unity."[22] Expanding on a Weberian notion, Leca and Vatin term the Algerian mode of governance as "sultanic," a system

> in which the leader seeks with more or less success to make himself independent of all groups having an autonomous base of power, whether these be institutional, political, administrative, or social.[23]

Quite clearly, this description could very well be applied to Libya, Tunisia and Morocco as well as Algeria; quite clearly, the suggestion is that religious norms play a major part in legitimizing this style of leadership; and quite clearly, the style is a major buttress of the centralization of state authority and power.

THE COLONIAL ADMINISTRATIVE INHERITANCE

Three of the four countries covered in this study were colonized by France. At the time of writing, a socialist government in France is embarking on a series of mildly decentralizing measures. The out-of-the-ordinary nature of these measures is conveyed by a statement in *Le Monde:* "The government's plan to call into question the ancestral practices of the French civil service, which since the time of Louis XI has constantly striven to put more power into the hands of Parisian bureaucrats, is nothing short of revolutionary."[24]

This centralist French administrative tradition was thoroughly applied to the North African colonies and protectorates, most intensely and for the longest period in Algeria (1830-1962) and somewhat less so in Tunisia (1881-1956) and Morocco (1912-1956). Protectorate status in the latter two countries did not prevent the French from erecting "a veritable parallel administration of intervention which was progressively substituted for the administration of the protected state."[25] All three countries were subjected to "the same type of direct administration,"[26] which was as — if not more — centralized and centralizing than that which existed in the metropole. The colonial administrators' quest for a "rational" system was not hampered by calls for reform from elected representatives of the indigenous populations — there being none.

In short, in North Africa the French instituted, or at least reinforced, an attitude that regarded the citizen as existing to serve the state, and not the reverse. The colonial mode of governance in general and the colonial bureaucracy in particular were neatly, strictly hierarchical. The function of subsidiary units was to respond correctly to the center's directives; the function of the center was to direct. A centralist philosophy and style were strongly supported by administrative procedures and accounting systems that vested all authority and monitoring functions in the center.

In North Africa, in spite of considerable lip service in all three formerly French countries to the notion of decentralization (the special case of Libya is discussed below), and in spite of considerable restructuring in Algeria of administrative forms, the results until very recently have been to strengthen the inherited administrative traditions rather than to restrict or dismantle them. As one Moroccan social scientist put it: "We suffer from a *double défaillance;* we inherited a rigid and inappropriate system, and we have retained and indeed strengthened it, while the French themselves have tried to correct its obvious faults."[27]

Most studies that touch on any aspect of administrative behavior in any of the former French states note the excessively centralized nature of planning and implementation systems, the related patronizing, rigid manner in which superiors direct their subordinates on what to do and how to do it, and the equally lofty manner in which these subordinates pass on these instructions, eventually to the citizenry at large.[28] This syndrome cannot totally be blamed on the French tradition. Two of the three countries have now had more than twenty-five years to divest themselves of unwanted inherited patterns, and Algeria has had both the resources and the opportunities to bring about drastic change in its twenty years of independence. Certainly, much of the explanation for reinforcement of the inherited centralist system is found in internal causes, which are dealt with later in this chapter. Nonetheless, the basic framework for a paternalistic, condescending, authoritarian, and highly centralized system was created by the French colonialists. And the French, for a variety of reasons, have had greater success than other colonialists in leaving behind the conviction that French institutions and procedures are the very best, indeed the only, models to emulate.

INTERNAL FACTORS

The remaining centralizing influences can be dealt with in a composite fashion, since they are relatively familiar factors that are not unique to North Africa but are found in all Third World and most of the First and Second worlds as well. These factors or justifications are internal in the sense that they derive from the local conditions of the postcolonial period and are not the result of a regional culture, religion, or dealings with outsiders. They can be grouped together under two headings: the pressures of Maghrebian underdevelopment, and the political nature and economic self-interest of dominant elites in North Africa.

PRESSURES OF UNDERDEVELOPMENT

A frequently, widely cited justification for centralist policies is that crises legitimate centralized control of the state apparatus. Just as in time of war or national emergency the most industrialized and stable of countries have relied on governments of national unity, so too must

Third World countries — plagued by ethnic divisions, dismal economic performance, and myriad other system-threatening events — take firm steps to impose a modicum of national integrity on their weak and fragile polities. The state of underdevelopment itself is the poor country's "moral equivalent of war"; the enemies of poverty, ignorance, and disease are so apparent, so pervasive, that a quasi-military, hierarchical, centralized form of organization is seen as not only defensible, but absolutely necessary.

Admittedly, none of the four countries dealt with in this study ranks among the poorest or most fragile of Third World states. Libya and Algeria, for obvious example, are energy exporters and have benefited accordingly. Tunisian economic performance in the period 1960-1979 was a remarkable 4.8 percent average annual increase (in real terms) of GNP per capita.[29] Even Morocco, the poorest of the four countries, is a major exporter of phosphates and is not without some economic hopes. Nonetheless, the pressures of underdevelopment weigh heavily throughout the entire region. This includes Libya, which, with its vast resources of oil and very small population, must still deal with the issue that few of its citizens have any training or skills in industry or technology. The Libyan energy industry was managed by Americans and Europeans, and now by Europeans alone, and worked by Egyptians and Tunisians — in effect, a list of the putative enemies of the Libyan state.[30]

In Tunisia, good overall economic performance has been accompanied by intransigent regional disequilibrium, by a pervasive belief that the fruits of growth have been inequitably distributed, and by increasing, and increasingly strident, demands for political liberalization. Algeria's energy wealth and massive investments in state-run industrialization programs mask rural stagnation, agricultural decline, and increasing discontent with bureaucratic ineffectiveness. Morocco has exhausted itself on an apparently unwinnable war to control the former Spanish Sahara. The country witnessed severe urban riots in June 1981 as people protested unemployment and high prices for basic necessities. In sum, none of the four countries' regimes can rest easy: There are Tunisian and Libyan dissidents in exile; the Algerian rulers must keep one eye on the army and the other on radical militants; and the remarkable feature of the Moroccan regime is not the number of its enemies but its surprising capacity to persist.

These general circumstances are sufficient to rationalize a centralizing ethos of control. When one adds to the list such factors as pressures for greater recognition of Berber language and culture in Algeria, the growth of fundamentalist Islamic movements of a somewhat antiregime tint in Tunisia and Morocco, the aura of instability that spills over into the region from its African, Near Eastern, and northern Mediterranean neighbors, and the intraregional bickering and outright destabilization efforts of one Maghrebian state against the other, one has a situation in which anything other than strong central rule is nearly unthinkable.

Still the list of centralizing factors is incomplete: Since the Maghreb countries have difficulty finding a sufficient number of competent people to staff their centralized administrative systems, how could they staff decentralized mechanisms, which almost certainly would require a larger number of skilled personnel? What incentives can reasonably be offered to move officials away from relatively comfortable capital or urban postings into rural or small-town assignments? The arguments supporting decentralization tend to be normative, or based on plausible but unproven scenarios. What precise, proven decentralization mechanisms exist which would convince Maghrebian leaders to run the risks of change?

A central fact of underdevelopment, of poverty in general, is the lack of "complex redundancy"[31] in resources and human skills, a lack of "variety and competition which provide alternative ways of getting things done."[32] Pervasive scarcity leads to the centralization of decisions concerning the allocation of desperately short resources. That is, underdevelopment increases the importance of every "little" decision regarding resource allocation. Since no allocation is merely routine or lacking in political import, every decision must be invested with as high and as much authority as possible. Decisions that in wealthy systems would be regarded as minor are dodged and passed along; central officers and offices become overloaded but seem incapable of delegating responsibility — perhaps because to do so would be suicidal in a zero-sum administrative climate.

Clearly, this general and negative portrait resembles the Maghrebian reality. It would be difficult to find an observer of the region who would dispute the notion that Maghrebian administrations are both overcentralized and inefficient. One cannot deny either the tremendous centralizing forces of underdevelopment in general or the fact that underdevelopment is a condition in which the Maghreb states still find themselves.

SELF-INTEREST OF THE DOMINANT ELITES

Finally in this survey of centralizing factors, one must note the fact that centralization has been very much in the self-interest, both political and economic, of the elites controlling the postcolonial Maghreb states. Scarcity of resources and lack of national unity may justify centralized administration and control, but it is evident that this justification masks much elite behavior aimed at self-enrichment and perpetuation of their position of power. Centralization facilitates these aims. Partially due to centralizing policies, these systems contain few strong judicial, administrative, or political mechanisms able to constrain the self-seeking actions of the powerful. Thus, control over allocation of societal resources has frequently meant unjustified personal use of those resources. Centralization has also served to mute competition for leadership posts, or at least channel it in ways which do not threaten the status of the upper echelons — who are generally responsible only to the all-directing, all-powerful head of state. In the Maghreb, with the possible exception of post-Boumedienne Algeria, and in spite of the extraordinary steps taken in Libya, ostensibly to debureaucratize and decentralize the government, the pattern is one of semideification of the head of state and rich, unjustified, and often illegal rewards for those in the ruling group. "Centralization" can thus be a misleading neutral euphemism for the authoritarian, antidemocratic rule of a clique, a class, an oligarchy, or a person.

This is not to say that the other factors considered above are *only* a smokescreen for self-interest. Rather, it is to point out the cumulative and generally negative effects of the set of factors that have contributed to centralization. Maghreb societies are poor; they possess some linguistic divisions; they have varying, potentially destabilizing intensities of attachment to ideological dogma; they have inherited a divisive cultural framework; they lack a strong attachment to the notion of countervailing powers or institutions. Thus, they are led to rely on highly centralized, personalized, and more or less unchecked leaderships to provide the unity and stability they need. They contain few possibilities or incentives, other than religion, for the growth of an ethos of self-sacrifice, either in the leading strata or in the populace at large. Centralization of policy initiation, centralized control over resource allocation — these practices surely arise because of a variety of determinants. But the elite-serving possibilities of this centralization are quickly perceived and seized.

The most popular explanation for this whole range of phenomena, at least among North African intellectuals and European observers of the region, is a modified form of class analysis. In this view, centralization of political and administrative activity is seen as part of a larger process in which a coalition of bureaucrats and essentially petit-bourgeois populists have captured the control of the postcolonial Maghreb states. The policies they put forward — expansion of the central state's machinery and control, reliance on parastatal industries, deemphasis of competing sources of interest aggregation and articulation — are uniformly centralist. The perspective of the class analysts leads them to present a wealth of explanatory detail on how and why postcolonial regimes of the type found in North Africa rely on and benefit from centralization.[33] The thrust of the class analysts' position is that in all four Maghreb countries the state is not dominated by a "true" bourgeoisie. If the bourgeois were dominant they would likely rely on the private sector, competitive parliamentary political mechanisms, and generally pluralist forms of competition and control to regulate the state and guarantee or "reproduce" their position of dominance. Obviously, these mechanisms would be decentralizing in their cumulative effect; equally obviously, such mechanisms have been generally absent or severely downplayed in the Maghreb. For the class analysts, the statist, centralized, not overtly competitive systems one finds in North Africa stem from the petit-bourgeois nature of the dominant strata. This class does not and cannot own the means of production, but it can control them by using the state apparatus — which it directs — to centralize and regulate the economy.[34] In this view, it follows logically that decentralization would run the risk of devolving power to the peasants and workers, or to the "real" bourgeoisie, which somehow has managed to survive. In short, the petit-bourgois control the state and must continue to control the state in a centralized manner if they are to perpetuate their dominance. One does not have to accept the revolutionary implications of this argument to realize that it presents a plausible explanation of Maghrebian centralization.

In sum, it is easy to find factors in North African history, culture, and present socioeconomic conditions to account for the pervasive emphasis on political and administrative centralization as the proper mode of governance and development. These factors are numerous and powerful, so much so that what is surprising is the strength of the recent pressures for decentralization.

PRESSURES FOR DECENTRALIZATION

The intellectual merits of the case for decentralization in general, and decentralized forms of administration and development policy implementation in particular, have been covered by Rondinelli and Cheema in their introductory chapter in this volume.[35] The arguments they advance apply to the situation found in North Africa. That is, in the Maghreb, starting roughly in the early 1970s, there has been a growing realization that the centralized policies pursued have not resulted in adequate levels of economic production or distribution and have not contributed to administrative effectiveness and efficiency. Writing in 1976, for example, F. Rivier labeled the period 1962 to 1974 as the era of "hypercentralization" in Algeria and offered examples of how excessive centralization stifled local initiative, reduced output, and, by rigidly applying national policies, failed to make the most of Algerian physical and human resources.[36] The Algerian case is the best documented, but it is clear that similar attitudes and assessments began to surface elsewhere in the region at roughly the same time. By the end of the decade, interests and agencies that would normally agree on very little — the international aid agencies, international business actors, European radical left critics, North African intellectuals, foreign observers of a technocratic or liberal persuasion, opposition politicians, and middle- and low-level field bureaucrats in all four countries — had informally coalesced into an increasingly vocal lobby for the presumed benefits of decentralization.

What all these disparate actors have in common is a negative opinion of past governmental performance and a conviction that one major explanation for poor performance has been the excessive centralization of power and control. Aid agencies and private business interests would prefer to deal with more efficient and fast-acting bureaucracies, which decentralization might conceivably create. Showing their distance from old left dogma, radical European observers of the Maghreb are among the most committed proponents of decentralization, which they claim and hope would increase the prospects for participation, democratization, and eventually radicalization of North African societies.[37] Younger North African intellectuals and students are moved by many of the same concerns and are decreasingly swayed by appeals to recall the glorious centralized unity of the anticolonial struggle — the days of which they cannot personally recall — or to honor the debt owed to the founding fathers — who appear to them rather well repaid already. Decentralization appears to offer hope to foreign technocrats and indigenous bureaucrats in middle and low positions — persons whose major concern is "getting things done" and who are daily faced with the delays and inaction spawned by centralist policies and habits. Opposition politicians in the region identify with decentralization as a desirable form of political and organizational arrangement. Whether this concern would survive a stint in power is largely untested.

This nonconstituted lobby has nowhere yet succeeded in overcoming the forces supporting centralized rule. Given the power of those supports, especially in the political realm, they may never do so. Still, the number and intensity of critical voices has succeeded in placing decentralization on the public agenda throughout the region. The concept is now a part of official North African discourse, with the Libyan and Algerian regimes leading the way and those in Tunisia and Morocco not far behind. It is true that, to date, claims to be applying the concept have only rarely been backed by concrete action. Programs based on thoroughly decentralist principles have been started, but their implementation has been halfhearted or actually turned to centralizing ends.

Nonetheless, it would be unwise to discount entirely the prospects for decentralization. To reiterate, these pressures stem from the increasingly widespread assessment that the development policies pursued in the region have been shown by experience to be inadequate if not disastrous. The evidence for this judgment is poor or modest economic performance, the persistence and growth of inequities, the readily apparent self-seeking behavior of most of the present elites, the failure of centralized rule to satisfy the political aspirations of large sections of the populace, and the growing sentiment that the models pursued have not spoken to the still potent spiritual and cultural roots of North African peoples. Since it seems unlikely that any of these conditions will be remedied quickly, decentralization will continue to serve as an attractive alternative, especially since it is an alternative sufficiently vast and vague to appeal to everybody who is dissatisfied with present events. Antimonarchists in Morocco, Algerian farmers stifled by government paperwork, Tunisian labor leaders, Libyan businessmen — all can envisage a benefit from decentralization. Added to the breadth of appeal is the stamp of intellectual respectability attached to the concept by its being espoused by the European left and by the local intelligensia — an important consideration in the formerly French countries, at least. This combination of discontent with the existing situation and the existence of a broadly appealing alternative organizational form, one that is sanctioned by intellectual opinion, makes it likely that decentralization will have a long run in the region.

IMPLEMENTATION OF DECENTRALIZATION POLICIES IN LIBYA

Fascinating and far-reaching experiments in decentralization have taken place in Libya. Indeed, "decentralization" is not an adequately strong term to describe what is, in theory, the dismantlement of the entire apparatus of the Libyan state and its replacement by the *jamahiriya* — a term that can loosely be translated as "things" or "era of the masses" and that connotes active, demonstrating masses practicing direct democracy.[38]

Though Libya is usually included in any definition of the Maghreb area, it possesses a number of features that distinguish it from the other countries of the region and from the perspective of this study. Libya was brutally, but at a relatively late date and for a brief period (1911-1943) colonized by Italy, the administrative style of which was certainly centralist but which possessed neither the time nor the resources to make much of a centralizing dent on the territory's geographically divided population centers[39] or its largely nomadic people. Thus, while Libya has been subject to the same set of historical, cultural, and religious factors influencing centralization, it was not subjected to an enduring centralizing colonial experience, nor have the regimes of King Idris or Muammar Qadafi attempted the centralizing feats of their Western neighbors. Nonetheless, the unusual, and unusually revealing, nature of the recent politico-administrative experiments in Libya persuade one that its situation be surveyed.

In 1969 the Libyan army overthrew the monarchy. Colonel Qadafi came to power supporting a then curious but now more familiar blend of ideological components: Nasserism, Pan-Arabism, nationalism, socialism, and Islam. The country's massive oil deposits had been discovered only in 1959. The oil had brought about "a period of unmanageable abundance";[40] the wealth generated had not been used for societal transformation or broad-based development. The new regime promised to alter this state of affairs.

From the outset Qadafi's interest in populist, direct democracy was evident. As early as 1970 he informed the people that they had the right and the duty to demand an accounting from government ministries.[41] In the earliest official pronouncements of the ruling Revolutionary Command Council, the formal administrative system inherited from the monarchical and colonial periods was portrayed as a self-seeking, illegitimate intermediary between the people and their revolutionary leaders. Qadafi's criticisms of the bureaucracy grew increasingly more heated, as from 1970 to 1974 the administration failed to satisfy the leaders' demands for a workable form of direct democracy. In April 1973, Qadafi made a speech launching the "popular revolution," the goal of which was the imposition of correct governance (and Pan-Arab unity) through what might be termed radical Islamic corporatism. The speech contained five major policy points:

(1) All existing laws were to be suppressed, as they dampened the creativity of the people. Henceforth, Islam would be the only accepted source of laws.

(2) All elements opposing the Libyan revolution would be eliminated.

(3) The masses would be armed and given total liberty.

(4) There would be an administrative revolution, and wrong-minded civil servants would be eliminated.

(5) There would be a cultural revolution, and all imported ideas contrary to Islam would be eliminated. A policy of complete Arabization was imposed.[42]

Qadafi then invited the public to implement this revolution. Between April and August 1973, some 2,400 "popular committees" were formed to undertake the revolutionary tasks.[43] The purpose of the popular committees was to take over all public administration from the discredited official Libyan bureaucracy. Mass demonstrations supported by these committees removed, nonviolently it seems, officials from their offices. The casualties went far beyond petty obstructing functionaries and touched grand (obstructing?) functionaries as well. Those removed included airline executives, oil industry managers, radio/television personalities, six regional governors, an entire municipal council, and the rector of the university.[44] The removals had the predictable results; the economy slowed to a halt. As in other instances of revolutionary enthusiasm, the traditional bureaucracy substantially righted itself and settled back to old patterns. But not quite, for the popular committees continued in existence, supported — after late 1974 — by Part I of Qadafi's *Green Book,* a neo-Koranic defense of direct, participatory democracy.

From 1974 to 1977 the institutional situation was one of even greater than normal confusion and fluctuation, as the theoretically powerful popular committees coexisted with at least portions of the normal administrative apparatus. By early 1977 Qadafi — no longer colonel, no longer head of the disbanded Revolutionary Command Council, but now the " Guide of the Faithful" — had done away with older forms of representation and created a General People's Congress. The 1977 deliberations of this body produced the concept of jamahiriya, the key organizational points of which are as follows:

(1) All citizens are members of "basic popular congresses" (BPCs). One source states that people are assigned to particular basic popular congresses on the basis of their "professional categories" — with laborers, peasants, students, and employees belonging to different BPCs.[45] A second source says more simply that people are assigned on the basis of locality of residence and estimates that in the whole country there are some 186 BPCs.[46]

(2) Each BPC chooses democratically a directing "working committee," led by a secretary and an assistant secretary.

(3) The BPCs choose "directly"[47] the people's committees (which we shall call pop coms, for short); the pop coms now officially and completely replace the traditional civil service, which has been disbanded. The BPCs have the power to fire workers and officials of the pop coms.

(4) Each of the corporate categories allowed by the regime — workers, peasants, students, merchants, craftsmen, officials, and professionals — has its own union or professional organization distinct from the BPC or pop com.

(5) The BPCs, the pop coms, and the professional organizations all send delegates to an annual meeting of the General Peoples' Congress, the purpose of which is to synthesize into national policies the expressions of the BPCs. Each BPC has one vote at the General Congress.

(6) Policies approved are then implemented by the pop coms on a completely decentralized basis. Implementation is supervised and regulated only by the BPCs. There are, it seems, no longer any ministries, central offices, directors, and the like. There remains but the General Secretariat of the General People's Congress, with responsibilities in national affairs such as defense, oil pricing, and so on.

(7) In 1978, dissatisfied with the performance of the BPCs, Qadafi instituted yet another type of local body, the "revolutionary committees," ostensibly to assist the pop coms in decision making and popular mobilization. Very little information exists on the composition or regulations of these committees, but it is rumored that Qadafi sees these bodies as the most important units in the country, as their task is to be revolutionary watchdogs over the actions of the more operational units.

Clearly, what is described here goes beyond any normal definition of decentralization; this is, in principle, an extreme case of the devolution of power. Note immediately that every observer of the Libyan reorganization is at pains to stress that "we do not know the details of the organization,"[48] and there is a "virtual lack of objective data pertaining to the inner workings of the various people's congresses and committees."[49] Thus, one has but the most sketchy of information regarding the implementation of these policies. It does seem likely that in spite of the new institutional arrangements and despite the lack of an official post, Qadafi still personally makes policy for the country as a whole. Moreover, the neat outline of institutions given above probably lends an air of spurious clarity and rationality to what is, on the ground, a very confused situation. Struggling to make sense of the chaotic situation — in which organizations are officially abolished but somehow continue to exist, in which different organizations are given the same responsibilities, in which those few and inadequate offices that in the past tried (ineffectually) to impose coordination have been eliminated — Bleuchot and Monastiri are reduced to complaining:

> In Libya, one really understands things only after they have been completely swept away. Moreover, the Libyan logic is not ours. It is more Anglo-Saxon and very pragmatic. General looseness and contradictions do not bother anybody in Libya.[50]

Aside from general, unsubstantiated assertions that the new system has brought managerial chaos to the country[51] and one or two articles on the unusual social theory being attempted,[52] there is a dearth of information on what precisely takes place in these decentralized institutions. Some few indirect insights on the inner workings of the jamahiriya system are revealed in Bleuchot's review of the Third Session of the General People's Congress. The proceedings of the Congress noted high-level concern with the lack of participation in local institutions. Qadafi's address to the Congress criticized the BPCs for overloading the General Secretariat with trivial problems and unreasonable requests for resources. The difficulties of the system were most graphically revealed in discussions on the national budget. Asked to consider the budget documents before the session, it appears that some of the BPCs simply ignored the request. Of those that responded, many simply added to the budget sizable demands for social services and supplies in their locales, especially roads, housing, health dispensaries, and water systems.[53] Most of the discussion was spent trying to persuade delegates of the necessity to take an overall, societal view and of the limitations on government's resources. The seeming ease with which this view was imposed indicates that Qadafi and the General Secretariat have so far had little difficulty controlling the theoretically decentralized jamahiriya.

Overall, there is not yet enough evidence to form a definitive judgment on the Libyan experiment. It does seem clear that the jamahiriya system is a form of imposed-from-the-top decentralization and that it is operating in the absence of human resources sufficient to make the experiment work. Skepticism seems justified. Still, the rare combination of Qadafi's central position, his populist/Islamic ideology, and the country's great wealth make it likely that the experiment will continue to be tolerated — indeed, fostered and subsidized — regardless of its practical achievements on the ground. Libya's hydrocarbon reserves are estimated as lasting from twenty to thirty years; few observers would be as specific regarding the future of the Libyan leader or the jamahiriya.

The apparently poor practical performance and modest prospects for the jamahiriya approach to decentralization should not prevent one from acknowledging the audacity of the venture. Qadafi's idea of a people practicing direct democracy through popular initiative and an antiformal bureaucracy — guided by a moral and austere Muslim leadership — generates considerable enthusiasm. The issue here is not whether this extreme form of decentralization works well, would apply to more developed societies, or would long survive in societies not having Libya's wealth. The point is that Qadafi's views are probably authentic representations of what people in Libya, and no doubt elsewhere in the region, regard as proper social organization. Conditioned by history, the outside observer finds it easy to dismiss the applied prospects of a concept seemingly as naive as jamahiriya. Nonetheless, Qadafi's views reveal some of the force that can be generated for notions of decentralization.

DECENTRALIZATION IN ALGERIA

Algeria offers a more typical approach to the concept of decentralization. To simplify matters further, and unlike the case of Libya, Algerian decentralization efforts have been under way for some time and have received considerable scholarly attention.

Having suffered the most intense and exploitative colonial experience on the African continent (save for South Africa) and having experienced a brutal war of liberation in which one-tenth of the Algerian male population lost their lives, it is natural that Algerian postcolonial leaders have frequently attempted to call into fundamental question their inherited forms of governance. (That they have not been totally successful is a crucial portion of this section's discussion.) In the great majority of African and Asian anticolonial struggles, it was the Western-educated elites who negotiated independence, inherited the reins of power, and proceeded to place themselves and people like themselves in the vacated positions of administrative leadership. In these circumstances institutional change was more often discussed than carried out. The inheriting elite was generally content to localize the state apparatus, not alter it. In the majority of postcolonial states this was the administrative path of least resistance; following the path has contributed to a maintenance of inherited centralist policies.

In Algeria, however, the educated elite failed in their efforts to negotiate political rights for Arab Algerians. The reason was the intransigence of the powerful settler community. Thus, after World War II and further demonstrations of the futility of nonviolent approaches, nationalist leadership passed to younger, less educated, more radical persons. This group led Algeria to independence in 1962, and it is the group that has furnished most of the top leadership of the Algerian state to the present. This relatively radicalized leadership has been more willing than most Third World ruling groups to consider the possibility of far-reaching institutional change.

Added to this ideological predisposition is the fact that a form of decentralization was thrust on Algeria in 1962. The immediate departure, at independence, of 90 percent of the nearly one million *colons* who had owned and managed most of the private sector and who had staffed the colonial government down to very low levels created an economic and administrative vacuum. Moreover, the French army had succeeded in substantially destroying the nationalist fighting organization within the country. The result was that the summer of 1962 witnessed a prolonged power struggle between the groups that had conducted the liberation movement from exile in Tunisia and Morocco. Little, if any, attention was paid to coherent governing policies.

The rapid flight of the French, especially from the rural areas, and the initial absence of a clear-cut inheriting group opened the door to local, spontaneous, decentralized efforts. Foremost among these was the well-known *autogestion* (self-management) activity, in which rural peasants and landless workers took over the vacated French farms and attempted to run them as democratically managed collectives.[54] Some few urban workers did the same in vacated factories, but urban/industrial autogestion was minuscule compared to the rural actions. Since the rural peasantry had been the main source of support to the liberation organization, and since this peasantry regarded the recuperation of their land as a major goal of the revolution, and, furthermore, since their attempt at self-managed collectivization fit so neatly the radical views of the ruling groups, the independent regime accepted the existence of the autogestion sector and indeed raised the concept to the level of official ideology.

The heyday of decentralized autogestion was brief; as early as 1963 the more secure Ben Bella regime created a National Office of Agrarian Reform, which appointed technical directors — ostensibly to advise, actually to control — to the self-managed farms.[55] Leftist critics of the Algerian regime have interpreted the ensuing bureaucratization of the autogestion farms as a splendid example of how petit-bourgeois technocrats suppress decentralized actions giving power to the workers and peasants.[56] Other observers emphasize the extremely poor production performance of the autogestion sector,[57] both before and after the appointment of technical directors, and point out the economic costs of declining internal food production to rapidly growing Algeria.

The first Algerian regime was overthrown by an army coup in June 1965. This brought to power Houari Boumedienne, whose thirteen-year period of rule can be divided into roughly equal portions. From 1965 to 1971 the Boumedienne regime concentrated on unabashedly centralist policies — building up the state planning and fiscal control machinery; opting for heavy industrialization as the key development policy; increasing the size and adding to the training of the central public service; nationalizing most foreign-owned business and financial ventures and replacing them with an elaborate constellation of centrally directed state enterprises; isolating or eliminating the supports of decentralization in the autogestion sector, the unions, the party, and the student movement; and appointing officials of a technocratic orientation to replace those associated with the first regime's stress on spontaneity and mass mobilization.[58] Though severely criticized for these activities, Boumedienne and his close associates consistently defended their actions on the grounds that they were laying the necessary economic and administrative base on which Algeria would proceed to build a socialist, self-managed, decentralized — and above all, economically powerful — state. The position of the new regime was that

> socialism is not this incoherent collection of improvised measures and personal reactions that for three years gave the people only an erroneous idea of socialism. Socialism is a long and laborious process of construction that requires the elaboration and application of a comprehensive plan.[59]

As for self-management, the official view was:

> We are for self-management, but a viable self-management that yields a profit, that results in an efficient organization of work and an increase in production. To liberate the worker is a revolutionary principle . . . but to produce is also a necessity.[60]

Most external observers dismissed this *reculer pour mieux sauter* reasoning as mystifying rationalizations for the imposition of either an autocracy or a state capitalist regime, the conclusion varying with the ideology of the critic.

Immediately on seizing power, the coup leaders had disbanded the Algerian National Assembly. Until 1967 they ruled without even the semblance of consultative, much less legislative, elected bodies. In January 1967 an official decree established communal popular assemblies *(assemblées populaires communales* — APCs) in the more than 700 communes in the country. This was followed in 1969 by the setting up of provincial popular assemblies *(assemblées populaires de wilaya* — APWs).[61] In the first elections to these bodies, voters merely ratified by a yes or no indication the single slate of candidates chosen by the sole official political party. More recently, a form of competition has been allowed, and voters now choose from a party list twice as large as the number of seats to be filled. Candidate selection remains firmly in the hands of the party, and no active campaigning is tolerated. Until the early 1970s these bodies were just what they appeared to be — essentially powerless "consultative" bodies giving the illusion but not the substance of representation and decentralization. In the succinct assessment of Wilfrid Knapp, "they lack political life."[62]

But their very creation, and more tellingly, the slow, cautious, but perceptibly increasing manner in which they have been charged with meaningful responsibilities, is quite indicative of what the Boumedienne regime long claimed to be its essential approach — that of providing Algeria with a solid institutional framework and then "schooling" the population in the democratic, decentralized use of these institutions. High officials in the Boumedienne regime frequently expressed a rather tutorial view of government; that is, they regarded the citizenry as a sort of pre-proletariat, "recently and violently torn from its peasant origins and culture, and in need of a lengthy and closely supervised apprenticeship before it can be entrusted with the full range of powers envisaged by the new system."[63] Speaking in 1974 of the slow evolution of power of the APCs and APWs, the then minister of the interior stated the reasons the regime had begun at the base, and why it had not fulfilled its promise to recreate a national assembly:

> There has been a pause in the process of setting up the institutions of the country. First, it must be said that on 19 June 1965 we committed ourselves to the construction of national institutions while choosing an original path, but also a difficult path. This does not consist of organizing institutions by starting at the summit — as has been done in many countries — but we opted for construction at the base level, because we wanted the people to participate in the management of the whole country, through their elected representatives.[64]

Clearly, there was a fair amount of self-serving cant involved in these views, but in the light of subsequent events the cynical or uniquely materialist interpretation of the regime's position has been proven inadequate.

1971 witnessed a shift in emphasis for the Boumedienne regime. It was the year in which the potentially dangerous nationalization of French-owned oil interests was completed. Having successfully re-captured control of the economy, and enjoying a period of political stability after having suppressed or eliminated dissenting voices, the regime evidently felt sufficiently secure to embark on some of its long-promised efforts at "democratization, deconcentration, and de-centralization." In late 1971 the government put forward two "char-ters" — not laws, but rather statements of intended new policies — of a participatory and decentralizing nature. These dealt with workers' participation in the nationalized industrial sector and what was called "the agrarian revolution," or land reform.[65]

The socialist management charter stated the regime's intention to decentralize control of industry to the level of the workplace. This was to be done by dividing each nationalized industry into units, in which the workers would elect an assembly. These workers as-semblies *(assemblées des travailleurs)* were to be endowed with considerable powers of supervision, fiscal consultation, and outright control in some areas, such as worker discipline. In keeping with the regime's tutorial perspective, the workers' authority was always matched and often exceeded by the powers of management and the reviewing civil service. Nonetheless, it was a start. The land reform program went even further. What was envisaged was not merely a redistribution of seized assets. Going beyond this, this charter called for the formation of strong cooperatives on all reformed lands, and at the level of the commune. Working closely with the APCs, the new cooperatives would be more than production points; they would be centers of decentralized planning and administration.

The ringing declarations of the charters[66] and the enthusiastic official publicity that accompanied their publication were not im-mediately followed by concrete efforts at implementation. The land reform started to take effect in June 1972, but only on uninhabited communal or religious lands. The first efforts at expropriating land from large or absentee landlords did not take place until mid-1973. This was the start of what was called the "second phase" of the reform. Writing in 1978, Jönsson noted that "it is important moreover to underline that this phase is not yet completed, and that there remain a very great number of agricultural lands to nationalize."[67] Im-plementation in the workers' participation program also moved at a leisurely pace. Though the charter had stated that the first-priority step was the production of enabling *textes d'application,* these were not published until December 1974, well *after* the first elections of workers' assemblies had been held. Nonetheless, the program grew swiftly after 1974, and the most recent available figures indicate that by mid-1976 the workers' participation scheme was in effect in 550 units of some 40 state enterprises, and touched about 150,000 workers.[68]

The most recent figures summarizing the land reform program came from government surveys conducted in 1979. They indicate that about two million hectares have been "recovered," of which 1.14 million are good agricultural land.[69] Some 91,000 heads of households have been given plots; these *attributaries* have been divided into 5,890 basic or pre-cooperatives. The most common form of basic cooperatives are the CAPRAs — *coopérative agricoles de production de la Révolution Agraire,* or agricultural production cooperatives of the Agrarian Revolution. CAPRAs number 4,205 and group some 52,000 people.[70] One step up the administrative ladder, in every commune, the government established CAPCS — *coopérative agricoles polyvalentes communales de service,* or multiservice communal agricultural cooperatives — which service the CAPRAs with machinery, seeds, advice, and credit and send up agricultural produce to the provincial cooperatives and offices of the government-controlled commercialization network. On paper, CAPCS have broad responsibilities, for they are supposed "to undertake at the communal level, within the framework of the national plan, operations of development, of economic exploitation, of employment generation, and of improvement of living and working conditions."[71] Though both the CAPRAs and the CAPCS possess elaborate formal arrangements for participatory management by the constituent farmers, observers are united in concluding that their decision-making powers are quite limited; moreover, these units are seen as dominated by large landowners and civil servants.[72] Once again, the Algerians created the institutional framework for participatory decentralization but seemed either unable or unwilling to put the institutions into effective action.

The hesitant pace of implementation of the cooperative program and the continuing dominance of nonpeasant interests in the directing bodies lend support to those who dismiss as rhetoric this effort. Still, one cannot entirely neglect the regime's countering view: that the new institutions are schools in which the Algerian population is learning the skills essential for local self-regulation. Solid evidence to support this view is sketchy, but some is offered by the workings of the "communal popular assemblies." From their inception in 1967 to the beginnings of the second phase of the land reform effort, in 1973, the communal assemblies were virtually without meaningful function. With the start of the second phase, the assemblies were enlarged to include representatives of the mass organizations of Algeria (the union movement and the youth, women's, veterans', and peasants' organizations) and local representatives of the party, the *Front de Libération Nationale* (FLN). The enlargement regulations specified that representatives of the National Union of Algerian Peasants (UNPA) must henceforth constitute a full half of the members of each assembly; moreover, two-thirds of the peasants' union representatives were to be landless farmers or seasonal laborers.[73] These bodies were then renamed the "enlarged communal popular assemblies" (or APCEs, to use the French acronym).

Far more important than this tinkering with the name or membership was the next step. The government surprised most observers by living up to the proposals in the land reform charter. It actually turned over to the APCEs the important tasks of deciding which lands were subject to nationalization and which farmers would be given plots on the newly formed CAPRAs. Admittedly, in terms of decentralization, this was not quite the same as handing over broad taxing and unsupervised spending powers to the communal level, but in Algerian terms the step was a major innovation and was definitely seen as such by local people.

Given a well-defined task and concrete resources to allocate, the APCEs took on new life. Though their task consisted mainly of applying nationally set norms on landowning limits, kinds of land to be nationalized, and making lists of those who would be struck by or benefit from these norms, a fair amount of adaptation of national directives to local conditions was required. Not all of the APCEs undertook these tasks well, and in a number of instances acceptable performance was attributable to civil servants' direction and not to the participatory nature of the body as a whole.[74] Be that as it may, this was the first instance in postindependence Algeria in which a nonnational, at least partly elected agency implemented an important decision. As Leca and Vatin noted in their 1975 study, this may have been a less than wholehearted decentralization exercise. They speculate that the regime sent this particular issue back to the communal level precisely to avoid responsibility for a program that could have raised powerful opposition.[75] The important point, still, is that the decision was taken and the exercise carried out.

From 1974 to the end of the Boumedienne period (he died of natural causes in December 1978), official statements laid increasing stress on the goal of decentralization. The term was frequently employed in the Second Four Year Plan of 1974-1977.[76] This national plan announced that in the future every commune would produce a local plan, which would be implemented and managed by the APCEs.[77] The communal plans were to be the principle expression of decentralization in the country. Unfortunately, little information is available on how, or even if, this intention has been carried out. As is often the case in the Maghreb, one must rely on fragmentary indicators and secondary sources to obtain some idea of what is taking place in the field.

After 1974 no government pronouncement was complete without a reference to decentralization. The concept became enshrined as dogma in the 1976 National Charter (a very important document that summarized past failures and accomplishments and established an ideological blueprint for the future of Algerian society). Stated the Charter:

> The state must not be a structure where the centralization of powers creates a very heavy system, which secretes a bureaucracy paralyzing and annihilating all spirit of initiative at the base. . . . The socialist state in Algeria bases therefore its conception and its organization on decentralization. . . . Decentralization must confer to the provinces and the communes full competence on all problems of local or regional interest. . . . It must reach into all fields — social, economic, and cultural. Decentralization aims at giving to localities the means and the responsibility of promoting themselves the development of their region, complementing the efforts undertaken by the nation.[78]

The Charter said that the key structures of decentralization were the communal and provincial assemblies, and it stated that "a fiscal reform will be implemented in order to transfer certain fiscal receipts now used by the national budget to the benefit of the communes and the provinces."[79]

Early 1977 was the high point of Boumedienne's liberalization campaign, of which decentralization was an important part. This campaign sent Algerians to the polls four times in a period of eight months, to vote on accepting or rejecting the National Charter, to approve a new constitution, to approve or reject Boumedienne as president of the Republic (he had been, prior to this, president of the Revolutionary Council), and to elect a new National Assembly. It is impossible to judge whether Boumedienne actually intended to implement fully his policies of decentralization and democratization and was prevented from so doing by declines in internal economic productivity, changes in the international situation because of Algeria's support of anti-Moroccan guerrillas in the former Spanish Sahara, and his rapid and fatal illness, or whether, in the absence of these factors, others would have been found to justify caution and inaction. Whatever the reasons, and despite the flood of official phraseology supporting the idea of decentralization, at the end of the Boumedienne period concrete achievements remained very modest.

Without providing detailed information on how the APCEs and APWs work, on whether the promised fiscal reform has been put into effect, or on how the supposedly decentralized communal planning system is or is not working, a 1979 study by Benakezouh argued generally that the whole range of local activities cannot be graced with the name "decentralization" but is rather an example of a much weaker process, that of "deconcentration." By this term Benakezouh meant that local authorities have no powers to initiate or end actions, despite official statements. They can only undertake or modify slightly those tasks directly assigned to them by national-level officials. Writing of central control, he stated that "nothing practically can be conceived and executed without its previous agreement: at the communal level the regulatory role of the central officials, which should normally be only to supervise the legality of actions of the decentralized agents [the APCEs and the APWs], has become debased and synonymous with hierarchical control."[80] He concluded:

> To speak of decentralization [is] to create an illusion, because it is in the sense of deconcentration that one acts in fact, as prerogatives theoretically accorded to decentralized local governments are in practice recovered, thanks to multiple administrative channels, by deconcentrated agents [bureaucrats representing the central ministries at the local level].[81]

The 1978 analysis by Leca and Vatin supported this contention. They noted that the official view of the role of the member of the communal and provincial assembly was resolutely nationalist; that is, the proper function of the elected representative was to serve the totality of his constituency within the framework of accepted national goals. Anything short of high-minded dedication to the general interest was viewed as particularism or, worse, "seizing upon local problems in order to build a national career."[82] APCEs, APWs, and a National Assembly composed of members basing their behavior on this ethos hardly constitute a dynamic lobby for decentralization.

There is not much information available on post-Boumedienne decentralization events. What little is known indicates that there has been no major change under the regime of President Chadli Benjedid. A long-promised and much delayed congress of the party, the FLN, was held in June 1980; the resolutions and statements of the Congress show clearly that decentralization remains a key policy — or at least slogan — of the Algerian leadership. But the wording of the resolutions indicates that implementation is as slow and as distant as ever. For example, the Congress's summary statement, entitled " Decentralization and Democratization of the Economy," noted that "the communal and provincial plans constitute, *in the future,* the framework of expression of social aspirations and of development of the initiatives at the local level, *in conformity with the objectives of the national plan.*"[83] Or again: decentralization is a process that "will be concretized" *(se concrétiseront).*[84] Or finally: "The congress recommends putting at the disposition of localities the human, material, financial and administrative means appropriate to the nature and the size of their new missions."[85] These phrases make it appear that the decentralization process remains stuck at the level of rhetoric, as something that will come about in the future, as something for which the resources are not currently available. Indeed, it is the admittedly "imperfect application of decentralization in the field of economic management"[86] that is partly responsible for poor levels of production. Who or what is to be blamed for this "imperfect application" is not specified.

As is so often the case in Algeria, one could construct a plausible explanation excusing the inactivity and delays — for example, by noting the necessity of the third regime to establish itself solidly before turning its attention to decentralization. The problem, of course, is that in any underdeveloped country, especially one in which the factors tending toward centralization are so powerful, one can always, under all imaginable conditions, find a plausible reason to maintain central-level dominance. There is literally always some troubling regional demand or dissident group; there is always an international crisis of one sort or another; there is always some system-threatening issue. Thus, the signs for implementing decentralization are never sufficiently auspicious. The threat of regime instability and personal loss is so apparent that even leaders sincerely committed to the idea find that the moment is never quite right to undertake wholeheartedly the process. Moreover, it is quite likely that the constant delays are not at all upsetting to large numbers of middle-level administrators, who are content with their present position and who see little but potential loss and extra work from decentralization. This certainly appears to be the Algerian case.

Still, the regime leaders, party ideologues, representatives of the mass organizations, and the state-controlled press continue the flow of statements attributing poor governmental performance to excessive centralization and recommending that decentralized planning and administration be set in place. If one argues that this is nothing but window-dressing, then one must also argue that the Algerian leaders have been totally lacking in imagination, since they have for so long dressed the window with the same material, and that the Algerian population is extremely gullible, since it continues to return to the window. Without being able to refute totally the negative interpretation, the conclusion of this section is that possibilities for decentralization remain alive in Algeria. As a number of past occasions have shown — for example, the socialist management program and the matter of elections to the communal and provincial assemblies — the Algerian regimes possess a quite long time horizon for policy implementation. This may yet prove the case with decentralization. Moreover, one must take very seriously the existing obstacles to the concept, for even the critics of regime actions have noted the severe difficulties involved in quickly changing largely illiterate and deferential peasants into democratically organized self-managers.[87] What may thus be surprising is not the tardiness of implementation of decentralization, but the very fact that it remains on the Algerian policy agenda.

Libya and Algeria are examples of an imperfect decentralization of planning and implementation functions. In principle, they seem well advanced on the route to subnational policy initiation and follow-through; in practice, the supposedly decentralized units are still thoroughly subject to central direction and close supervision. "Central direction" may be too charitable a term to describe the Libyan situation, given the frequent and personal intervention of Qadafi and his closest associates in all areas of public activity. This kind of control is both more and less than centralization: more, because unfettered personalized leadership can and does intervene on any issue, at any time, to any extent; yet it is also less, because — given the reasonable assumption that the central leadership group is hopelessly overburdened — the basic popular congresses may actually have at their disposal a certain amount of decentralized initiative, at least until their actions catch the disapproving eye of the National Secretariat or the Guide of the Faithful. In Algeria, the constraints are more rational and obvious. The chances are few for the APWs and APCEs to exceed the limits of national directives. In both countries, moreover, the crucial financial powers remain firmly in the hands of central decision makers. The argument cautiously advanced in previous sections of this chapter is that, irrespective of continuing informal centralization, the formal commitment to decentralization — even very poorly implemented — is significant in itself, since it creates a framework and a pressure for the enlargement of decentralized devices.

This is a modest and strictly qualified conclusion. Nonetheless, it is a conclusion that has to be even more tightly qualified to make it apply to Tunisia or Morocco. It is in these countries that the pressures for centralization were the most acute. Libya's special circumstances of a relatively weak form of colonization and Algeria's institution and limit-destroying war of liberation do not apply. In these last two cases to be considered, the main thrust of postindependence policy was to localize an acceptable mode of governance.

DECENTRALIZATION IN TUNISIA

Both Tunisia and Morocco possess regimes of remarkable stamina: Habib Bourguiba led Tunisia to independence in 1956 and has been its principal ruler ever since; Hassan II inherited the Moroccan throne from his father in 1961, five years after independence, which was, again, in 1956. Both regimes, the Moroccan much more seriously, have been periodically threatened. The threats have balanced, or have been used to balance, the fluctuating but substantial internal pressures for liberalization and decentralization. The result is two regimes sufficiently strong, and at the same time sufficiently insecure, consistently to have solidified their inherited centralized administrations and political systems, at least until the mid-1970s.

This is certainly the Tunisian case. For example, Sbih's 1977 study of the formal/legal aspects of Maghrebian administrative systems noted that the Tunisian legal texts regarding local government decentralization were either more vague or more constricting than the Moroccan, much less the Algerian, codes.[88] Thus, even in formal/legal terms, the Tunisian decentralization situation compared unfavorably to other regional actors. In 1975, the United Nations' FAO commissioned a former French cabinet minister to analyze the administration of the Tunisian Ministry of Agriculture; his report characterized the organization of the Ministry as based on "a heritage of the past: Napoleonic rationalism."[89] The report stated that "all powers are concentrated in Tunis," resulting in "a very great clumsiness in management, principally on the financial level."[90] There is no reason to believe that the Ministry of Agriculture was any worse in this regard than other branches of the government.

The Tunisian provincial administration is organized on hierarchical lines, familiar to any student of colonial government. The country is divided into twenty *gouvernorats,* each headed by a centrally appointed *gouverneur (wali,* in Arabic). Each gouvernorat is subdivided into betweeen three and six *délégations,* headed by a *délégue (matamad).* These officials are also central appointees. The *délégations,* in turn, are divided into four or five *secteurs,* which are directed by an *omdah,* who is always a nontransferable local. At the gouvernorat and délégation levels there are consultative assemblies to advise and oversee the administrative officials. These have been in existence since independence, but it is only recently that members of these bodies have been subject to any meaningful electoral check; until 1980 the sole official political party simply put forward a list of names that the public could approve or reject. The formal administrative divisions are matched by a parallel party organization at every level, complete with supposedly consultative and representative assemblies. Several early studies of the country placed optimistic emphasis on the participation and representation potential of the party units;[91] more recent analyses conclude that neither the local councils nor the party units have played any substantial decentralizing role — though the November 1981 national elections allowed for the first time a limited form of multipartyism that may lead to major changes.

Field administration of the Tunisian line ministries — agriculture, education, health, public works, and so on — is remarkably chaotic. Each ministry is internally divided into many competing, overlapping, ill-coordinated sections, most of which are managed as nonaccountable "fiefdoms" by powerful directors. The large and important Ministry of Agriculture, for example, is composed of twelve central sections, five separate research units, five quasi-autonomous "boards," two "national centers," three "professional groupings," and it directly oversees (is the *tutelle*) of twelve *offices,* equivalent to the English "authorities" or parastatals.[92] In each gouvernorat there is a "regional commissar for agricultural development," much of whose time appears to be spent in boundary disputes with the many other quasi-independent directors of his own and other ministries. The plethora of agencies is superficially reminiscent of Caiden and Wildavsky's notion of "functional redundancy"; but in practice the result is poor, due to the intense personalization of authority and lack of cooperation between components — all of which increases centralization, as disputes can only be resolved at higher levels.

A 1978 report to the USAID mission in Tunis, on the question of optimal administrative arrangements to promote an integrated rural development project, is instructive in this regard. Written by an expert in development administration, James Mayfield, it stated that decentralization in general and even local administrative control of selected development projects were at the time of writing beyond the reach of Tunisia. The main reason for this was the lack of competent, skilled personnel. For example, Mayfield found that most gouverneurs lacked one or two, and sometimes three, of their called-for seven key supporting staff.[93] In one particular rural gouvernorat, the total civil service establishment was 67 people; at the time of Mayfield's inquiry only 41 posts were filled.[94] Levels of competence and experience among those in post were low. Mayfield's conclusion was that the local administrative system was "often inefficient, unreliable, slow in decision making, inconsistent in allocating funds, and subject to local pressures and central government demands which make effective policy implementation almost impossible."[95] Mayfield regarded firm centralization as inevitable, given the Tunisian government's constraints and emphasis on establishing legitimacy and control. He therefore opted for a parastatal arrangement for the proposed development project, as local direction was out of the question.

However, as noted earlier, tight centralization seems inevitably to generate counterpressures for decentralization and participation. The peak period of centralized planning approaches in Tunisia was during the late 1960s, when both comprehensive planning and collectivized agriculture were being pushed from the center. The inefficiencies and injustices carried out in the name of central planning spawned considerable protest. At the end of the 1960s Bourguiba dropped the rural cooperative program and the minister most closely associated with the "socialist" effort. One of the first concrete responses to the anticentralist feeling was a decree of 1973, establishing the Rural Development Program *(Programme de développement rural,* or *PDR).* This program, a block grant activity, is still very much in effect; it works as follows: Each of the twenty gouvernorats receives annually a modest set sum. Poor and rural units receive twice the normal sum. Funds must be spent on locally generated and supervised projects, with community development and employment-generating actions favored. Gouvernorat-level civil servants are charged with the tasks of identifying projects, studying their feasibility and potential payoff, "harmonizing" the proposed action with nationally conceived operations in the region, and supervising implementation. The government made much of the decentralization aspect of the program when it was announced, claiming that it was an "apprenticeship of new responsibilities in the field of planning"[96] and a prelude to full regionalization. A 1976 government report noted glowingly the money spent, projects initiated, and jobs created and indicated the government's intention to increase the resources of the PDR.[97] This was done; each rural gouvernorat now receives over $3.5 million annually through this program. Still, and in spite of the local emphasis, all projects must be put forward according to a detailed schedule imposed by the central Ministry of Plan, and all projects must be approved by Tunis before funds can be spent. Tunisian informants state that this is not a *pro forma* vetting operation; projects can be and have been turned down.

Given the central officials' close control of the program, it is clear that the PDR is but a limited measure and far from a model of complete decentralization, enthusiastic official descriptions notwithstanding. But, as in the Algerian case, one should recognize the limitations of the field staff and the rural population and accept somewhat the rationality of the government's view that one must start small, with a closely supervised effort. The PDR was a significant first step.

Indeed, it is hard to describe the extent to which the PDR, and other seemingly halting steps toward decentralization described below, are radical departures from past Tunisian practice. Centralization of authority and control is so deeply enmeshed in the Tunisian system that even writers arguing for relaxation are moved to note that "in an underdeveloped country where reconstruction can only be nationally and state controlled, the phenomenon [centralization] is thus in the nature of things."[98] The same authors note that Tunisian local councillors find it "unthinkable" that they can do anything but implement central directives, for they all accept the dictum that the role of the locality is to execute that which the center conceives.

What, then, does decentralization mean in Tunisia? The most recent and exhaustive study of the issue, by Ben Achour and Moussa, views the concept as a "political myth" used by the aging leadership to "offset criticism of their centralized single party rule." Talk of decentralization is a seemingly progressive but less than radical defensive position for a regime that "cannot or does not want to reconsider fundamentally its own norms of political behavior."[99] Having a strongly positive connotation and lacking a crystalline definition, the term "decentralization" can mean anything and everything that takes place outside the capital, including the normally scheduled routine administrative meetings of three or four gouverneurs. All this is an inexpensive way to soften the reality, which is: "All sectors of social activity are regulated by the center in their least detail."[100]

This regulation was supposedly weakened in 1975, when, with the usual burst of effusive fanfare, the government announced that the finances and powers of the local councils would be increased. Texts were drafted and regulations enacted to transfer some managerial and fiscal responsibility to the communal level. There are two points to note here: (1) The specific nature of what powers were transferred or enlarged is not completely clear from available materials. (2) The 158 communes in Tunisia are electoral units based on cities, towns, villages and are — confusingly — not the same as the administrative delegations. The bulk of the rural population is covered by the gouvernorat councils and thus is *not* touched by the reforms. Bearing this in mind, the main innovation of the reforms appears to have been the regulation obliging the central government to consult the municipal councils on matters of local concern rather than simply recommending consultation, as before. This hardly seems a revolutionary change.

Without specifying the details of the reforms, Ben Achour and Moussa claim that the municipal councils are now legally empowered to take action in many fields that formerly were the preserve of central authorities. The problem is that the promised financial transfers are still incomplete, and even more importantly, the councillors are prevented — by culture, custom, and self-interest — from undertaking the roles allowed by law. The councillors were, up to 1980, not chosen by competitive election but were placed in their posts because of their contacts with and loyalty to party leaders. Tunisia being a very small country, local party leaders are in most cases also national figures. Councillors were thus "accountable" to central leaders and not to local concerns; this encouraged a centralist perspective. Second, the councils were well accustomed to being dependent bodies, with all their financial and technical needs filled by central agencies. When the councillors realized that they would have to take the responsibility of imposing taxes and making technical decisions, they became "the most active lobby in favor of [central] assistance, and thus, in effect, of centralization."[101]

The lack of decision-making experience and technical expertise was touched on, if not dealt with, in the 1975 reforms. A secretary general was appointed to each municipal council by the Ministry of the Interior, to serve as a permanent civil servant. While these officials may well assist the councils in raising and spending money, as appointees of a central ministry they will look to Tunis rather than to the councils for advancement and direction. Still, the general lack of trained personnel was recognized, and the reforms called for the creation of a training school for local officials of the Ministry of the Interior.[102] In theory, as more trained people become available, at least some of the technical problems will be eliminated. Perhaps more important were the electoral reforms instituted in time for the 1980 municipal elections, the first in which competition was allowed (two members of the party contested each council seat). It is possible, though not terribly likely, that this form of competition will increase a localist viewpoint among councillors. This will depend on how the party chooses candidates and on what sort of an electoral campaign is allowed. It is also possible that these initial stages of competition will be expanded by the introduction of a two- or multiparty system after the death of Bourguiba. The national elections in November 1981 pointed in this direction. All this is speculation about the future; there is little one can say with assurance.

What one can say is that since 1975 the "decentralizing discourse" has grown enormously in Tunisia, mostly in response to the regime's perception that the old rigidities could not be justified to the postindependence generation. The new "discourse" is rather similar to that espoused in Algeria, despite the differences in the guiding ideologies of the two states. The official claim is that the communes will be made the centers of socioeconomic development activity, by gradually increasing their responsibilities, means, and expertise. The rationale is that this is "the means of bringing about the participation of the citizen in economic planning"; behind this lies the assumption that "decentralization accelerates the economic takeoff."[103] To recall Algeria one final time, there is even talk of devolving the planning function to the communal level. And all this talk has increased following the 1980 appointment of Mohammed Mzali, an avowed proponent of liberalization, as prime minister.

Again, what one can witness are laudable and popular intentions, combined with painfully slow implementation. Once more, to judge the causes of slow implementation one must balance the obvious benefits of the present system to those on top of Tunisian society with the equally obvious truth of the assertion that Tunisian local governments can only gradually assume their new responsibilities. Which of these sets of factors accounts for the creeping pace of performance to date? Some evidence supporting the view that decentralization will for some time remain in the realm of wishful thinking comes from a review of the Central Tunisia Development Project. This action was aimed at transforming the poorest populated section of the country. The idea was to carve up three central gouvernorats, placing their poorer dryland portions under the control of a quasi-autonomous body, l' Office de développement de la Tunisie centrale, the Central Tunisia Development Authority, or CTDA. On paper, and as usual, the CTDA is well endowed with the legal powers to plan, initiate, coordinate, and implement actions in agriculture, water management, social services, health, and so forth. Launched in 1979, it has its own Evaluation and Planning Unit in the field, fairly well staffed and very well equipped.[104] It has been the recipient of substantial amounts of financial and technical assistance from USAID. Its called-for operations included a number of innovative, localized development efforts. Among these was the creation of an "experimental fund," which would identify small, promising but high-risk ventures shunned by central planners and then both set them in motion and evaluate them locally. The underlying idea was that by eliminating the constant to-ing and fro-ing between local initiation and central approval processes, one could gain solid implementation experience for untried field staff, while at the same time one might hit upon inexpensive, high payoff projects. Other components of the project were equally innovative; all aimed at building decentralized planning and local implementation capacities.

As of mid-1981, admittedly a very short two and a half years into the project, the results were slim. Planned project outputs had not been achieved. The Evaluation and Planning Unit was disorganized. Some officials of normal line ministries dismissed the project and the

CTDA as an expensive, inappropriate, American-inspired idea. Within Tunisia, the normal line of explanation for the poor performance so far was problems of management and the lack of experience and competence of junior personnel. These factors are very important, but they are not the whole story.

Decades of ingrained centralization directly contribute to the CTDA's difficulties. That is, the regional planning and spatial, as opposed to microeconomic, implementation approach of the CTDA is completely alien to Tunisian sensibilities. Lacking control of its finances, the CTDA must submit all its subprojects to Tunis for funding approval. The central officials in the ministries of the interior, planning, and finance do not understand the CTDA or its approach, and they continually ask why its actions are not proposed in the normal manner, through normal channels, or why the Authority is engaging in tasks that are normally the responsibility of the line ministries? (The problem is severely compounded by the fact that the CTDA is new; it is the only development authority in Tunisia. There are eleven other "authorities," but they are technical, mainly irrigation, units, without major planning responsibilities.) Delays, demands for further justifying information, and refusals to allow expenditure are the frequent result.

Interviewed officials on all levels indicated that the proper role of a subnational unit is to execute directives given from above. American technical assistance to the CTDA's planning unit ran into great difficulty by proposing a regional plan (they had been expressly charged with this task by the project agreement) that assumed the CTDA was precisely what the law said it was: an independent planning and implementation body, able to act without close central supervision and committed to the notion of a regional locus of planning and power. But when the rhetorical bluff was called and a preliminary strategy produced expressir these assumptions concretely, the central-level Tunisians withdre.v in alarm. They claimed the CTDA and its advisers were exceeding their authority, and they characterized the draft strategy as "premature" and as not based on existing political realities.[105] Eventually the Tunisian central officials sent a second team into the area to produce an acceptable plan, that is, one that discussed the mobilization of local resources to fit the Tunis-set objectives of the national plan.

Strengthening regional and local responses to centrally set goals — that is as far as "decentralization" goes in Tunisia today. As elsewhere in the region, the Tunisian decentralization picture is not currently as bleak as it was a decade ago. Because of the evident shortcomings of previous centralist policies, decentralization pressures have increased, personalities have changed, and strategies have become more flexible. All these developments constitute some grounds on which a reasonably optimistic scenario for change can be built. But they are merely hopeful signs, not evidence that change is about to take place. As Ben Achour and Moussa concluded, what one finds in Tunisia at present is a spirit of reform, but not the reforms themselves.[106]

DECENTRALIZATION IN MOROCCO

The decentralization situation in Morocco resembles that found in Tunisia. Morocco, too, inherited and strengthened a centralized institutional framework. Moreover, postindependence political and administrative outcomes have generally and ultimately depended directly on the personal decisions of the heads of state, King Mohammed V and the present ruler, Hassan II. Morocco does differ from other North African states in many important ways — for example, in its linguistic/cultural divisions, in the persistence of the traditional political leadership, and in its long-standing, if limited, tolerance of multiparty political competition. But in the first twenty years of independence the crucial powers of fiscal control and policy initiation were consistently retained at the center. Moreover, and in line with developments in the rest of the region, it was in the mid-1970s that the first official announcements were made concerning a new policy of decentralizing responsibilities through a revitalization of the local government system. Since 1976 a great many efforts have been set in motion that, if carried through to fruition, will greatly change the location and focus of government activities in Morocco.

Morocco is currently divided into 7 economic planning regions (created in 1971), and 43 provinces or *préfectures*, each headed by a powerful *gouverneur*. The préfectures are administratively subdivided into *cercles*, each headed by an official called a *super caid*. Cercles are made up of *communes*. There are 45 urban communes, 40 "autonomous communes," which are semiurban in nature, and 761 rural communes. Administrative figures called *pachas* in the urban areas and *caids* in the rural areas oversee the operations of two or more communes, the number depending on population density. All of these officials are part of the national civil service; Sbih notes that all "represent the executive power"[107] and that their perspective has tended to be centralist. As shall be seen, there are now some signs that this is changing.

Very little written information is available on the functioning of the lower administrative units. The lack of published materials reflects the simple fact that until the recent past the attention of the central government has been focused on the upper levels of the administration. In a 1980 interview, the then director of the Moroccan National School of Public Administration stated that he had repeatedly been struck by the lack of the most basic information on the lower units of the country, particularly the rural communes.[108] He hoped to start a final-year field internship for his students, in the course of which teams of senior students would visit rural communes and establish inventories of government services, obtain facts and figures on population and production, gain a general picture of the agricultural or livestock situation, and discuss economic possibilities. That the head of the national civil service training institute was in need of such fundamental data and had to propose such an ad hoc method to obtain them indicates the depth of the need.

In June 1975 King Hassan announced an intention "to enlarge to the maximum the attributions and the responsibilities of elected representatives, and to accord to them in the future the means giving them the power to control local efforts."[109] This was to be accomplished by reconstituting the elected municipal and rural communal councils and endowing them with expanded resources, powers, and competence. (That the rural communes were included in the reform sharply distinguishes the effort from the similar, and similarly timed, Tunisian action.) In the following twelve months, enabling texts were drawn up, without which no Moroccan (or Algerian or Tunisian) government action can be implemented. The result, in September 1976, was a series of royal decrees that were gathered together and published under the title, *Communal Organization: Organization of the Finances of Local Governments*.[110] The decrees established revised communal elected assemblies and described in great legal detail their organization, the attributions of communal council presidents (legally dominant figures), and the manner in which the budgets of both the communes and provinces would be formed, and created a Local Government Development Fund, run by the powerful Ministry of the Interior. Based on the principles of these decrees, in November 1976 competitive elections were held in all rural and urban communes, and over 13,000 local councillors were chosen.

In principle, these elected communal councils and the indirectly elected provincial councils above them possess great powers. By law, they must be consulted by central authorities when any action of local concern is under consideration. The communal councils are theoretically responsible for the delivery of local social services. In time, communal councils are expected to become centers of local planning. Unlike the provincial councils, the budgets of which are financed totally from central subsidies, the communal councils possess some legal prospects of generating their own funds — though these are currently so limited that, for the moment, they too depend almost totally on central subsidies and centrally controlled block grants.

The texts mentioned the key need to overhaul the fund-raising powers of the local governments, both provincial and communal. Until the late 1960s, certain national Moroccan taxes were legally tied for the use of local governments; that is, the revenues generated by certain taxes were designated solely for the use of local authorities. These funds were insufficient for the local governments' needs; the system was ended at the close of the 1960s and replaced by direct subsidization. After the mid-1970s reforms, direct subsidization has continued, but it is now supplemented by the reserving of income generated from forest reserves to those very few communes possessing such resources, and by the availability of three central funds that loan money to local governments for infrastructure investments. These are the Special Regional Development Fund, the Communal Equipment Fund, and the previously mentioned Local Government Development Fund. The sums available in these three funds have grown tremendously since the early and mid-1970s. For example, the Local Government Development Fund grew from a 100 million dirham appropriation in 1977 to 1.1 billion dirhams in 1979.[111] Direct transfers from the treasury to local governments are also on the increase; in 1973 direct transfers totalled 100 million dirhams; by 1979 the sum had reached 270 million.[112] Accompanying the monetary increase was a substantial enlargement in the number of civil service staff attached to local governments, and the most recent five-year plan, of 1981-1985, forecasts a continuing and sizable growth in both funds and personnel for the local government system.[113] All of this represents a substantial Moroccan commitment to the concept of decentralization.

It is true that the formal conditions of decentralization are not yet being met; that is, the local governments, with rare exceptions, do not raise their own funds and dispense them as they see fit. Again, one must acknowledge the harsh realities. The rural countryside is so poor that there is simply no tax base for local self-reliance. The rural local councillors are inexperienced and uneducated. A Moroccan official interviewed in March 1982 estimated that as many as half of the communal council presidents were illiterate. On the reasonable assumption that many councils would tend to choose their more educated members to serve as presidents, it seems likely that the level of illiteracy of the councillors as a whole is far greater than 50 percent.[114] In such circumstances, complete local self-reliance would likely result in rapidly increasing inequities between well-endowed and less well-endowed areas.

To assist the councils in their expanded tasks, the government created, in 1977, a special new civil service corps for posts in the local council system. Each urban and autonomous communal council is currently provided with a centrally trained and paid chief civil servant called a secretary-general; this assistance is being expanded as the new corps feeds secretaries-general (SGs) and other technical officers to the rural local governments. The first group of about eighty SGs for rural communes was graduated from a special six-month course in mid-1982. Probably it will take four or five years to train SGs for all 761 rural communes. These officials are vital, since it is their ability to formulate project proposals in a manner acceptable to central fund dispensers that will allow the rural communes to tap the resources available in the centrally controlled investment funds.

Up to 1980, the bulk of approved expenditures under the three investment funds has been in productive infrastructure fields — roads, public works, rural water, irrigation facilities, and training.[115] Not surprisingly, the Southern Economic Region, which presumably includes the newly incorporated but still contested Saharan territories, has received close to a third of all the funds dispensed by the Special Regional Development Fund.[116] To move to social expenditures, with a higher level of involvement of local officials and people, will require even greater increases in the number of skilled personnel at the provincial and communal levels. It is recognized that local staff must be trained in local finance, accounting, planning, and economic appraisal of projects. To implement decentralization fully, the locally elected representatives must also gain a basic familiarity with at least the principles of these operations. In 1981, a new Directorate of Training was created in the Ministry of the Interior and charged with the tasks of assessing the staff needs of local governments, training these officials, *and* providing short-term "information" courses to communal councillors. The new directorate is moving rapidly to expand the number of training institutions and courses devoted to local government needs. Interviews and observations in March 1982 revealed an impressive amount of energy and resources being committed to the local government training programs. Neither the ultimate success nor even the short-run continuation of these efforts is assured; Morocco's very difficult present economic position could well lead to the curtailment of funds, personnel, and commitment. But at the moment, prospects are bright.

Of course, the usual cautions are in order. What one has here is a situation akin to the tutorial perspective found in Algeria. An unskilled, unstaffed, and very poor local council system is being provided with a few trained advisers and civil service workers and is being given access to earmarked national funds — provided the councils can produce acceptable project proposals, the definition of "acceptable" remaining in central hands. Is this decentralization? Given Moroccan past practices, it is something very close to it. As the king said in introducing the reforms in 1975:

> It is, for the elected representatives, a school where one learns how to manage a budget, to organize action and to execute plans, a school which trains citizens conscious of the true priorities and sensitive to the needs of the population.[117]

Will it work? The 1978 study by André Baldous was pessimistic; he stressed the passivity of the rural Moroccan population and the "indifference" of local councillors, as both groups have grown used to direction from the "incomparably more well-endowed" national government.[118] Moreover, Moroccan councillors are not paid for their services. Only the commune president, chosen by fellow councillors, and a very few heads of standing committees receive a salary. This weakens the council in general and its participation/decentralization aspects in particular. Lack of a cash incentive further reduces the already meager likelihood that ordinary farmers and workers will run for office. Moreover, though it is logical to assume that those who run for office are doing so for reasons other than immediate material gain, still the rate of absences from council meetings is very high.

Councillors who do attend meetings are often ignorant of their powers and tend to defer to the opinions of the administrators, either those serving the councils or the pachas and caids. Baldous notes an absence of precise information on how one goes about implementing the new powers and states that at every step the councillors are overwhelmed by the myriad forms, policies, and procedures that must be completed before the central government will allow expenditure to take place.[119] The official counterargument is that these admitted deficiencies will be corrected as the councillors receive training and become more familiar with their responsibilities and as the local civil service system expands. For the moment, however, what one has in Morocco is more decentralization of powers to local-level officials, and not yet to elected representatives.

CONCLUSION

In the Maghreb region, four governments are moving to deconcentrate and decentralize their modes of government and administration. With the exception of Libya — and here the situation is confused and the information incomplete — decentralization policies have been implemented at a very slow pace. The Maghreb governments claim that cautious, step-by-step implementation is natural and necessary, given the social context and human resource levels with which they are working. Repeatedly they state or imply that time is needed to build up skills and competencies, to change attitudes, and to perfect new patterns of administration and behavior. They point to the fact that, though local governments are legally empowered to take action in many fields, they frequently fail to do so because of their own timidity and ignorance, not because of central government control. (The governments fail to note, however, that having the legal power to take action means little unless it is accompanied by financial powers, which are generally absent or very limited and, even where present, are still ultimately controlled by the center.) Despite qualifications, the governments' argument has merit. Full immediate transfer to the local level of policy initiation and implementation powers would very likely result in costly inefficiencies at best and destabilizing breakdowns at worst.[120] Even partial transfers require money, skilled people, and a receptive populace — unless the goal is simply to increase involvement of local officials, in which case a receptive populace is somewhat less important. Thus, when North African governments say they are constrained in what they can propose and how rapidly they can put into effect that which they do propose, they are putting forward a plausible argument.

But clearly, the argument is also a rationalization for inaction, a justification for maintaining the ultimate power of decision in central offices. The gap that exists between the fulsome official rhetoric of decentralization and the meager nature of the powers actually transferred to noncentral agencies is sufficiently wide, and sufficiently visible, to allow critics to dismiss most efforts as propaganda for the gullible, masking the retention of power by the dominant elites. One can therefore find in the literature complete rejections of the Maghrebian governments' claims to decentralization, and to democratization and participation efforts in general.[121]

This dismissal carries considerable weight. In North Africa, as elsewhere, it is evident that issues of power and self-interest are never absent from the calculus of policy, and one can readily construct an explanation of events based on the assumption that elite self-interest is the major determinant of outcomes. But one must also realize that decentralization is a particularly complicated and indeed contradictory undertaking, and that ostensibly decentralizing policies — sincerely attempted — can have an ultimately centralizing impact. For example, both Tunisia and Algeria are officially committed to policies of regional equilibrium, aimed at correcting potentially destabilizing economic imbalances between poor and rich sections of the countries. These programs are offered as evidence of decentralization. But as Ben Achour and Moussa point out, such policies are naturally centralizing, as only the national government can channel resources away from the comparatively well-off regions and toward the deprived.[122]

The same authors also argue that all financial transfers, even those supposedly aimed at decentralizing goals — such as the Tunisian PDR — have a centralizing effect, as long as the center retains the final financial say. A more paradoxical Algerian example of the difficulties involved is the negative effect of a recently announced industrial decentralization program on the long-standing effort to devolve power to the rural cooperative system. A number of observers have noted the large number of Algerian farmers who have given up the plots of land and positions in cooperatives assigned to them by the agrarian reform movement. It has long been obvious that they were leaving the land in order to seek employment in the urban sector, but only recently has it been realized that the decentralizing policy of shifting industrial plants to outlying towns has dramatically increased the rural exodus, as prospects for nonagricultural employment are now found so much closer to home.[123] This may be good development policy, but the important rural decentralization program has suffered. Particularly in this last instance, this is not a case of central officials blocking the initiative or power of decision of local people; this is one decentralization effort having an unanticipated, negative effect on another.

The point is this: Along with the shortage of skills and the difficult cultural context, these unanticipated complications strike one as very important in the explanatory equation of why Maghrebian decentralization moves at such a creaking pace. It is not possible to sort out precisely whether these factors are as important as the pursuit of self-interest on the part of elites. What one can say is that they are of significance.

What one is wrestling with here is a judgment on the utility or futility of offering prescriptive recommendations of an incremental nature. If one concludes that elite self-interest is the only meaningful explanatory factor, then it does not make much sense to discuss minor reforms. The only logical conclusion would be a call for total societal transformation, as a necessary condition for the creation of a democratic, participatory system of decentralized policy initiation and implementation. If, on the other hand, one interprets the currently less-than-satisfactory Maghrebian decentralization situation as being shaped by a range of determinants — of which elite dominance is only one, albeit an important one — then it is legitimate to retain hopes of effecting progressive change within the boundaries of the existing political/administrative system.

One major point of this study has been that one must not underestimate the strength or the intransigence of established North African elites. But equally, it would be unwise to treat the elites as a monolithic force, united in their determination to prevent change. Moreover, the amount of attention that the Maghrebian governments have recently paid to the decentralization theme demonstrates a modicum of responsiveness — partly to their own populations and partly to the evolving constituency of local intellectuals, middle-range officials, and interested foreign parties that attempts to influence policy outcomes in the region. In sum, and admitting the absence of conclusive objective evidence to support the view, I assert that the possibility remains for progressive internal reforms.

What could be done? In Algeria, Tunisia, and Morocco a fundamental first step would be an attack on the concept of *tutelle* — the practice of supervision, especially fiscal supervision, by central authorities, of the actions of local or subordinate units. This was a keystone of the inherited system, and it has been polished and buttressed ever since independence, though not in Libya. The concept is deeply embedded in the Maghrebian legal and administrative framework; it is unthinkable that it could be eliminated totally or rapidly. But it is conceivable that tutelle supervision could be relaxed or abolished, on a trial basis, for a limited range of actions — of the type such as the PDR in Tunisia, for example. The added responsibilities might stimulate local endeavor. Competent local performance, in turn, might persuade national officials of the feasibility of further relaxation. Agreed, it is equally possible that local officials, freed from higher-level review, might channel resources toward goals that conflict with national priorities or, worse, that local authorities might manage programs so poorly as to call into question the entire venture. These are real risks. It is precisely because of these risks that one must start small, with limited arenas of action. These efforts must be treated as an experiment and supported by additions of trained staff. In this regard, the Moroccan situation appears especially promising.

The range of needs and actions necessary to bring about meaningful change is, obviously, very broad. Even in the small-scale experiments suggested here, there are many points at which the process could be assessed by central decision makers as failing — or, perhaps worse, threatening — and brought to a halt. It can be seen from this that decentralization is not a limited tactical "solution" to perceived problems. It is an entire alternative strategy in itself. A realization that this is the case is discouraging for those who would like to view decentralization as an easily imposed technique. At the same time, the realization lends weight to the North African governments' insistence that only a slow-moving tutorial approach can put decentralized policies into effect.

A second conclusion is that an area needing study — prior to any consideration of decentralizing reform — is the local public finance situation in all four Maghrebian states. The dearth of solid information on local revenue generation, on local council or administrative subunit budgeting, and on the central governments' grant and loan process to subnational units limits the discussion of decentralization to what are essentially secondary and indirect matters. The heart of the matter — money — is placed on the edge and not at the center of the discourse. It is true that what information is available indicates a centralization of all fiscal authority; but a consideration of where changes could be effected demands more precise and detailed information on how the present systems function. Such a study would most likely indicate that the central grant and loan process remains of paramount importance, yet it would still be revealing to have knowledge of the strategies used by subunits and councils to secure central funds. All that one currently possesses are tantalizing hints: For example, Hugh Roberts's study of the Kabylia region of Algeria noted in passing that the local APW "decided" to embark on a large construction program that included post offices, housing, two hospitals, schools, and even a factory.[124] This "decision" reflects both resources and the power to allocate them. But one is not told where the resources came from or who had to approve their expenditure. The implication is that the Assembly controls the issue, but it is only an implication. Harder data are required.

Third, one might offer the following argument: Though it is not possible to state exactly where and how North African decentralization will be further advanced, advanced it certainly will be — because of the pressures accumulating from the reforms already set in motion. These reforms, no matter how halting and imperfect, have launched a process extremely difficult to reverse. Though central leaders and officials will no doubt be reluctant further to transform their rhetoric into reality, eventually they will be pushed into action by the several and growing forces that favor decentralization. To repeat, these forces include the reconstituted local councils and assemblies, opinion makers in the region's political parties and universities, at least some middle-level officials, and most of the international agency and donor community in the region. The thrust of the argument is that the concept of decentralization, in its various forms, has gathered significant momentum in North Africa and that rational leaders will perceive the costs of trying to slow or stop the process as outweighing the benefits.

The problem with this argument is the ease with which one can sketch an opposing view, based on the defensible contention that what has been set in motion so far can still be reversed. In the event of an economic crisis, in the event of an external threat, in the event of an assessment that decentralized units are acting contrary to the national interest (however and by whomever defined), then recentralization would be a likely response of alarmed governments. At the very best, they would be likely to freeze the situation in its present state. One can make a case that the half-formed constituency of clients and interests in favor of decentralization is not sufficiently well defined or powerful to counter such action (or inaction). It is thus plausible to argue that the incipient decentralization efforts could be allowed to stagnate or actually be repressed. The latter would be most difficult to effect in Libya, only somewhat less difficult in Algeria, and least difficult of all in Tunisia and Morocco. All in all, to state that the process of decentralization is irreversible would be to misread the strength of the contending parties, as well as to misread the grip within the region of the notion of the organic unity of the state.

In sum, it is not at all difficult to construct and defend opposing interpretations of what is likely to happen regarding decentralization in North Africa. This is hardly an exceptional situation in policy analysis studies, especially those dealing with underdeveloped countries. The data base is weak; trends are not well established; patterns of action are not set. Thus, it is not unusual for conclusions of studies to take the safe route by listing the questions the next study should ask, rather than risk flagrant error by proferring guestimates that prove incorrect. The risks of speculation notwithstanding, the final assessment is that one can be guardedly optimistic concerning the prospects for decentralization in the Maghreb. That is, the study accepts the premise of the optimistic argument — that efforts to date have activated a clientele of some significance, a clientele that cannot be totally ignored or indefinitely put off with rhetoric. Decentralization has achieved a difficult-to-reverse status in the region.

But a weighing of the number and intensity — and increases in both — of the voices in favor of decentralization is only a part of the assessment. There is also the less substantial but still important factor that the development strategies pursued since independence are widely viewed as inadequate, even or especially among the younger generation of the ruling elites. Perhaps precisely because of its vague and untested nature, the concept of decentralization appears to offer a progressive way out of present problems, and it does so without shaking the foundations of the established postcolonial systems. Therefore, North African regimes will continue to tinker with minor decentralizing reforms. In so doing, they launch an accumulating process that will eventually result in decentralized policy initiation and implementation.

NOTES

1. Martin Walker, "Gadafy — The Magnificent Child of Wrath," *The Guardian*, September 13, 1981, p. 8. (No two sources spell the Libyan leader's name the same way.)

2. Lucette Valensi, *On the Eve of Colonialism: North Africa Before the French Conquest* (New York: Africana, 1977), p. 73.

3. Andrew C. Hess, *The Forgotten Frontier* (Chicago: University of Chicago Press, 1978), pp. 21-22.

4. *Ibid*. See also J. B. Wolf, *The Barbary Coast: Algiers Under the Turks – 1500 to 1830* (New York: Norton, 1979), who notes that "no strong power emerged in the central Maghrib. By the opening of the fifteenth century, there was no real central authority. [In the area now known as Tunisia the regime was weak] . . . and largely unable to control the powerful Arab tribes, or to govern the towns over which it pretended suzerainity . . . in Morocco, too, decadence rather than political vigor best describes the government of the land. The central Maghrib, the territory we know as Algeria today, was without any government that could even pretend to speak for the entire land" (p. 3).

5. Robert Montagne, *The Berbers: Their Social and Political Organization* (London: Constable, translation of 1931 edition published in 1973), p. 82.

6. L. Carl Brown, *The Tunisia of Ahmed Bey – 1827-1855* (Princeton, NJ: Princeton University Press, 1974), pp. 197-200.

7. Raphael Danziger, *Abd al-Qadir and the Algerians* (New York: Holmes & Meier, 1977), Ch. 1, *passim*, especially p. 23.

8. Valensi, *On the Eve of Colonialism*, p. 119. Valensi's appendix, pp. 111-120, offers an excellent summary of the various reasons that have been put forward to account for the rapid submission of Algeria, Tunisia, and eventually Morocco to French colonial rule.

9. *Ibid*., p. 80.

10. *Ibid*., p. 117.

11. Ernest Gellner, *Saints of the Atlas* (London: Weidenfeld & Nicolson, 1969), p. 41.

12. *Ibid*., p. 43.

13. *Ibid*., p. 42.

14. Brown, *Tunisia*, p. 190.

15. *Ibid*., p. 192.

16. *Ibid*., p. 196.

17. *Ibid*., p. 200.

18. Bruno Etienne, *L'Algérie, Cultures et Révolutions* (Paris: Editions de Seuil, 1977), p. 31. (This, and all other translations from the French, are made by this author.)

19. *Ibid*.

20. *Ibid*., p. 29.

21. Something of this sentiment persists. During the 1976 public debate on the ideological direction to be followed, many Algerians supported the idea that "we want a Muslim regime, whether it be capitalist or socialist" (quoted in John Nellis, *The Algerian National Charter: Content, Public Reaction and Significance* (Washington, DC: Center for Contemporary Arab Studies, Georgetown University, 1980), p. 32.

22. Jean Leca and Jean-Claude Vatin, "Le Système Politique Algérien (1976-1978): Idéologie, Institutions et Changement Social," *Annuaire de l'Afrique du Nord,* vol. XVI (1977), p. 20. (A 1977 publication reports on 1978 events because the *AAN* is running late; this issue was put together and published in 1979.)

23. *Ibid*., p. 27.

24. Thierry Brethier, "Decentralization Bill: Power to the Regions," *Le Monde,* July 15, 1981, translated and reprinted in the *Manchester Guardian Weekly,* July 26, 1981, p. 11.

25. Missoum Sbih, *Les Institutions Administratives du Maghreb* (Paris: Hachette, 1977), p. 13.

26. *Ibid.*

27. Personal interview with a Moroccan sociologist, Rabat, Morocco, May 1980.

28. For one example from each of the three francophone countries, see Raymond Apthorpe, "Peasants and Planistrators: Rural Cooperatives in Tunisia," *Maghreb Review,* vol. 2, no. 1 (January/February 1977), whole study, but especially p. 8; Paolo DeMas, *Marges Marocaines: Limites de la Coopération au Développement dans une Région Périphérique: Le Cas du Rif* (The Hague: Remplod, 1978), whole study; and Abdelkrim Elaïdi, "Le Processus de Constitution d'une Organisation Paysanne dans le Cadre de la Révolution Agraire," *Revue Tiers-Monde,* special issue on Algeria, vol. XXI, no. 83 (July-September 1980), pp. 627-647.

29. Figure taken from World Bank, *World Development Report, 1981* (Washington, DC: Oxford University Press, 1981), p. 135.

30. Libyan dependence, and, parenthetically, the skills of its leader, Muammar Qadafi, were revealed in 1978 after the General People's Congress passed a resolution demanding the expulsion of all foreigners residing in the country. Qadafi seized the main microphone, smashed it to bits on the head table, and then shouted to ask if there was anyone in the gathering who could fix it. Silence. Qadafi said that when Libyans could produce and maintain their own technology, then the foreigners would go. Reported in Hervé Bleuchot et Taoufik Monastiri, "Libye: L'Evolution des Institutions Politiques," *Annuaire de l'Afrique du Nord,* vol. XVI (1977): 181.

31. Naomi Caiden and Aaron Wildavsky, *Planning and Budgeting in Poor Countries* (New York: John Wiley, 1974), p. 49.

32. *Ibid.,* p. 50.

33. There is a very substantial literature interpreting North African events from a class perspective. See, for example, Ruth First, *Libya: The Elusive Revolution* (London: Penguin Books, 1974); Jean Poncet, *La Tunisie à la Recherche de Son Avenir* (Paris: Notre Temps/Monde, 1974); Marnia Lazreg, *The Emergence of Classes in Algeria* (Boulder, CO: Westview Press, 1976); the articles by Jean-Jacques Regnier and Werner Ruf in CRESM, *Introduction à l'Afrique du Nord Contemporaine* (Paris: Editions du CNRS, 1975); and the eleven articles in Sections II, III, and IV in the special edition, "Du Maghreb," *Les Temps Modernes,* no. 375 BIS (October 1977).

34. For a discussion of this issue, see John R. Nellis, "Algerian Socialism and Its Critics," *Canadian Journal of Political Science,* vol. XIII, no. 3 (September 1980), especially pp. 493-496; 502-506.

35. Dennis A. Rondinelli and G. Shabbir Cheema, "Implementing Decentralization Policies: An Introduction," in this volume.

36. F. Rivier, "L'Autonomie des Unités Agricoles du Secteur Socialiste," *Revue Algérienne des sciences juridiques, economiques et politiques (RASJEP),* vol. XIII, no. 2 (June 1976): 380.

37. Thus, Ruth First on Libya: "Change can, however, not be bureaucratically imposed from above without the mobilization of the masses of the people, and without their assertion of their need for social control of the productive forces and political systems of their countries" (*Libya,* p. 257); and Marnia Lazreg argues that one of the main reasons for dismissing the Algerian claim to socialist status is that Algerian workers, even in the public sector, "do not participate in the management of the finances of the enterprise . . . nor do they market the product of their labor" (*Emergence of Classes,* p. 10).

38. For definitions and discussions of the term *jamahiriya,* see Sami G. Hajjar, "The Jamahiriya Experiment in Libya: Qadafi and Rousseau," *Journal of Modern African Studies,* vol. 18, no. 2 (June 1980): 181-200; and Bleuchot et Monastiri, "Libye."

39. Libya's 2.5 million people are scattered thinly over a very large area; historically the territory was a nonunified amalgam of three distinct regions: Cyrenaica, Tripolitania, and Fezzan. For a brief summary of how the Libyan state emerged from these three units, see Omar I. El Fathaly, "Libya: The Social, Economic and Historical Milieus," in Omar I. El Fathaly *et al., Political Development and Bureaucracy in Libya* (Lexington, MA: D.C. Heath, 1977), pp. 21-23.

40. *Ibid.,* p. 16.

41. Bleuchot et Monastiri, "Libye," p. 150.

42. *Ibid.,* p. 156.

43. Bleuchot et Monastiri give the 2,400 figure on p. 156 of their article; Hajjar writes that 450 popular committees were in existence in 1973 ("The Jamahiriya Experiment, p. 185).

44. Bleuchot et Monastiri, "Libye," p. 157. See also Valerie Plave Bennett, "Libyan Socialism," in *Socialism in the Third World,* ed. Helen Desfosses and Jaques Levesque (New York: Praeger, 1975), pp. 115-116, for a discussion of these events.

45. Hajjar, "The Jamahiriy Experiment," p. 186.

46. Bleuchot et Monastiri, "Libye," p. 169.

47. Hajjar, "The Jamahiriya Experiment," p. 186.

48. Bleuchot et Monastiri, "Libye," p. 169.

49. Hajjar, "The Jamahiriya Experiment," p. 198.

50. Bleuchot et Monastiri, "Libye," p. 141.

51. Economist Intelligence Unit, *Quarterly Economic Report, Libya, Tunisia and Malta,* Fourth Quarter, 1980, p. 2 states: "Administration by revolutionary people's committees is giving rise to confusion, frustration, shortages, harassment, corruption, waste and inefficiency."

52. See Omar I. El Fathaly and Fathi Abusidra, "The Impact of Socio-Political Change on Economic Development in Libya," *Middle Eastern Studies,* vol. 16, no. 3 (October 1980): 225-235; and Hajjar, "The Jamahiriya Experiment."

53. Hervé Bleuchot, "Libye: Chronique Politique," *Annuaire de l'Afrique du Nord,* vol. XVI (1977): 493-495. Bleuchot offers lengthy quotations revealing exchanges between Qadafi and the congressional delegates.

54. On *autogestion,* see Gérard Duprat, *Révolution et Autogestion Rurale en Algérie* (Paris: Armand Colin, 1973); Claudine Chaulet, *La Mitidja Autogerée* (Algiers: S.N.E.D., 1971); Thomas Blair, *The Land to Those Those Who Work It* (Garden City: Anchor, 1970); Ian Clegg, *Workers' Self-Management in Algeria* (New York: Monthly Review Press, n.d.); Sergé Koulychizky, *L'Autogestion, l'Homme et L'Etat* (Paris/The Hague: Mouton, 1974); and for a brief summary, John Nellis, "Workers' Participation in Algeria's Nationalized Industries: La Gestion Socialiste des Entreprises," Occasional Paper no. 30 (Ottawa: School of International Affairs, Carleton University, 1976), pp. 5-11.

55. Keith Sutton, "Algeria: Centre-Down Development, State Capitalism and Emergent Decentralization," in *Development from Above or Below?* ed. W.B. Stohr and D.R. Fraser Taylor (New York: John Wiley, 1981), p. 356.

56. This is the opinion of Lazreg *(The Emergence of Classes)* and Clegg *(Workers' Self-Management),* for example.

57. Duprat's careful study states that yields declined in wine, citrus, and cereals after autogestion. (*Révolution et Autogestion*, p. 240).

58. The steps in this process are reviewed in J. R. Nellis, "Socialist Management in Algeria," *Journal of Modern African Studies*, vol. 15, no. 4 (1977): 530-532.

59. Houari Boumedienne in 1965, quoted in John Waterbury, *Land, Man and Development in Algeria*, Part III (Hanover, NH: Reports of the American Universities Field Staff, 1973), p. 1.

60. Houari Boumedienne in 1968, quoted by David and Marina Ottaway, *Algeria: The Politics of a Socialist Revolution* (Berkeley: University of California Press, 1970), p. 270.

61. Prior to 1974 there were fifteen wilaya; in that year the number was expanded to thirty-one, as a decentralizing measure to bring government closer to the people. There are thus now thirty-one APWs.

62. Wilfrid Knapp, *North-West Africa: A Political and Economic Survey*, 3rd ed. (New York: Oxford University Press, 1977), p. 117.

63. Nellis, "Socialist Management in Algeria," p. 549.

64. Interview with the late Ahmed Medeghri, in *El Moudhahid* (French-language daily of Algiers), February 17-18, 1974, p. 3.

65. See *Charte et Code de la Gestion Socialiste des Entreprises* (Algiers: Imprimerie Officielle, November 1971); and *Charte de la Révolution Agraire* (Algiers: Ministère de l'Agriculture et de la Réforme Agraire, Novembre 1971).

66. For example, the opening paragraph of the socialist management charter states: "Having recovered its sovereignty, established solid foundations for the institutions of the state, improved the health of the economy, and recovered its national riches, Algeria is setting out henceforth on the process of construction of the material bases of socialism. The new socialist organization of enterprises marks a decisive stage of revolutionary construction" (*Charte et Code*, p. 5).

67. Lars Jönsson, "La Révolution Agraire en Algérie: Historique, Contenu et Problèmes," Research Report no. 47 (Uppsala: Scandinavian Institute of African Studies, 1978), p. 25.

68. Nellis, "Socialist Management," p. 547.

69. Omar Bessaoud, "La Révolution Agraire en Algérie," *Revue Tiers-Monde*, vol. XXI, no. 83 (July-September 1980), p. 607.

70. *Ibid.*, p. 618. 52,000 divided by 4,205 equals 12.37 persons on average; the CAPRAs are obviously quite small groupings.

71. Official Algerian document, quoted in Jönsson, "La Révolution Agraire," p. 38.

72. This is the opinion of Jonsson ("La Révolution Agraire"), Bessaoud ("La Révolution Agraire"), Rivier ("L'Autonomie"), and Elaïdi ("Le Processus").

73. Figures given in Jönsson, "La Révolution Agraire," p. 33.

74. Jönsson discusses the workings of the APCEs; *ibid.*, pp. 51-53.

75. Leca and Vatin, *L'Algérie politique*, p. 201.

76. République Algérienne Democratique et Populaire, *IIe Plan Quadriennal, Rapport General* (Alger: Imprimerie Officielle, May 1974), p. 242, for example.

77. The basic ideas of the communal planning system are discussed in Sutton, "Algeria," pp. 363-364.

78. Front de Libération Nationale, République Algérienne, *Project de Charte Nationale* (Algiers: El Moudjahid, June 1976), p. 10.

79. *Ibid.*

80. Chabane Benakezouh, "De Quelques Aspects du 'Controle Populaire,'" *Revue algérienne des sciences juridiques, économiques et politiques,* vol. XVI, no. 3 (September 1979), p. 536.

81. *Ibid.,* p. 537.

82. Leca and Vatin, "Le Système Politique Algérien," p. 34.

83. "Résolutions Adoptées par le Congrés Extraordinaire du Parti, Juin, 1980," *Revue algérienne des sciences juridiques, economiques et politiques,* vol. XVII, no. 3 (September 1980), p. 450, emphasis mine.

84. *Ibid.*

85. *Ibid.,* p. 451.

86. *Ibid.,* p. 445.

87. See Elaïdi, "Le Processus," p. 644; and Bessaoud, "La Révolution Agraire," p. 621.

88. Sbih, *Les Institutions,* pp. 137-139, 147.

89. Michel Cointat, *Pour Une Administration Efficace* (Tunis: Programme de Développement de Nations Unies, June/July 1975), p. 44.

90. *Ibid.,* p. 46.

91. This argument was advanced by Clement Henry Moore, *Tunisia Since Independence* (Los Angeles: University of California Press, 1965), and especially Lars Rudebeck, *Party and People: A Study of Political Change in Tunisia* (Stockholm: Almquist & Wiksell, 1967).

92. Cointat, *Pour une Administration Efficace,* pp. 33-40.

93. James Mayfield, "Governmental Structures and Administrative Strategies for an Integrated Rural Development Program in Tunisia" (Unpublished report submitted to USAID/Tunis, July 1978), p. 32.

94. *Ibid.*

95. *Ibid.*

96. Government of Tunisia, "Programme de développement rural," unpublished mimeographed report, Tunis, n.d. but obviously written in 1976, p. 1.

97. *Ibid.,* p. 11.

98. Yadh Ben Achour and Fadhel Moussa, "Réformes, Elections Municipales et Discours Décentralisateur en Tunisie," *Annuaire de l'Afrique du Nord,* vol. XVI (1977): 349. Note that vol. XVI has a 1977 date but was actually published in 1979. Thus, studies in this volume cover events through 1978.

99. *Ibid.,* p. 348.

100. *Ibid.,* p. 349.

101. *Ibid.,* p. 350.

102. *Ibid.,* p. 358.

103. *Ibid.,* p. 359.

104. Information on the Central Tunisia Development project was obtained in personal interviews in Tunis and Kasserine, Tunisia, May-June, 1981. The author was a member of a Tunisian/American team evaluating a subproject of the CTDA, and spent ten days in Kasserine interviewing all members of the CTDA's Evaluation and Planning Unit. All opinions expressed are those of the author and are not necessarily shared by other members of the Evaluation Team, the Government of Tunisia, or USAID.

105. The American advisers presented their strategy in October 1980; Tunisian reaction is obtained from interviews with participants at the presentation session and by a reading of notes on the meeting kept by one participant.

106. Ben Achour and Moussa, "Réformes," p. 377.

107. Sbih, *Les Institutions,* p. 121.

108. Personal interview with the school's director, Rabat, Morocco, May 1980.

109. André Baldous, "La Reforme Communale au Maroc," *Annuaire de l'Afrique du Nord,* vol. XVI (1977): 283.

110. Royaume du Maroc, *Organisation Communale – Organisation des Finances des Collectivités Locales et de leurs Groupements* (Rabat: Imprimerie Officielle, 1976).

111. World Bank data.

112. *Ibid.*

113. Royaume du Maroc, *Projet de Plan de Développement Economique et Social,* vol. I (Rabat: Ministère du Plan, Avril, 1981), pp. 66-68.

114. Personal interview with officials in the Moroccan Ministry of the Interior, Rabat, March 1982.

115. Royaume du Maroc, *Project de Plan,* pp. 65-69.

116. *Ibid.*

117. Quoted in "La décentralisation au Maroc," *Cities Unies,* no. 104 (Fall 1981): 18.

118. Baldous, "La Réforme," p. 306.

119. *Ibid.,* p. 300.

120. One can think of qualifications to this statement. Yugoslavia survived an attempt to combine decentralization and development; if the two were compatible in this instance, why not elsewhere? See Cyrus Ardalan, "Workers' Self-Management and Planning: The Yugoslav Case," *World Development,* vol. 8, no. 9 (September 1980): 623-638. Libya may be a North African example of "elsewhere," though one does not know enough about the workings of the jamahiriya to reach a conclusion.

121. This is the summary opinion of Lazreg *(Emergence of Classes)* on Algeria, Poncet *(La Tunisie)* on Tunisia, and First *(Libya)* on Libya, for example — though it is admitted that these studies are now somewhat dated.

122. Ben Achour and Moussa, "Réformes," p. 351.

123. Bessaoud, "La Révolution Agraire," p. 616.

124. Hugh Roberts, "Kabylia in Transition," *The Maghreb Review,* vol. 3, nos. 7-8 (May-August 1978): 17.

CHAPTER 6

CENTRALIZATION AND DECENTRALIZATION IN LATIN AMERICA

Richard L. Harris

Government decentralization is a complex and multifaceted issue in Latin America. Analysis of recent attempts at decentralization requires an understanding of the contradictory forces at work within the political systems, and particularly the bureaucracies, of Latin American countries, in which strong centralizing tendencies coexist with particular forms of bureaucratic decentralization. Centralizing tendencies remain predominant, and decentralizing forces both are caused by and serve to reinforce them.

Concentration of decision making within central government ministries, often referred to as overcentralization, is a fundamental characteristic of Latin American governments.[1] Thus, it is no accident that the deconcentration of decision making has become an objective of contemporary administrative reforms. The term "decentralization" frequently refers to efforts at deconcentrating or delegating decision making from the headquarters of central government ministries to their lower echelons or field offices. However, other forms of decentralization have been tried in Latin America, and the term is often used to refer to those as well. They include (1) the transfer of functions and decision making authority from the central government to local units of government, (2) the establishment of relatively autonomous public organizations in specific functional areas (such as the creation of a "decentralized" public enterprise to produce steel), and (3) the transfer of public enterprises to private ownership and control (often referred to as "debureaucratization" or "privatization"). Examples of all these forms of decentralization can be found in most Latin American countries and, to a lesser or greater degree, are incorporated in contemporary administratve reforms.[2]

The traditional tendency to concentrate decision making at the upper levels of central government ministries has spawned recent attempts to establish a wide variety of relatively autonomous central government agencies outside of the ministries' direct control. These "decentralized agencies," as they are called in most of Latin America, tend to have their own funds and property and are directed by special governing boards. The inflexible bureaucratic sructure has required the creation of more flexible forms of organization and management, modeled quite often on those of the private sector, particularly for government activities that parallel or substitute for private enterprise. With the rapid expansion of the state's role in the economy over the last three or four decades in Latin America, there has been a proliferation of these decentralized agencies.[3]

Thus, a bewildering array of relatively autonomous public enterprises, institutes, foundations, and other organizations now coexist with traditional central government ministries. The relative autonomy of these agencies, the haphazard manner in which many have been established, and their tendency to assume new functions and responsibilities have given rise to serious problems of coordination and control. To overcome the lack of coordination and the overlapping between these agencies and the central ministries, most recent administrative reforms in Latin America have emphasized *sectorialization,* the grouping and coordination of agencies by related functions, and *regionalization,* the coordination of all government agencies operating within a designated geographical area.

In essence, both sectorialization and regionalization are "centralizing" reforms in that they attempt to coordinate or consolidate diverse government agencies operating in various functional sectors or geographic regions. However, regionalization is often claimed to be decentralization, and in fact some form of decentralization may be involved, but most often only through the deconcentration of decision making from the pinnacle of the central government ministries in the capital to regional offices. Nevertheless, the general direction of such reforms tends to be toward greater centralization because they centralize coordination and control over the diverse, and previously uncoordinated, operations of government agencies in each region.[4]

Another response to the proliferation of decentralized agencies and the problem of coordinating and controlling them is the establishment of "horizontal" interagency commissions and boards that employ a collegial style of decision making and seek coordination through cooperation and joint planning. This is a pattern that is particularly pronounced in Brazil, where there is a strong tendency toward bureaucratic fragmentation and autonomy among the numerous agencies that have been created at the federal and state levels.[5] While this type of structural innovation is intended to extend the control of the central government, the collegial and horizontal nature of coordination appears to reinforce the autonomy of the participating agencies.

Against this backdrop of strong centralizing tendencies and reforms aimed at curbing the power and discretion of decentralized agencies, the general conditions have not been favorable for decentralization policies that devolve or transfer power from the central to local units of government. Nearly everywhere in Latin America, the hypertrophic expansion of the central government bureaucracy is a result of the state's increased involvement in the development of the economy and society and has prejudiced the development of local government. The political and administrative development of local government has tended to be severely retarded by a combination of factors, inducing their lack of financial resources, their shortage of adequately trained personnel, their antiquated structure of government, pervasive corruption, and the predominance of central government agencies operating at the local level.[6]

To a limited degree, current administrative reforms in Latin America are concerned with strengthening the administrative capacity of local governments to permit decentralization of some functions and local participation in development projects. However, the underdevelopment of local government and the reluctance of political leaders at the center to relinquish power have greatly inhibited such efforts and made real devolution rare.

In sum, both centralizing and decentralizing tendencies coexist in the governments of contemporary Latin American countries. In a complicated and often seemingly confused manner, these tendencies combine and conflict with one another, with the centralizing tendency remaining unquestionably dominant. However, this tendency results in the overconcentration of decision making at the top of the hierarchical structure and in turn generates decentralizing efforts aimed at decongesting the overloaded apexes of decision making within central ministries. In this environment, the possibilities for the devolution of power from central bureaucratic agencies to local units of government are not very favorable. Decentralization, where it exists, has taken other, more subtle forms, such as indirect administration and regionalization.

INDIRECT ADMINISTRATION

The proliferation of autonomous agencies at the center of government has given rise to what is sometimes referred to as "indirect administration" (as distinct from the "direct administration" of the traditional ministries).[7] The number and variety of public organizations that can be categorized under this label vary among Latin American countries, but certain general patterns can be identified. Since this type of decentralization tends to be the dominant form in Latin America, it is important to consider briefly the nature and significance of the variations of autonomous agencies that can be found in the region.

Mexico probably has the largest number of autonomous government agencies. The Mexican federal government has created an expanding array of public corporations, mixed enterprises with both state and private capital, marketing boards, credit and loan institutions, research organizations, state holding companies, social service agencies, educational institutions, and regional development commissions. They vary in size from the giant national petroleum corporation, which is almost a government itself, to small institutes and public improvement funds for localities. The federal government groups these autonomous agencies into two general categories: *decentralized organizations* and *parastatal enterprises*.

There are over 100 decentralized organizations, including the giant state petroleum corporation, Petroleos Mexicanos (PEMEX); the national railway corporation, Ferrocarriles Nacionales; the major social assistance agency, Instituto Mexicano del Seguro Social; the major national university, Universidad Nacional Autonoma de Mexico; the state coffee marketing board, Instituto Mexicano del Café; and the national science foundation, Consenjo Nacional de Cinencia y Technologia.[8]

There are also over 400 parastatal enterprises have been established by the Mexican federal government, sometimes with private capital. These include banks, hotels, sugar mills, automobile factories, steel mills, airlines, mines, food industries, insurance companies, clothing manufacturing plants, construction companies, public transportation corporations, the national telephone company, television channels, paper mills, newspapers, and publishing companies.[9] These parastatal enterprises operate under commercial law much like private corporations, except that they have government representatives on their governing boards and their activities are subject to the general oversight of the federal government. The decentralized organizations have their own legal personality, property, funds, and special governing boards, but they fall under special provisions of administrative law instead of the commercial law that regulates parastatal enterprises.[10]

In addition to these two, there is a third form of public organization that has considerable autonomy, although it is not usually considered decentralized. This category includes over 800 independent commissions and councils, including such important bodies as the National Commission for the Development of Arid Areas, the National Council of Cinemagraphic Art, the Federal Commission on Electricity Rates, the National Council of Agriculture, the National Council on Tourism, and such important development agencies as the Commission for the Development of the Papaloapan River Valley.[11] By "independent" it is meant that these agencies are autonomous, separate from central government ministries, although under recent Mexican administrative reforms, they have been grouped by functional sector, like the rest of the federal agencies, and placed under the general coordination of one of the ministries.

One of the main objectives of the current administrative reforms in Mexico is the consolidation and reduction of the number of autonomous agencies and the coordination of those that remain by grouping them and placing them under the supervision of a federal ministry. Eleven sectors have been established, and a single ministry has been assigned responsibility for coordinating sectorial planning, standardizing budgetary, and administrative procedures, and programming their activities. The Ministry of Agriculture and Water Resources, for example, has been assigned responsibility for coordinating and supervising the activities of all the autonomous agencies (decentralized organizations, parastatal enterprises, and commissions) involved in agriculture, fisheries, forestry, irrigation, dams and flood control, hydroelectric projects, and inland waterways.[12] Although it is too early to determine the success of sectorialization, some available data suggest the extent to which the federal government has been able to consolidate and reduce the total number of autonomous agencies. In 1979, 150 were eliminated and 43 new agencies were established,[13] although this three-to-one ratio is somewhat inflated by the fact that some of the new agencies are combinations of two or more of the organizations that were abolished.

In Brazil, the Administrative Reform Act of 1969 and its subsequent amendments have attempted to give some order to the confusing assortment of autonomous agencies that have been created by the federal government. The Act divides the federal bureaucracy into *direct* and *indirect* administrative bodies. The latter are grouped into three categories: (1) autonomous institutions, (2) public enterprises, and (3) mixed enterprises and societies.[14] *Autonomous institutions* encompass a large number of entities that have their own legal personality and earmarked funds. They carry out typical public administration activities, but with some managerial autonomy and financial independence. This category includes the national social security agency, Instituto Nacional de Previdência Social; the central bank of Brazil, Banco Central do Brasil; and the majority of federal universities and technological institutes. The second category, *public enterprises,* includes entities that have a legal personality under private law and their own property. They have been created to carry out economic activities, and their capital is exclusively public, but indirect administrative entities from the federal, state, or municipal levels may participate. By law, the federal government must have a majority of the capital and voting membership on their governing boards. The main difference between these public enterprises and the third category, *mixed enterprises and societies,* is that the latter have access to both public and private capital. Nevertheless, even in the case of mixed enterprises, the federal government generally controls a majority of the voting capital, and in the case of those that are a monopoly, such as Petrobras (the Brazilian state petroleum corporation), the majority of voting capital *must* belong to the federal government.

The magnitude of indirect administration in the Brazilian economy is tremendous; public and mixed enterprises together account for close to 50 percent of the total liquid capital invested in nonagricultural activities in Brazil, whereas nationally owned private enterprises account for 28 percent and foreign-owned enterprises represent 22 percent.[1]

In addition to these three categories of indirect administration there is a fourth type in Brazil that is officially defined as neither a direct nor an indirect administrative entity. These agencies are called *fundacões* (foundations) and perform specific services. Although they are governed by private law, they have been created by the federal government and as such represent something of a contradiction in terms; they are "public foundations."[16] At least one-third of their financial resources must come from private sources, but they are subject to ministerial supervision if they receive any funds from the federal government. They include such important agencies as the Conselho Nacional de Desenvolvimento Científico e Technológico (the National Council for the Development of Science and Technology), the Instituto Brasileiro de Geografia e Estatística (the Brazilian Institute of National Statistics), and the prestigious Fundacao Getulio Vargas (Getulio Vargas Foundaton), which was set up after the death of President Getulio Vargas to serve as a source of technical assistance and training for the reform of the Brazilian federal bureaucracy. In reality, these foundations have a status similar to that of the autonomous institutions in terms of their degree of discretion and their relationship to the rest of the federal government.[17]

Ironically, the autonomous institutions possess the least autonomy of all indirect or decentralized federal administrative agencies. During the 1930s and 1940s, when most of these agencies were created, they enjoyed considerable independence, but over time they appear to have lost much of it and today they are controlled by the same regulations regarding classification of positions, salaries, promotions, and purchasing that apply to the regular departments of the federal government. Those agencies that have maintained their earlier autonomy have since been made public enterprises or foundations.[18]

The degree of autonomy enjoyed by the public enterprises and mixed enterprises and societies appears to be directly related to their size and economic importance. The largest and economically most important enterprises, such as Petrobras, the Companhia Siderúrgica Nacional (the National Metalurgy Company), and the Companhia Vale do Rio Doce (the important regional development corporation for the Rio Doce river valley), tend to have much greater autonomy that their legal charters indicate. Their supervising federal agencies, such as the national petroleum council for Petrobras, are supposed to establish general policies but in practice it appears that the enterprises impose or at least obtain the adoption of the policies that they want.[19] However, under the administrative reforms initiated during the 1970s, the expansion of this important sector of the federal administrative system appears to have been contained. They have been consolidated by sector in an effort to strengthen the control of the central ministries over them.[20] The sectorialization program that has been launched in

Brazil had been much like that in Mexico, and with the same centralizing aims.

The Brazilian government provides an excellent example of the coexistence of centralizing and decentralizing tendencies mentioned earlier and of the problems and results of the interaction of these tendencies. As elsewhere in Latin America, centralization manifests itself in both the overconcentration of decision making at the top of central government ministries and in efforts aimed at coordinating and consolidating the many public organizations that have mushroomed at the central government level. Decentralization, on the other hand, manifests itself in the creation of relatively autonomous agencies and enterprises that can carry out specific functions with greater flexibility and speed than the traditional ministries. It also manifests itself in the efforts of such agencies and enterprises to perserve and extend their separate spheres of influence in opposition to systemwide planning and interagency coordination. Carried to its logical extreme, this tendency gives rise to bureaucratic expansionism through the extension of jurisdictional spheres of influence to the point where overlapping and duplication of functions among autonomous organizations becomes commonplace and a source of almost constant conflict, as has happened at the central level in Brazil, Mexico, and Venezuela.[21]

These coexisting and conflicting tendencies cannot adequately be understood outside their political context. In fact, they appear to be directly related to one of the determining structural conditions of the Latin American political systems, namely, *premature bureaucratization*.[22] That is, the general pattern of political development in Latin America has been one in which the formal bureaucratic structures have developed more rapidly and with greater strength than arrangements for political representation. This results in weak and underdeveloped political interest groups, ineffectual legislative institutions, and unstable political party systems.[23]

In particular, the relatively underdeveloped structure of political interest groups provides a political environment in which centralizing bureaucratic tendencies are not restrained by powerful private groups intent on preserving the autonomy of the bureaucratic agencies that they have captured or that they consider to be sympathetic to their interests. In the absence of countervailing power, the government agencies tend to act as special interest groups. However, they seek to preserve or advance their own influence rather than the interests of other groups in society.[24]

It could be assumed that the development of a variety of powerful interest groups outside of the bureaucracy would strengthen the decentralizing tendencies within the bureaucratic system. This could well be the case, but under the present circumstances, in which very few powerful private interest groups exert pressure on the bureaucracy, centralization is unhindered by external pressures. Moreover, bureaucratic centralization is consistent with the interests and tactics of the political elites in Latin America, whereas decentralization tends to be inconsistent and even threatening to elite rule. When decentralization does take place, as in the establishment of relatively autonomous public enterprises, it is because it is consistent with bureaucratic interests. Decentralization tends to be viewed as a "technical solution" to problems of bureaucratic inflexibility and the overconcentration of decision making in central government ministries.[25] Thus, what has been generally referred to as "indirect administration" appears to be largely a bureaucratic innovation in response to a bureaucratic problem.

REGIONALIZATION

Recent administrative reforms in Latin America have emphasized regional deconcentration of both traditional ministries and autonomous administrative entities. This form of decentralization has been implemented in varying degrees in nearly all the larger Latin American countries, particularly in Argentina, Brazil, Mexico, and Venezuela.

As mentioned earlier, regionalization actually tends to be a centralizing reform aimed at achieving greater coordination among various government agencies operating in a region. However, it can and often does involve some genuine decentralization. Considerable variation can be found among countries in the degree to which power is actually decentralized.

Venezuela's regionalization reforms are the most ambitious. They go beyond the mere deconcentration of the central government's agencies to the regional level and seek to establish a new level of government between the center and the states and municipalities that can plan and coordinate the activities of all government units within each region.[26]

While the Venezuelan approach is primarily aimed at coordinating and consolidating the activities of the central, state, and municipal governments by a strong regional government and at integrating the regional planning process, it also seeks to develop the administrative capacity of state and municipal governments so that certain functions can be delegated or devolved to them.[27] The obstacles confronting this regionalization strategy, however, cast doubts on its ultimate success. First, the coordination and integrated planning envisaged in this reform have been seriously obstructed by the slowness of many central government agencies in deconcentrating their activities to the regional level. Some ministries have delegated decision making to their regional representatives, but others continue to make their decisions at the center.[28]

Another major problem is the central officials' lack of confidence in the ability of officials in the regions. It is difficult to determine whether this is a product of what has been refeerred to as the "centralist mentality" of national officials or is a well-founded concern over the shortage of highly skilled and trained officials in the regions. But the result is a widespread reluctance on the part of the central government officials to delegate power to regional and subregional levels. This has resulted in a yo-yo process of delegation and withdrawal of delegation, depending on whether the central officials are satisfied with the decisions and actions taken by officials in the regions.[29]

Municipal administrative development is promoted through limited training programs and through the establishment of *fundaciones municipales* (municipal foundations). With financial assistance from the central government, these foundations promote municipal development projects in such areas as housing, social assistance, tourism public works, and public transportation.[30] The central government also encourages *concentración participativa* (participative concentration) between municipal governments through *mancomunidades,* or intermunicipal agreements, in which two or more municipalities consolidate a service or activitiy, such as public transportation, police, or urban planning. This participative concentration at the municipal and state levels is seen by the architects of Venezuela's administrative reforms as a prerequisite for integrated regional planning and the delegation of functions to state and municipal governments.

In Mexico and Brazil the primary thrust of regionalization is the deconcentration of federal administrative agencies from the capital to major regional centers. However, some effort has also been made to coordinate the activities of the government agencies operating in the states and regions. In Mexico, for example, an effort is being made to improve the coordination between state and federal administrative agencies. In each state, the federal government has established a committee that includes representatives of all the federal agencies operating within it. These committees are responsible both for linking federal activities and programs with those of the state governments and for coordinating federal and state development efforts in each state.[32]

In both Mexico and Brazil, large regional development projects continue to be undertaken by national governments. The Mexican pattern involves the development of irrigation and hydroelectric power in a major river valley through a special commission with wide authority to plan and implement major economic and social transformations in the region. The structure resembles a TVA type of multipurpose regional development scheme. Tight federal control is exercised over the projects, and there is little input from state and municipal governments.[33]

The most comprehensive examples of regional planning and coordinaton undertaken by the federal government in Brazil involve the country's two most underdeveloped regions: the Northeast and the Amazon. In both cases, the federal government has placed these regions under a special *superintendência* (superintendency), which is responsible for coordinating the activities of the federal and state governments in each region in accordance with an integrated regional development plan.[34] The Brazilian federal government has also used regional development corporations — mixed enterprises — to channel public and private capital for economic development to the region. The Venezuelan government has used the same kind of structure to promote agricultural and industrial development in its least developed regions.[35] However, these forms of regional development tend to strengthen the presence of the central government in these regions at the expense of the local governments to assume the activities initiated by central government agencies, once the project or development process has been established.[36]

Argentina offers an interesting example of the devolution of functions to provincial governments, an approach quite unlike anything that has been done in Venezuela, Mexico, or Brazil. In the last three years, the federal government in Argentina has embarked on a dramatic program of transferring federally provided public services, such as public health, education, public utilities, and public works, to the provincial governments. It is also in the process of transferring federal personnel, facilities, and equipment to the provinces. This is part of the military regime's efforts to reduce the predominance of the central government, cut federal expenditures and the size of the federal bureaucracy, and strengthen provincial governments as a potential power base for future political party development. A striking feature of this example of decentralization is that it has been initiated by a highly centralized military regime, which is imposing the devolution of central government functions on largely unwilling and unprepared provincial governments.[37] Whether this process of "forced decentralization" will be successful can be determined only later; however, it represents a dramatic reversal of the overcentralizing tendencies that have characterized the Argentine administrative system until very recently.[38]

The Argentine federal government is also encouraging the provincial governments to cooperate in long-range regional planning and to avoid the unnecessary duplication of new projects and programs that could be provided on a regional instead of a provincial basis. However, it has not attempted to establish regional governing bodies or to force the provincial governments to engage in integrated regional planning.[39]

The critical issue in the Argentine case is the financing of new functions, which the provincial governments must now assume. As an interim measure, the federal govenment is distributing revenues it collects to the provincial governments to cover new operating costs. There is general confusion over how this should best be accomplished and anxiety over whether in the future the federal government will decide drastically to reduce its subventions and leave the provincial governments with insufficient funds to finance their newly acquired functions.

It should also be noted that in addition to being financially dependent on the federal government for operating and capital expenditures, the provincial governments are supervised by the federal government through military governors who have been appointed to head the provinces by the ruling military junta in Buenos Aires. Thus, the autonomy of the provincial governments is greatly limited by both their financial dependency and Argentina's system of military rule.[40]

DECENTRALIZATION AND LOCAL GOVERNMENT
IN LATIN AMERICA

Devolution of power from central and intermediary levels to local units of government has *not* been a major feature of contemporary administrative reforms in Latin America. Lip service is frequently paid to the need for increased citizen participation through the reform of municipal government, but in practice very little has been done to improve the financial and administrative capacities of the municipalities or to increase citizen participation at the local level.

What one Mexican observer has called an "administrative vacuum" exists at the local level throughout most of Latin America.[41] The development of local government has been severely retarded by the lack of financial resources and by the steady encroachment of central government agencies that carry out programs and provide services at the local level. In fact, local governments have been barely able to survive.

In a very real sense, the proliferation of central government bureaucracies has taken place at the expense of local government in Latin America. The central governments have absorbed an increasingly greater portion of the financial resources available to the public sector, leaving very little to the already poor local governments.

Over the last several decades in Brazil, for example, the proportion of total fiscal resources going to municipal government has steadily declined as federal government revenues have increased. Tax receipts of municipal governments in Brazil have declined from 6.9 percent of the total in 1949 to only 2.0 percent by 1973 (the last year for which data are available). Meanwhile, the proportion of total tax receipts going to the federal government has risen from 62.2 percent to 71.9 percent during the same period.[42]

It is important to note that the financial resources of Brazilian municipal governments have been reduced as a result of the tax reforms of 1967, which have favored the federal government over state and municipal governments.[43] As a consequence, the administrative capacity of municipalities has been seriously limited by their shortage of funds.

The financial imbalance in Mexico is even worse. The total amount of the budgets of all state and municipal governments is *less than 10 percent* of the federal government's budget.[44]

A vicious circle of administrative underdevelopment and fiscal poverty exists among local governments in Latin America. Because of their lack of financial resources, local governments have difficulty covering their basic operating expenses, let alone training their personnel, purchasing modern office equipment, financing organizational improvements, hiring technical consultants, and expanding the range and quality of public services. Their limited funds make it impossible for them to improve their administrative capacity. Their limited administrative capacity, in turn, discourages the allocation of new functions, for fear that they will not be able to carry them out effectively or use the funds given to them efficiently. Finally, their limited administrative capacity greatly hinders their ability to levy and collect taxes or mobilize their own sources of revenue.[45]

Unless the fiscal capacity of the municipal governments in Latin America is significantly increased, there is no way for them to break the vicious circle that retards their administrative development. Without reforms in the system of government taxation and distribution of public funds among different levels of government, municipalities will continue to be eclipsed by central governments and reduced to an even more insignificant role in the political process.[46]

The reforms that have been made in recent years at the local level largely appear to be token efforts. For example, in Mexico, the federal government has recently made some effort to strengthen the role of municipal government in local development by reducing its pervasive involvement in local affairs. Thus, the federal government has abolished the local Juntas Federales de Mejoras Materiales (federal councils for physical improvements); and has allocated the funds that previously went to these federal entities to the municipalities. However, this will not significantly improve the status of municipal governments in Mexico, as long as they continue to lack adequate financial resources, trained personnel, and sufficient political support from other levels of government. Federal agencies continue to drill local wells, build local roads and bridges, conduct local surveys, plan local development projects, construct local schools, and carry out a multitude of other local services and functions.[47]

Moreover, nominal efforts to promote the participation of the population in construction of rural roads and drainage systems do not appear to have a significant impact. Local civic improvement and construction programs, in which voluntary local labor and materials are mobilized to construct public works, are usually planned and directed by federal or state administrative agencies rather than by the local government and citizenry. Furthermore, due to the nature of these projects, no lasting improvement in the organizational or technical capacity of the participants is left behind after the project is completed. No attempt is made to leave an ongoing self-help organization.

Local officials are not trained in how to design and manage the construction of such projects, and there is rarely any continuing support provided by federal or state agencies to ensure that the projects are maintained and repaired after they have been constructed.[48]

In Venezuela, one of the stated goals of the regionalization reforms is to promote local participation in regional planning and policy implementation. However, in practice citizens are frequently not even informed that development projects are being planned for their areas. When they are informed thay are often given only perfunctory roles in planning such projects. Here again, only nominal participation appears to be desired, and local government is ignored as a channel for eliticiting it.[49]

Sustained social and economic development in the rural areas of Latin America, where the majority of the population live, requires strengthening local government and mobilizing the active and responsible participation of citizens. As the Cornell rural development studies have revealed, local governments in the developing areas can play a critical role in promoting rural development by providing an effective channel between the local population and higher levels of government, providing basic public services and utilities, mobilizing local resources and self-help efforts, and coordinating public and private development efforts. They can also contribute in an important way to integrated rural development by planning and managing local projects.[50]

However, the strong tendency toward centralized bureaucratic control and paternalistic dependence on the national government to finance, plan, and manage development efforts presents serious obstacles to integrated rural development in Latin America. For example, in Colombia a large-scale experiment in integrated rural development has been under way since 1976, with considerable international support.[51] Despite relative success in improving agricultural productivity, this program has been beset by the typical problems of centralized bureaucratic control and lack of local participation that appear throughout Latin America. Thirteen central government agencies are involved in the program as well as various international organizations. The individual farmer is surrounded by government technicians and advisers. Local committees, which were initially intended to elicit farmer participation, have been set up at the municipal level. But these committees have become forums for the reports of the bureaucratic agencies involved, and little or no farmer participation is solicited. Decision making rests with the National Planning Department and its regional representatives, while management at the local level is in the hands of central government officials. Thus, the farmers become totally dependent on the bureaucratic agencies that plan, supervise, and assist in the implementation of the program. As one observer has noted, "As long as the *parceleros* have no control over decision making they seem to have insufficient incentive to maximize the return from project investments."[52]

In sum, self-sustaining social and economic development in the rural areas of Latin America appears to demand the decentralization of decision making to the local level and the creation of effective mechanisms at this level to encourage the active participation of the local population in planning and managing the development process. The reform of local government is necessary to establish local control over and participation in the development process. Municipal governments must increase their local revenue-raising capabilities, obtain greater political autonomy from higher levels of government, gain a greater share of the revenues collected from local sources by the central government, greatly improve the training and working conditions of local officials, eliminate widespread corruption and graft, and provide for effective citizen participation. The strengthening of local government appears to offer a more viable means of accomplishing decentralization and increased local participation than efforts to create alternative structures.

THE PROSPECTS FOR DECENTRALIZATION IN LATIN AMERICA

Because of the dominant centralizing tendency and premature bureaucratization of the Latin American political systems, the prospects in general are not very favorable for the successful implementation of forms of political and administrative decentralization that are based on the devolution of power from the national to the local level. This does not necessarily mean that devolution of authority to local government will not be attempted or that, if attempted, it will not succeed. The contemporary political scene in Latin America is very complex, and in seemingly the least likely circumstances, decentralization is being attempted. Argentina is a case where a highly centralized military regime is forcing the provincial governments to assume responsibility for important public services that were previously carried out by the national government.

The influence of international agencies is an important factor bearing on the prospects for decentralization in Latin America. In recent years, the United Nations as well as certain other international assistance agencies have begun to promote administrative decentralization and increased local participation in development planning and implementation.[53] The influence of these international organizations appears to be stimulating greater interest and awareness of the need for decentralization among the Latin American governments.[54]

Recent efforts to promote integrated rural development in Latin America have brought home the need for both decentralization and efffective local participation in the planning and implementation of rural development projects. Recognition appears to be growing at the international and national levels that integrated rural development necessitates the active participation of the local population and local institutions in the design and management of rural development efforts. It is also increasingly clear that centralized bureaucratic control of rural development programs has been an important factor responsible for the failure of many of these programs.[55]

Finally, it is important to note that several national political systems in Latin America are undergoing a process of transition from nondemocratic to more democratic forms of governance. Countries such as Ecuador, Brazil, and Peru (and perhaps Argentina in the near future) are in stages of transition from military to civilian rule. As reforms are undertaken, it is not unreasonable to expect that local bases of power will develop and give rise to increasing pressure for decentralization.[56] If this trend toward greater political democratization continues and is supported by complementary social and economic developments, the prospects for greater political and administrative decentralization in Latin America may prove to be much more favorable in the near future than they are at present.

NOTES

1. For a discussion of this problem of excessive centralization and the need for deconcentration, see Aliysson Darowich Mitraud, "Panomara de Administracão Federal Brasileira e Reforma Administrative," *Revista de Administracão Pública* (Rio de Janeiro; hereafter referred to as *RAP*), vol. 11, no. 4 (October-December 1977): 187-188; Mark Hanson, "Decentralization and Regionalization in the Ministry of Education: The Case of Venezuela," *International Review of Education,* vol. XXII, no. 2 (Summer 1976): 157-159; Adalberto Saldaña Harlow, *Observaciones sobre Practicas Administrativas – en México* (Mexico City: Instituto de Administración Pública del Estado de México, 1974), p. 53-54; and Wilburg Jimenez Castro,

"Estrategia de Reforma Administrativa en la America Latina," in United Nations, *Report of the Interregional Seminar on Major Administrative Reforms in Developing Countries,* ST/TAO/M/62 (1971), pp. 79; 84-85.

2. See Beatriz Wahrlich, "Reforma administrativa na América — Latina; semelhancas e diferencas entre cinco experiências — nacionais," *RAP,* vol. 8, no. 4: 5-47.

3. See Santiago Ruiz Granadino and Victor Valle Monterosa, eds. *Casos de la Administración de entidades Publicas Decentralizadas del Istmo Centroamericao* (San Jose de Costa Rica: Instituto Centroamericano de Administración Pública, 1979), *passim.*

4. For example, the centralizing objectives of regionalization are quite explicit in the basic documents of the Venezuelan administrative reforms. See Venezuela, *Informe Sobre la Reforma de la Administración Pública Nacional,* vol.I (Caracas: Comisión de Administración Pública, 1972), pp. 389-391.

5. See Renato Raul Boschi and Eli Diniz Cerqueira, "Burocracia, Clientela e Relacoes de Poder: Un Modelo Teorico," *Dados* (Rio de Janeiro), no. 17 (1978): 104-105.

6. For a discussion of the conditions of local government and the extent to which the development of local government has been prejudiced by the hypertrophic expansion of the central government in Mexico, see Saldaña Harlow, *Observaciones,* pp. 135-138.

7. For a discussion of *indirect administration,* see Beatriz-Wahrlich, "Organizacão Governamental e Administrativa: O Caso Brasileiro," *RAP,* vol. 13, no. 2 (April-June 1979): 26-33.

8. Alejandro Carrillo Castro, *La Reforma Administrativa en México* (Mexico City: Instituto Nacional de Administración Pública, 1975), pp. 98-99.

9. *Ibid.*

10. Pedro Ojeda Paullada, "El Marco Juridico de la Administración Públic en México," *International Review of Administrative Sciences,* vol. XXI, no. 1 (1974): 10-11.

11. Castro Carrillo, *La Reforma,* pp. 98-99.

12. *Ibid.,* p. 131.

13. Moises Ochoa Campos, "La Reforma Administrativa no es de technocratas," *Jueves* [Mexico City] (December 27, 1979): 6.

14. Wahrlich, "Organização Governmental," p. 26-28.

15. *Ibid.,* pp. 32-33.

16. *Ibid.,* p. 31.

17. *Ibid.,* pp. 28-29.

18. *Ibid.*

19. Enrique Saravia, "Aspectos gerais do Comportamento das Empresas — publicas brasileiras," *RAP,* vol. 11, no. 1 (January-March 1977): 67-68.

20. Wahrlich, "Organização Governmental," p. 33.

21. For Brazil, see Boschi and Cerqueira, "Burocracia," pp. 104-107; for Venezuela, see *Informe Sobre la Reforma,* pp. 337-346; and for Mexico, see Saldaña Harlow, *Observaciones,* pp. 129-130.

22. For an application of this concept to Brazil, see Boschi and Cerqueira, "Buocracia," pp. 106-113. Basicaly, this is Fred Riggs's thesis as developed in his *Administrative Reform and Political Responsiveness: A Theory of Dynamic Balancing* Sage Professional Papers in Comparative Politics, vol. 1, series no. 01-010 (Beverly Hills, CA: Sage, 1970), pp. 567-606.

23. For a general theoretical perspective on this problem, see Guillerrmo O'Donnell, "Reflections on the Patterns of Change in the Bureaucratic Authoritarian State," *Latin American Research Review,* vol. XIII, no. 1 (1978): 1-27.

24. See Boschi and Cerqueira, "Burocracia," pp. 106-113; O'Donnell, "Reflections," p. 13.

25. *Ibid.*

26. See Venezuela, *Informe Sobre la Reforma,* pp. 453-462.

27. *Ibid.,* pp. 422-429.

28. See Hanson, "Decentralization and Regionalization," pp. 164-165.

29. *Ibid.,* pp. 166-167.

30. Venezuela, *Informa Sobre la Reforma,* pp. 394-395.

31. *Ibid.,* pp. 428-429.

32. Ochoa Campos, "La Reforma Administrativa," p. 6.

33. See David Barkin and Timothy King, eds., *Desarrollo Economico Regional* (Mexico City: Siglo XXI, 1970), pp. 103-104.

34. Wahrlich, "Organização Governmental," p. 21.

35. Venezuela, *Informe Sobre la Reforma,* pp. 446-449.

36. See Adalberto Saldaña Harlow, *Apuntes Sobre Desarrollo Urbano, Regional y Nacional* (Mexico City: Instituto de Desarrollo Urbano y Regional, 1974), pp. 145-162.

37. These observations are based on the author's interviews with provincial and federal officials in Argentina, between July and December 1979.

38. For a discussion of the centralizing tendencies in the Argentinian administrative system, see Oscar Juan Callazo, *Administración Pública en Argentina* (Buenos Aires: Macchi, 1974), pp. 109-118 and *passim.*

39. At present, the federal government encourages the provincial governments to enter into regional agreements or *convenios,* but there are plans to institute interprovincial regional commissions.

40. These observations are based on the author's field research and conversations with officials of the national institute of public administration in Buenos Aires (1979). Moreover, the situation is frequently commented upon in the major daily newspapers in Argentina.

41. See Saldaña Harlow, *Observaciones,* p. 136.

42. *Conjuntura Econômica* (Rio de Janeiro), vol. 29, no. 6 (January 1975), pp. 82-90.

43. Wahrlich, "Organização Governamental," pp. 15-18.

44. Ignacio Pichardo Pagaza, "Futuro de la Administración Públic Estatal y Municipal en México," *International Review of Administrative Sciences,* vol. XXI, no. 1 (1974), p. 24.

45. Saldaña Harlow, *Observaciones,"* pp. 136-138.

46. *Ibid.*

47. Ochoa Campos, "La Reforma Administrativa," p. 6.

48. Saldaña Harlow, *Apuntes,* pp. 146-157.

49. See Robert Chesterfield and Kenneth Ruddle, "Venezuelan Campesino Perceptions of Extension Agents," in *Educational Alternatives in Latin America,* ed. Thomas La Belle (University of California, Los Angeles, Latin American Center, 1975), pp. 149-168.

50. See Norman Uphoff and Milton Esman, *Local Organization for Rural Development* (Ithaca, NY: Cornell University Press, 1974), *passim.*

51. Michael Taussig's "Peasant Economics and the Development of Capitalist Agrigulture in the Cauca Valley of Colombia," *Latin American Perspectives,* vol. V (Summer 1978): 62-91

52. Eleanor Howard, "The Approach to Agrarian Reform in Colombia," mimeographed (Ph.D. diss., Harvard University, 1978), p. 165.

53. See United Nations, *Interregional Seminar,* pp. 21-22.

54. See comments by representative of Brazilian governemnt Alberto Fonseca-Pimental, "La Experencia Brasilena," in United Nations, *Interregional Seminar,* vol. II, pp. 1-10.

55. See Dennis Rondinelli and Kenneth Ruddle, "Local Organization for Integrated Rural Development," *International Review of Administrative Sciences,* vol. XLIII, no. 1 (1977): pp. 20-30.

56. See Wanderly Guilherme dos Santos, *Cidadania e Participação,* (Rio de Janeiro: Editora Campus, 1979), *passim.*

CHAPTER 7

THE ROLE OF VOLUNTARY
ORGANIZATIONS

G. Shabbir Cheema

The implementation of development programs has proven to be extremely difficult in most developing countries during the last three decades, despite centrally controlled planning. As a result, the gaps between rich and poor and between those living in urban and rural areas have widened. The number of people living in poverty has increased and landlessness has become more widespread, while popular participation in the process of development remains minimal. The rural poor in most developing countries have little access to services, facilities, and resources that would improve their living standards and increase their incomes and many lack such basic human needs as shelter, health care, and adequate nutrition. Economic disparities among regions have become greater in many countries and the plight of the poor has worsened.[1]

The current emphasis in many countries on decentralization of development planning and administration can be attributed to the consequences of past development strategies. These attempts to decentralize planning — the Provincial Development Assistance Program in the Philippines, the Changwat Development Program in Thailand, and the Decentralized Budget Program in Sri Lanka, for example — are designed to meet the developmental challenges of the 1980s: accelerating economic growth and greater social equity, expanding participation in decision making, increasing the access of the poor to social services, providing for the basic human needs of a majority of the population. Both governments in developing countries and international organizations are increasingly advocating decentralization to meet these objectives more effectively.

In this chapter, an attempt is made to examine the role of nongovernmental, voluntary organizations in facilitating decentralization.[2] The following section identifies the possible tasks or functions which *could,* under favorable circumstances, be performed by voluntary organizations in implementing decentralization policies and programs and accelerating the pace of local development. In the second section, various types of voluntary organizations existing in rural areas of developing countries are identified. The next four sections deal with the characteristics and the actual functioning of these organizations: specifically, their genesis and growth, objectives and activities, management and leadership patterns, and organizational structure and linkages. The next section deals with the membership and involvement of the rural poor in the activities of these organizations. Finally, policy implications for strengthening the role of voluntary organizations are described. The scope of the analysis is limited to nongovernmental, voluntary organizations in the rural areas, and illustrations from selected developing countries are given to substantiate the arguments.

FUNCTIONS OF VOLUNTARY ORGANIZATIONS

Decentralized development involves the transfer or delegation of authority from the national government to four types of organizations at the regional or local levels: (1) government agencies and departments in the field; (2) semi-autonomous public corporations, including regional and functional authorities; (3) local authorities; and (4) nongovernmental, voluntary organizations. Each type of organization can perform functions that help to implement local development programs and projects. The effective performance of these functions depends, of course, on the characteristics and capabilities of organizations involved as well as the dynamics of the political, social, and economic environment in which they operate. In any case, it is assumed that the institutional capability of a country effectively to implement development policies and programs, including those dealing with decentralization, is reflected in the extent to which these four types of organizations are able to perform their assigned tasks at various levels of government.

Voluntary organizations can play many roles in facilitating decentralized development.[3] An organization could perform these roles simultaneously or play different roles at different times. Before analyzing how well voluntary organizations actually perform these functions in developing countries, it would be helpful to identify their possible roles.

To begin with, voluntary organizations can act as vehicles for popular participaton and mobilization, and the extent to which they are successful at this influences the success of decentralization policies. For example, farmers' associations, youth clubs, local branches of political parties, women's organizations, and peasant groups can give people a sense of involvement and thus increase local support and legitimacy for government intervention. Without these organizations, local groups might adopt a passive attitude toward government initiatives, thereby indirectly sabotaging them.[4]

Local planning and goal setting are other functions that voluntary organizations can perform. Although in most cases the final responsibility for goal setting and planning rests with government or quasi-government organizations, there are several ways voluntary organizations can facilitate these tasks. They might provide relevant information about local conditions to the central and regional agencies, identify local priorities, and assist in the allocation of local resources. The existence of viable agricultural cooperatives and functional groups in an area, for example, could lead to more appropriate strategies for using resources and for integrating government facilities and programs. Realistic local planning often depends on the degree to which nongovernmental organizations become involved.

Voluntary organizations can also contribute to providing services. Most local projects in developing countries involve social welfare, infrastructural facilities, and agricultural inputs. These organizations can make the government's delivery system more effective by identifying target groups, increasing the accessiblity of these groups to the services, and assisting government organizations in ensuring the timely availability of inputs. The government's delivery system cannot be effective without the cooperation and support of recipients. Cooperative societies and organizations of small farmers, for example, could be used to deliver agricultural inputs such as credit and fertilizer; farmers' organizations could be consulted to identify those who need assistance, the most accessible location for government facilities, and the views of leaders and members of other organizations concerning the effectiveness of the programs.

The mobilization of local resources is another important task that could be performed by voluntary organizations. Funds transferred from the central and regional governments must be supplemented by local human and material resources. Their familiarity with the local situation and ability to exert social pressure place voluntary organizations in a good position to mobilize local resources, and they can often identify projects that can be financed either entirely on a self-help basis or in partnership with an appropriate government organization. In any case, when local people contribute human or material resources to a project, they are more likely to have a greater interest in its outcome and to lend their full support to its implementation. Those communities with nongovernmental organizations such as cooperatives, youth clubs, village development committees, and village welfare organizations are more likely to be able to mobilize local sources and to have a greater capacity to change their environments.

Voluntary organizations can define and express local needs and demands, which can then be incorporated into government development programs. Since there is often no harmony of interest among various groups within rural communities, this role is extremely important for local development. Indeed, the heterogeneity of interests requires organizations strong enough to prevent the benefits from government development projects being captured entirely by the local elite. The multiplicity of voluntary organizations representing diverse interests can help to ensure that government agencies take their needs and demands into consideration in allocating resources. Such organizations can help to balance conflicting interests in an area for the collective good of the community. Cooperative societies and organizations of subsistence farmers and sharecroppers have a greater likelihood of being heard by government agencies than do individuals, and government agenices may find it more convenient to respond if local claims are channeled through voluntary organizations, especially those that have the support of the government.

Another role these organizations can play is to influence local administration. It is through units of field administration that government services are provided to the people, but in most developing countries red tape and political influences restrict the access of disadvantaged groups to local government services. Therefore, voluntary organizations, in particular those that represent the rural poor and disadvantaged, are essential to ensure greater responsiveness of local administrations to their needs and aspirations. The evidence suggests that local administrators in those areas where influential voluntary organizations exist are more likely to respond to requests and complaints from their members.[5]

Finally, voluntary organizations create political awareness among people at the local level. The poor are often not in a position to safeguard their interests or to make claims unless they are first aware of their own situation and have faith in their ability to change their environment. Nongovernmental organizations can facilitate the creation of political awareness by providing disadvantaged groups with an opportunity to make collective decisions. Thus, individually, landless laborers might be afraid to make a claim for higher wages, but through an organization, they gain more faith in their ability to transform those relationships in the village that negatively affect them.

TYPES OF VOLUNTARY ORGANIZATIONS

There are many kinds of voluntary organizations in developing countries. They differ in objectives, activities, recruitment of members, management, leadership, geographical area of coverage, and linkages with government, and therefore classifying them is often a complex task. Several attempts have been made to categorize them on the basis of their manifest functions. Wanasinghe, for example, classifies peasant organizations into the following types: those that are formed to agitate for government response to local needs for infrastructure, energy, and social services; those committed to obtaining social and economic benefits, such as security of land tenure and land redistribution through group action; those organized to protect the interests of weaker groups of rural people; those formed to carry out functions related to production, such as the provision of credit, processing and marketing of produce, and maintenance of irrigation systems; and finally, those directly involved in communal production or the regulation of production activities.[6]

Ralston and others have used "basis of recruitment" and "specificity of purpose" as criteria for classifying voluntary organizations.[7] Those organizations that attempt to promote rural development are divided into two categories: (1) those providing significant services on a regular and continuous basis and that play a vital role in ensuring community solidarity, and (2) those that emerge in response to more specific tasks and disband when the goals are achieved. The first type of organization, in most cases, includes most of the adult population in a community, while the second type is likely to have limited membership. The multipurpose, inclusive organizations are those based on kinship, age, or gender. Such organizations also include friendship societies, welfare associations, and trade unions. The single-purpose inclusive organizations include irrigation associations, mutual aid work groups, and rotating credit associations. The exclusive organizations are those based on caste, ethnicity, religion, or shared beliefs.

Hilhorst identifies two types of nongovernmental organizations: (1) those working directly with the poor, such as the Sarvodaya Movement in Sri Lanka, and (2) those that occasionally support them either financially or in other ways, such as Christian churches, employers' organizations, and foundations. His classification is concerned primarily with those voluntary organizations that attempt to remove constraints on the development of human potential within disadvantaged groups.[8]

Hollnsteiner identifies two categories based on methods used by rural organizations to mobilize peasants: (1) the Community Development (CD) type, and (2) the Community Organization (CO) type.[9] The CD organization seeks to promote harmony and cooperation and to extend government services through the active involvement of the CD worker who is assigned to monitor activities in a community. The CO organization attempts to initiate a dialogue between conflicting groups, on the one hand, and the authorities and people at the local level, on the other. The emphasis in these organizations is on creating membership awareness, involving members in decision making, making leaders aware of members' needs, and eliciting participation of the rural poor in community projects that will meet their needs.

Voluntary organizations within villages have also been classified into two categories: (1) production-oriented, such as agricultural cooperatives, and (2) welfare- and maintenance-oriented, such as village welfare associations.[10] In Cheema's analysis of rural organizations in Malaysia, three criteria were used to classify them: (1) government-sponsored versus nongovernment-sponsored, (2) institutionalized versus noninstitutionalized, and (3) formal versus informal.[11] The first criterion assumes that the source of sponsorship of a voluntary organization has a significant impact on its actual functioning. The word "institutionalized" is used to imply durability and continuity in the organization's operation. Formal organizations are those that are legally registered.

In a Food and Agriculture Organization (FAO) report based on a survey of rural organizations in Asia, Africa, and Latin America, two types of organizations are identified: (1) "Standard" organizations are defined as those that are usually funded and sponsored by a government agency; they are formal and official, have a relatively more rigid organizational structure, and are dominated by the elite. (2) "Participatory" organizations are started by the people themselves rather than by the government and are more flexible in their objectives and structure. Furthermore, leaders and members of these organizations reach decisions after mutual consultation and discussion. The activities of these organizations are directly relevant to the needs of the rural poor, who are usually more inclined to join them.[12]

Thus, the multiciplicity of voluntary organizations in diverse environments makes it almost impossible to use one classification in comparative analyses. However, the classification by FAO offers several advantages in analyzing the role of voluntary organizations in the process of decentralized development. First, it identifies those organizations the rural poor are more likely to join. Second, it facilitates the understanding of both formal and informal, government-sponsored and nongovernment-sponsored, and enduring and ad hoc organizations. Finally, the classification is based on several factors — recruitment of members, leadership patterns, organizational structure, and scope of activities — that are helpful in understanding the way these organizations actually work in the rural areas of developing countries and the manner in which they affect local development.

One of the disadvantages of the FAO classification is that the distinction between "standard" and "participatory" organizations is sometimes questionable because some of the "standard" organizations are, at the same time, also participatory, particularly in those cases in which the local power structure is egalitarian. For this reason, it seems appropriate to modify the FAO's classification. In this study two types of voluntary organizations are identified: (1) standard organizations and (2) community organizations and peasant groups. Examples of the first type are cooperatives, village development committees, and government-sponsored farmers' associations. Examples of the second type are village-based small peasant groups, indigenous organizations, and ad hoc groups formed to perform specific tasks and to satisfy immediate local needs. The basic characteristics of the two types are assumed to be the same as those identified in the FAO's classification. It should be recognized, however,

TABLE 7.1   Classification of Voluntary Organizations

Standard Organizations	Community Organizations and Peasant Groupings
1. Cooperatives	1. Special organizations of rural disadvantaged groups, such as tenants' associations and organizations of agricultural laborers and landless women
2. Village development committees	
3. Government sponsored farmers' organizations	
	2. Village based ad hoc organizations formed to agitate for a specific and immediate local need
4. Trade unions	
5. Women's organizations	
	3. Village welfare associations
6. Youth clubs	
	4. Village funeral societies
7. Political party branches	
	5. Kinship associations
8. Development committees in new settlements	
	6. Caste associations
9. Other voluntary organizations sponsored by the government	7. Ethnic associations
	8. Irrigation associations
	9. Mutual aid work groups
	10. Rotating credit associations
	11. Religious associations

that within each category variations do exist. For example, among the standard organizations, government-sponsored cooperatives function somewhat differently from trade unions, and some of the community organizations are likely to be more hierarchical and formal than others.

Table 7.1 identifies voluntary organizations that exist in rural areas of Asian developing countries.[13]

GENESIS AND GROWTH

The genesis and pattern of growth of a voluntary organization are two of the most critical factors affecting their performance and the way they influence decentralized development planning and management. The Asian experience clearly shows the diversity in the ways that standard and community organizations came into existence.

In most Asian developing countries, cooperatives have been in existence for more than three decades, in most cases having been initiated and supported by government agencies.[14] Their growth has depended on the priority accorded by government to the cooperative movement. In Malaysia, for example, the significance of the cooperative movement was recognized as early as 1922. Credit cooperatives were the first to emerge, because of the increasing demand for institutional credit by farmers and fishermen. The second type that emerged under government sponsorship was the marketing cooperative, and finally, multipurpose cooperative societies and farmers' associations were established by Parliament. In 1973 the government restructured rural institutions. Farmers' associations and agro-based cooperative societies were integrated into "farmers' organizations." The historical evolution and growth of cooperatives in the country show the extent of government involvement in the initiation and sponsorship of the cooperative movement.[15]

An example of a standard organization is the *samahong nayon* precooperatives (SN, barrio associations), sponsored by the Philippine government after the declaration of martial law.[16] These cooperatives were tied to the government's land reform program, under which tenants of rice and corn landholdings of larger than seven hectares were to become owners of the land through a fifteen-year amortization scheme. A specified amount was to be paid to the landowners by tenant farmers. However, in order to become beneficiaries of the land reform program, tenant farmers were expected to acquire membership in a recognized cooperative, which, in the case of default by the tenant farmer, would guarantee payment. After the SNs completed their training courses and implemented their savings program, the second stage — full-fledged cooperatives *(kilusang bayan)* — would centralize all economic activities of barrio-based associations. During the third stage, consumer cooperatives would be organized in major urban areas. Integration of the system at the national level is to be accomplished during the fourth phase.

Trade unions and organizations for rural workers are usually initiated and sponsored by people who often either have substantial influence among policymakers or belong to the class of big landowners or both. Unlike cooperatives, however, there is no direct sponsorship by the government. As long as trade unions function within the existing sociopolitical framework, there are no legal barriers to their establishment. However, they are very likely to be declared "subversive" as soon as they challenge the owner elite at the national level. The case of the Federation of Free Farmers (FFF) in the Philippines provides an illustration of the initiation and sponsorship of trade unions.[17] In 1953 the FFF emerged as the largest nongovernment, voluntary peasant organization in the Philippines after the "communist-oriented" peasant organizations were dismantled. By 1974, it had a general membership of about 200,000 and branches in sixty provinces and subprovinces. The founders of the FFF were Catholics headed by a law graduate having strong links with the local landowning class. The constitution of the organization provided for political nonpartisanship. However, as the organization grew and the scope of its activities expanded, the leadership started to champion the members' interests more actively; following the declaration of martial law, the more radical elements in the organization were purged.

Another example of the standard trade union is the National Union of Plantation Workers (NUPW) in Malaysia. By 1948 there were about twenty trade unions in the plantation sector.[18] The Negotiating Committee for the Rubber Worker's Union (NCRWU) was established the same year and consisted of the six largest trade unions. By 1954 only a few larger unions of plantation workers were left in the country. It was at this time that the merger of different trade unions took place and the National Union of Plantation Workers emerged. The general secretary of the Union, P. P. Narayanan, played a significant role in its growth. Since he was considered to be anticommunist, he was acceptable to the planters as well as to local and national politicians, who began to recognize him as the sole bargaining agent for estate workers. Furthermore, the Union was able to identify and communicate to the employers the needs of estate workers, who did not have any other effective channel for this purpose.

The initiation and sponsorship of women's organizations and youth clubs follow almost the same pattern as cooperatives. In most cases, a relevant government agency encourages the formation of the organizations within villages; they are then coordinated at the regional and national levels. These organizations are not designed to agitate for a particular objective; rather, they provide vocational training and recreational facilities.

Compared to standard organizations, community organizations and peasant groupings emerge and grow in a different manner. This is illustrated by Hollnsteiner in her study of Kagawasan, a corn farming community in the Philippines.[19] Soon after World War II, several families began settling on the hilly slopes and engaging in subsistence agriculture, leading to the growth of nine barrios within two decades. Though the area had been classified as forest reserve, a large logging firm was able to get a permit from the Local Bureau of Forestry. In the late 1960s the settlers were continuously threatened by the forestry officials, who asked them to leave the area. While some were jailed, others allegedly bribed the rangers so that they were not evicted. In 1972 the settlers were informed by the mayor that the government wanted to undertake reforestation, and they were asked to move out. The settlers, realizing that there were vested interests involved, decided to organize themselves in order to exert pressure on the appropriate authorities. They learned from the Director of the Bureau of Lands that the area had indeed been classified as a forest reserve. The settlers became even more suspicious about the real intentions of the mayor and told him that none of them had any intention of vacating the land. From that time onward, the settlers started functioning as an organization, which grew as it attempted to surmount obstacles to the achievement of its goal.

Another illustration of the emergence of this type of voluntary organization, based on the conflict resolution model, is provided by Das and others in their case study of the Kisan Sabha in Jhakia village in Bihar, India.[20] The community in this village was characterized by dependency relationships because of the inegalitarian patterns of landownership. The landlords paid unfair wages to the rural poor, who, used to their traditional norms of behavior, would not openly challenge the traditionally recognized authority of the village elite. The impetus for change in the village emanated from a young man belonging to a medium-sized landowning family in the village who had been an active student leader and who had once been a member of the Communist Party of India (Marxist-Leninist). He decided to devote his full attention to organizing the oppressed peasants in his own village. He found an opportunity to organize the peasants when the Village Arbitration Committee, consisting of landlords, fined a poor peasant for adultery while, soon after, pardoning a landlord committing the same offense. By this time he had won the confidence of the poor in the village, who decided to organize themselves to safeguard their interests. The poor peasants refused to work for low wages. The landlords made several attempts to invite laborers from outside the village but were thwarted by the peasants. In most conflicting situations, the police intervened on behalf of the landlords, which gave further impetus to the oppressed peasants to work through their sabhas.

Another example of such organizations is provided by Ali's account of the emergence of the *Swanirvar* (self-reliance) movement in rural Bangladesh.[21] The movement began after the devastating floods of 1974. By that time, several relief agencies that had come to Bangladesh after independence were leaving. Left to their own resources, the people in several areas started self-help projects. In 1975, the Agricultural Research Institute at Joydevpur organized a seminar, inviting leaders of these self-help projects to evolve a uniform approach. Eventually, in most such villages, Swanirvar committees emerged. The movement encouraged the formation of interest and functional groups, such as those of small farmers, landless laborers, youth, and women. Youth, schoolteachers, social workers, and some members of Union Parishads were instrumental in organizing these groups. The movement was, of course, based on the assumption that there was no homogeneity of interests in the village. It went through several changes. In some areas government's role in the movement increased, while in others civil servants exercised little or no control. After 1976, attempts were made to integrate the *gram sarkar* (village government) initiated by the government into this movement. With this in view, the Ministry of Local Government, Rural Development, and Cooperatives proposed the "Swanirvar Gram Sarkar" constitution. However, after the death of the president in 1981, support for the arrangement declined, and no steps were undertaken to get the necessary legislation approved. In the meantime, Swanirvar committees continue to involve the people in local projects.

Brahme and others have analyzed the initiation and sponsorship of two such organizations in Maharashtra, India.[22] The Shramik Sanghatana (Toiler's Union) emerged in 1971 and is still active in the Shahad and Taloda blocks in Maharashtra. The factor that led to its emergence and growth was the recognition, by the leaders of the *Adivasis* (Indian aborigines), of the potentially significant role of peasant organizations in eliminating exploitative mechanisms in the area. An immediate reason, however, was an incident in 1971 in the area in which several aborigines were killed or injured. The idea of organizing the disadvantaged spread rapidly following a group meeting at the village meeting place, and the union emerged spontaneously without having as yet identified any specific goals. Soon after, the union organized a Land Liberation Conference. During that conference it was decided that Adivasis should take over land from the landlords if the former were the legal owners; that upon the expiration of a lease, land belonging to them should be immediately reclaimed; and that the Adivasis should insist on the timely implementation of the Employment Guarantee Scheme, which had been announced by the state government. The emergence in 1970 and growth of Bhoomi Sena in Palghar Taluka of Maharashtra, India, followed almost the same pattern as the Shramik Sanghatana. The gradual awareness of the Adivasis of their own social and economic conditions resulted partly from the interest of the organization's leader, who is a resident of the taluka and belongs to the Adivasis group. The leaders of Bhoomi Sena did not have any meaningful links with any political party at the national or state level. However, through constant dialogue with the aborigines, they were able to elicit their response and cooperation in the organization to achieve the immediately relevant common goal of recovering land alienated from the aborigines by local moneylenders.

Another illustration of the emergent, somewhat identical voluntary organization is provided by the Food and Agriculture Organization (FAO)-sponsored Small Farmers and Peasant Production (SFPP) groups in Bangladesh, Nepal, and the Philippines.[23] The FAO held various workshops in these countries under a regional project entitled Asian Survey of Agrarian Reform and Rural Development (ASARRD). Upon identification of basic problems in consultation with the rural poor and rural development officials, the ASARRD prepared guidelines for the experimental action and research project. In this project, an attempt was made to assist landless laborers and small farmers to organize themselves into self-help groups, that is, SFPPs for various income-generation activities, and for serving as receiving mechanisms for government facilities. In each participating area, two villages are selected as well as a full-time group organizer. The number of potential beneficiaries is determined on the basis of a household survey.

OBJECTIVES AND ACTIVITIES

The formally stated objectives of most standard voluntary organizations are quite comprehensive. In actual practice, however, their services and activities are restricted to the accomplishment of only a few of these. Their objectives are usually delineated by government agencies, but without first adequately consulting the rural people. Conversely, the objectives of community organizations and peasant groupings usually evolve as the organization grows. The organization becomes a mechanism for solving many kinds of problems.

The formally stated objectives of the cooperatives in Malaysia, for example, include organizing and utilizing the resources of the rural community, increasing farming productivity, providing farm services in an integrated manner, and encouraging savings and investment. To achieve these objectives, the cooperatives include among their main services credit, inputs, marketing, and processing.[24] Trade unions negotiate for better wages and provide social welfare services to members. In the case of the National Union of Plantation Workers (NUPW) in Malaysia, for example, the stated objectives are to obtain better wages for estate workers by negotiation with the employers, to provide educational facilities to estate workers and their children, to assist in legal matters, and to facilitate the establishment of NUPW cooperatives and other economic ventures. To achieve these objectives, the organization has provided several services. The organization has continuously bargained on behalf of estate workers, resulting in a 685 percent increase in their wages during the first twenty-five years of its existence. Other services provided by the NUPW include scholarships for workers' children, hostel facilities, securing work permits for members, conducting family planning classes, organizing annual sports, and running kindergarten classes for members' children.[25]

The formally stated objectives of Samahang Nayon (SN, Barrio Association) include capital building and savings and facilitating land transfer under the agrarian reform program.[26] These organizations, which were initiated after the declaration of martial law, are in effect "precooperatives" and are designed to provide an opportunity for barrio residents to learn the necessary skills and acquire the appropriate attitudes, eventually enabling them to assume greater responsibilities as members of full-fledged cooperatives.

Among the community organizations and peasant groupings based on the conflict resolution model, the Kisan Sabha in the village Jhakia has, in the past, undertaken activities such as organizing strikes for higher wages and preventing the eviction of sharecroppers.[27] The activities undertaken by Sharamik Sanghatana have included taking action to stop the illegal transfer of Advisasis' land to landlords, ensuring better wages for them, negotiating with landlords to ensure that they sell food grain at the price agreed upon, securing alternative jobs for Advisasis during a drought in 1972-1973, starting night schools that are regularly attended by the adults, and organizing women's groups.[28] Similarly, Bhoomi Sena has been campaigning for minimum wages and improved employment opportunities for the aborigines. Another activity of this organization dealt with bonded labor. Though this system was legally abolished in 1975, several such cases still existed, and the workers of Bhoomi Sena brought about one hundred cases to the courts. The leaders of the organization were also instrumental in the creation of grain banks in the area.[29]

The objectives of Small Farmers and Peasant Production (SFPP) groups have included raising the income of small farmers, tenants and landless laborers. The SFPP groups in Bangladesh have been engaged in several activities, including paddy cultivation, rice processing, potato growing, goat rearing, rickshaw pulling, and fishnet making. Various groups have used loan facilities provided by the government.[30]

Though the main objective of the Kegawasan community organization was to halt the eviction of settlers on the hilly slopes, the scope of its activities gradually expanded to include any community problems that could be resolved through collective effort. For example, the leadership negotiated with the department of education for a schoolteacher and successfully boycotted a bus company that did not pay adequate compensation to the family of a traffic accident victim. The women formed their own group to take care of their special needs, such as obtaining medical supplies, developing training programs, and starting home gardens.[31]

MANAGEMENT AND LEADERSHIP

The leaders of most standard organizations are older, relatively more educated people who belong to the upper socioeconomic strata of the village community. In theory, these leaders are elected. In practice, however, the key determinant of leadership positions within these organizations is usually the individual's socioeconomic status. This is the case especially in those rural areas that have highly inegalitarian patterns of landownership. In such situations, the styles of decision making in these organizations range from paternalistic to relatively participatory, depending on the background of the leaders. While some large-scale standard organizations have full-time professional staffs, work in others is undertaken on a voluntary basis. In most countries, facilities exist for training the leaders of these organizations. The patterns of management and leadership in community organizations and peasant groupings are significantly different. In peasant groups, leaders are more closely linked to members, and even when leaders are from outside the community, they have better rapport with the members. The procedures for managing such organizations are flexible, and the style of decision making is more informal. Face-to-face consultations are encouraged, and work is done on a voluntary basis.

An illustration of the general pattern of management and leadership of standard organizations in rural areas is provided by Haq's analysis of the cooperative movement in rural Bangladesh. He points out that cooperatives there are run by managing committees that are directly elected by the members. The members of these committees, in turn, elect officers such as the chairperson and the secretary. In the Comilla project, attempts were made to develop the skills of the leaders by giving them training. Studies undertaken by the academy at Comilla show that leadership in most cooperatives in Bangladesh is in the hands of wealthier farmers; that in some cases new leaders are also emerging; that the leaders of the cooperative movement want not only to safeguard their economic interests through the cooperative but also to advance their social and political status.[32]

An illustration of community organizations based on conflict resolution is provided by the case of Bhoomi Sena, described earlier. The key leader of the organization is a resident of the Taluka and belongs to an aborigine group. The Bhoomi Sena employs two paid workers; three others from the same area are also employed, but they do not receive any stipend. The organization has neither a written constitution nor party membership. It receives voluntary contributions, most of which are from the aborigines.[33] In the case of SFPP groups in Bangladesh, the organizers emphasized that leadership for different functions should be widely distributed to avoid the concentration of power in the hands of a few individuals. The members of each group select a chairperson, who conducts and guides the proceedings of the group, and a secretary-treasurer, who handles funds and maintains a register of numbers. Participation by all members in decision making is emphasized. Data on the background characteristics of the chairpersons and secretaries of the selected groups shows that twenty leaders are between 20 and 40 years old, while four are between 41 and 55. None of the leaders is illiterate. The groups do not have any full-time or part-time professional staff, and the chairpersons and secretaries work on a voluntary basis.[34] In the case of the Kagowasan community organization, those who had actively participated in mobilizing the settlers to agitate against their eviction from the area were eventually elected leaders of their respective barrios. The decision-making process in the organization is informal.

ORGANIZATIONAL STRUCTURE AND LINKAGES

There are significant variations in the organizational structures of government-sponsored voluntary organizations such as cooperatives and peasant groupings like Kisan Sabha and Bhoomi Sena. In the former, the organizational structure is imposed from above. There are apex bodies at the national level, followed by branches at the state, district, and village levels. In the decision-making processes of some of these organizations — cooperatives, for instance — government officials enjoy a predominant position. Since these organizations emerge under the initiative and supervision of government agencies, they have direct communication links with the national level and with their branches at the state and the district levels. At the local level, these organizations have informal communication links with one another. Finally, this type of organization has good communication links with other agencies of the government.

In the second type of organization, the set-up is relatively more informal and decisions are made by consensus. The relationships within the organization are less hierarchical, leading to more effective communication among members. In most cases, such organizations initially have a more or less antagonistic relationship with government agenices at the state and district levels. However, some organizations may eventually be forced to build more effective linkages with other voluntary organizations as well as relevant government agencies in order to gain greater acceptance and government support.

An illustration of the first type of organization is provided by the farmers' organizations (FOs) in Malaysia.[35] The apex body for the FOs is the Farmers' Organization Authority, which was created through an act of Parliament and has, therefore, relatively more administrative and operational autonomy than a government department. It has branches at the state and the district levels. In each FO, policy formulation is the responsibility of the "representative assembly." Subordinate to this is the board of directors, which is partly elected by the assembly and partly appointed by the Minister of Agriculture. The general manager is a full-time employee. Below the FO level, about ten small agricultural units (SAUs) exist, each of which is headed by a unit chief, who is directly elected by members of the unit. Though membership in these units is on a voluntary basis, farmers are eager to join them, since a significant portion of the agricultural input facilities provided by the government are channeled through the FOs. The farmers are aware that these organizations enjoy government support and resources, strong linkages with other organizations at the local level, and qualified staff. They are, therefore, interested in receiving inputs through FOs without, in most cases, considering them as their own organizations.[36]

Compared to cooperatives, trade unions have fewer links with and are less controlled by government agencies. In the case of the Federation of Free Farmers (FFF), for example, the basic unit of the organization is the barrio chapter. The barrio units are grouped into a municipal chapter and municipal chapters into a provincial association. Policy formulation is the responsibility of the National Policy Board (NPB), which is elected every year by a national convention. The NPB elects the members of the National Executive Council. The FFF has a total of thirty-eight nationally paid officers and staff. It is registered with the Ministry of Labour. Since the initiative in establishing the organization was taken in 1953 by a group of the leaders after a revolutionary movement had been crushed by the national government, the organization has been operating independently and has few direct links with the government.[37]

Among the community organizations and conflict resolution-based peasant groupings, two general patterns of organizational structures and linkages emerge. Organizations such as Kisan Subha, Bhoomi Sena, and the Toiler's Union have informal structures and few links with government agencies. They are able to elicit support from sympathetic individuals at the national or regional level. Other organizations in this category, such as Swanirvar groups and SFPP groups, enjoy greater links with the government; indeed, the latter are designed, among other things, to serve as receiving mechanisms through which government inputs and facilities can be delivered to disadvantaged groups. The organizational format of the Swanirvar movement includes Swanirvar Committees at the village, Thana, district, divisional, and the national levels. Similarly SFPP groups are expected to be federated in an association to facilitate the use of credit, processing, and marketing facilities.

The lack of viable linkages between most of the community organizations and government agenices has several implications. First, government services are not channeled through their organizations, and in some cases leaders find it difficult to sustain the interest of members who might be tempted to join these organizations that have government support. Second, after the immediate objectives of such organizations (such as land security) have been accomplished, the organization has to provide agricultural inputs and other facilties to keep the members interested in the organization. In the absence of viable linkages with government agencies, this sometimes proved difficult. Third, governments in most developing countries are likely to look with suspicion upon such organizations, with the result that they evoke a negative attitude from the bureaucracy.

MEMBERSHIP AND THE INVOLVMENT
OF THE RURAL POOR

Standard organizations have formal procedures for the recruitment of members. If they are government-sponsored, the local elite usually play a dominant role in eliciting the support of the rural community by exerting pressure on the disadvantaged and using their traditional leadership authority. In the case of nongovernment standard organizations, commonality of interest and persuasion by the leadership of the organization are critical factors in the recruitment of members. The membership of cooperative societies varies from country to country. The members of cooperatives usually are landowners and those who have higher socioeconomic status in the community. Landless laborers, tenants, and small farmers are not adequately represented. Even when they join, they remain inactive. The actual membership of cooperatives in most countries is far below the existing potential. Women and youth, for example, are not adequately represented in them. Compared to standard organizations, most community organizations and peasant groups do not have formal procedures for membership. Those directly affected by the issues raised by the organization become involved. The disadvantaged are more likely to be represented in these organizations and, indeed, most of such organizations are initiated by the poor.

One illustration of the standard organization is provided by the cooperatives in rural India, which were designed, among other things, to help the rural poor and others who did not have access to credit to improve their farm practices. The number of cooperative societies increased substantially during the 1960s. At the end of 1972, there were 97,000 cooperative farming societies. Between 1955 and 1968 average membership per society increased from 49 to 162. However, as Mathur points out, the disadvantaged groups, "whose need for their services is the most urgent, have suffered most where these institutions have failed and did not stand to gain where they proved successful."[38] Loans by cooperative societies are given in proportion to the ownership of land or other property. Due to the domination of powerful vested interests, there is little opportunity for the rural poor to become involved in the activities of cooperatives.

In the case of farmers' organizations in Malaysia, the membership increased from 15,864 in 1969 to 173,270 in 1974. This increase could be attributed to a decision by the government to use these organizations as one of the main mechanisms for the delivery of agricultural inputs to farmers. At the national level, data on the background characteristics of members of FOs are not available. However, a survey of selected FOs by Gan Wan Yee and others showed that the majority of members were in the 31-50 age bracket, 14 percent of the members and 24 percent of nonmembers had received no education, the average area of land owned by member farmers was significantly larger than that of nonmembers, about 40 percent of nonmembers were tenants, and the gross monthly farm income of members was relatively higher than that of nonmembers.[39]

The number of paying members in the FFF in the Philippines is approximately 10,000. However, the leadership of the organization argues that "general membership" is around 200,000. As in the case of other developing countries, the category of general membership includes those who joined in the past but subsequently ceased to pay their contributions. Small membership and a weak financial base have limited the capacity of the FFF to negotiate from a position of strength on behalf of the rural workers. Nevertheless, through personal relationships the leaders of the organization have been able to increase the influence and respect for the FFF.[40]

The membership of the National Union of Plantation Workers (NUPW) in Malaysia has been increasing rapidly.[41] The Union leadership made persistent efforts to recruit more members. In the second decade of its existence, the NUPW has been successful in maintaining a membership consisting of between half and two-thirds of the estate labor force. While in 1954 the number of paid-up union members was 35,700, it had increased to 137,100 by 1968. There are many reasons that some estate workers fail to join.[42] The nonresident labor force is discouraged by labor contractors from becoming unionized, and the NUPW is not authorized to extend its activities to the government-controlled Federal Land Development Authority estates. Moreover, the Industrial Relations Act contains many features that limit the pace of unionization; for example, the act includes compulsory postponement of strikes for an indefinite period in the public sector as well as in other essential services. Finally, the NUPW as been unable to pressure the government into enforcing labor legislation in the small holding sector.

Among conflict resolution-based voluntary organizations such as the Kisan Sabha in village Jhakia in Bihar, India, the peasants feel committed to the organization; they attend monthly meetings regularly and do not default on the payment of membership fees. Das and others point out three reasons for the active involvement of peasants in the Sabha.[43] First, peasants have significantly benefited from the considerably improved wages and security of land tenure. Moreover, democratic practices are used within the organization. Elections, for example, are held regularly and advance notice is given so that there is sufficient time for discussion before elections. The executive committee, consisting of nine members, meets regularly and is elected every year. In the meetings there is open discussion. This has enabled the peasants to identify themselves with the organization. Finally, homogeneity of members and common interests is a significant unifying factor. The analysis of Bhoomi Sena by Brahme and others shows similar determinants of the involvement of the members in the organization. These include encouragement of spontaneous action by the organization, its flexible and informal organizational structure, the smallness of the area, and the integration of cadres with the members.[44]

In the case of SFPP groups, the membership is open to all small farmers, sharecroppers, and landless peasants in the village. A survey in Bangladesh shows that 80 percent of all households in the three selected areas in which these groups were formed were either small farmers or landless tenants.[45] The groups, however, do not have adequate linkages with functionaries of the government and other organizations in the area.

Thus, this analysis shows that, with the exception of community organizations and peasant groups, the rural poor are not actively involved in voluntary organizations. This is particularly the case with standard organizations such as cooperatives. There are many reasons for the lack of adequate involvement of the disadvantaged groups in standard organizations:

(1) These organizations emerge under the initiative of the village elite who, subsequently, play a predominant role in their decision-making processes. The rural poor do not, therefore, regard these organizations as their own.

(2) The village elite who initiate these organizations assume leadership positions and, due to their traditional authority within the rural community, are rarely challenged by members, especially the rural poor, who show very little interest in the activities of the organization.

(3) The leaders and managers of standard rural organizations do not make any persistent efforts to recruit the rural poor, since the interests of the former conflict with the latter.

(4) The attitude of the government bureaucracy in most cases is paternalistic. As passive recipients of information and instruction, the rural poor consider the standard organizations as government agencies through which government facilities and services are distributed and to which they do not have adequate access.

(5) Standard rural organizations have specific goals and attract only a particular segment of the rural community, such as owner farmers for cooperative farming. This excludes landless laborers and artisans from many orgnizations.

(6) In several countries, rural power structures are characterized by patron-client and dependency relationships. Thus, the rural poor might join the standard rural organizations because of their personal loyalty to the leader rather than through commitment to and understanding of the goals of the organization. Indeed, they might serve as an instrument of the leader, who may be able to obtain credit on their behalf for his personal use.

(7) Many standard rural organizations do not reflect the priorities of the rural poor, whose needs might be quite different from those identified by the organizations.

(8) Members in standard rural organizations are usually not expected to evaluate organization activities. This is especially the case with the rural poor, even when they decide to join the organization. This, of course, eventually alienates them from all standard organizations.

(9) Most standard organizations emerge under the initiative and spon-sorship of government agencies. The goal of government officials is to show quick results by increasing the number of members of such organizations. The primary goal of the official is not to ensure the active involvement of the rural poor and disadvantaged groups.

The relatively greater involvement of the rural poor in community organizations and peasant groupings is due to several factors, which include the interest of leaders in mobilizing the rural poor, the organi-zations' holistic view of the issues and problems that face the rural poor, the evolution of some organizations from informal groupings to elected bodies, homogeneity between socioeconomic backgrounds of leaders and members, an organization's spontaneous action to fulfill a locally felt need, and efforts by most of those organizations to trans-form the local power structure by encouraging the rural poor to discard their traditional belief in the inevitability of dependency rela-tionships within the rural community.

CONCLUSION

The significance of decentralization is increasingly recognized by development planners, policymakers, and practitioners. It is being argued that in certain situations, decentralization encourages and promotes greater access to governmental facilities, increased in-volvement of the people in the development process, more efficient delivery of public services for meeting basic human needs, and in-creased accountablity on the part of government agencies. It is, moreover, being suggested that one way these goals can be achieved is by strengthening nongovernment, voluntary organizations at the grass roots. However, the multiplicity of these organizations, ranging from large-scale cooperatives and trade unions to informal peasant groupings, and the diversity of situations in which they function preclude the possibility of delineating a strategy applicable to all countries. Different types of voluntary organizations are performing their tasks in different ways. Each has a contribution to make. What is needed is to recognize the strengths and weaknesses of each in ac-celerating the pace of decentralized development.

Standard organizations are usually large enough to be used as viable mechanisms for the delivery of the government's agricultural input, social welfare, and infrastructural development facilities. Their organizational structures, linkages, management, and leadership are, in most cases, conducive to increased productivity through the greater infusion of new techniques and methods. Furthermore, these organizations can improve the accountability of government agencies. However, sufficient evidence suggests that in communities with inegalitarian power structures, these organizations do not increase access to government services, nor can the interests of the disadvantaged groups safeguarded through them. Consequently, these organizations can actually lead to a further widening of income disparities.

Community organizations and peasant groups play a vital role in creating awareness among the disadvantaged of their situation, agitating on behalf of the specific needs of the poor, and increasing the access of the poor to government facilties and programs. However, in some cases these organizations cease to be active once their immediate objective has been accomplished. Furthermore, they can generate greater conflict within the rural community, and for this reason some governments are unwilling to tolerate them. It is extremely difficult to replicate such organizations due to the special circumstances under which they emerge. Most are very small and focus only on a specific need; thus it is difficult for government agencies to use them to deliver government services.

Standard organizations as well as peasant groupings and community organizations have their respective roles to play in accelerating decentralization. Too much reliance on standard voluntary organizations to elicit popular response to government development efforts or to safeguard the interests of the rural poor is not likely to yield meaningful results. Similarly, the proliferation of conflict resolution-based peasant groupings and community organizations could lead to a degree of politicization at the grassroots that some national governments might be unwilling to tolerate and that could well impede agricultural productivity. The growth of both types of organizations should be encouraged to enable them to perform their tasks in local development; however, because constraints on the emergence and growth of peasant groupings and community organizations are much greater than those on standard organizations, the former merit increased attention and encouragement by governments seeking to promote decentralization.

NOTES

1. For a discussion of the impact of planning among others, see Dennis A. Rondinelli, "National Investment Planning and Equity Policy in Developing Countries: The Challenge of Decentralized Administration," *Policy Sciences,* vol. 10 (1978): 45-74; Albert Waterston, *Development Planning* (Baltimore: Johns Hopkins University Press, 1969); Naomi Caiden and Aaron Wildavsky, *Planning and Budgeting in Poor Countries* (New York: John Wiley, 1974); and Martin Rudner, *Nationalism, Planning and Economic Modernization in Malaysia* (Beverly Hills, CA: Sage, 1975).

2. The organizations to be discussed in this chapter are those in which membership is on a voluntary basis and which are nongovernmental. In actual practice, however, one finds several cases in which the rural people may be forced to join due to strong pressures and incentives by the government. To facilitate comparative analysis, both government-sponsored and nongovernment-sponsored voluntary organizations have been included.

3. Wanasinghe has identified five roles that peasant organizations play in rural development: identification of development goals, agitation for the achievement of the identified goals, formulation of action programs; mobilization of resources, and organization of the implementation of the action programme. See H. S. Wanasinghe, "Role of Peasant Organizations in Rural Development" in   Inayatullah, ed., *Approaches to Rural Development: Some Asian Experiences* (Kuala Lumpur: Asian and Pacific Development Administration Centre, 1979), pp. 320-321. Uphoff and Esman have identified six functions "rural institutional systems" can perform to facilitate rural development: planning and goal setting, resource mobilization, provision of services, integration of services, control of administration, and making claims. See Norman H. Uphoff and Milton J. Esman, *Local Organization for Development: Analysis of Asian Experience* (Ithaca, NY: Cornell University Center for International Studies, 1974), pp. 16-17.

4. Lenore Ralston, James Anderson, and Elizabeth Colson, *Voluntary Efforts in Decentralized Management* (Berkeley: Institute of International Studies, University of California, 1981), p. 31.

5. Muhammed Safiur Rahman, "Administration of Local Level Development in Bangladesh" (Paper delivered at the Senior Level Seminar on Institutional Capability for Regional Development: Focus on Coordination, Nagoya, August 16-20, 1980), pp. 15-45.

6. Wanasinghe, *Approaches to Rural Development,* pp. 317-318.

7. Ralston et al., *Voluntary Efforts,* pp. 80-145.

8. Jos G. M. Hilhorst, "NGO and Integrated Rural Development," mimeographed, pp. 1-2.

9. Mary Racelis Hollnsteiner, "Mobilizing the Rural Poor Through Community Organization," *Philippine Studies,* vol. 27 (1979): 404-408.

10. G. Shabbir Cheema, P. F. Kaplan, M. Nawawi, and S. A. Hussein *Rural Organizations and Rural Development in Selected Malaysian Villages* (Kuala Lumpur: Asian and Pacific Development Administration Centre, 1978), p. 10.

11. G. Shabbir Cheema, "Rural Organizations and Participation in Malaysia," (Paper prepared for presentation to the World Conference on Agrarian Reform and Rural Development [WCARRD], Food and Agriculture Organization, Rome, 1979).

12. Benard Van Heck, *Participation of the Poor in Rural Organizations* (Rome: Food and Agriculture Organization, 1979), pp. 24-25.

13. *Ibid.*

14. United Nations Research Institute for Social Development, *Rural Cooperatives as Agents of Change: A Research Report and a Debate* (Geneva: UNRISD, 1975), pp. 2-20. For a detailed analysis of the impact of cooperatives in Iran, Pakistan, and Sri Lanka, see Inayatullah, *Cooperatives and Development in Asia* (Geneva: UNRISD, 1972).

15. Cheema, et al., *Rural Organizations,* pp. 54-56. For a more detailed discussion of the cooperative movement in rural Malaysia, among other countries, see Ahmad Sarji Bin Abdul Hamid, *Farmers' Cooperatives: Institutions for Small Farmers in Malaysia* (Kuala Lumpur: Farmers' Organization Authority, 1976); and L. J. Fredericks et al., *The Role of Farmers' Organizations in Two Paddy Farming Areas in West Malaysia* (Wageningen: University of Agriculture, 1980).

16. Blondie Po, "Rural Organizations and Rural Development in the Philippines: A Documentary Study," in Inaytullah, ed., *Rural Organizations and Rural Development* (Kuala Lumpur: Asian and Pacific Development Administration Centre, 1978), pp. 340-354. For an in-depth analysis of two Samahang Nayon, see Christina Montiel, *The Role of Rural Organizations in Rural Development: The Philippine Case* (Kuala Lumpur: Asian Centre for Development Administration, 1977).

17. *Ibid.,* pp. 301-316.

18. Cheema, et al., *Rural Organizations,* pp. 72-90.

19. Hollnsteiner, "Mobilizing the Rural Poor," pp. 398-403.

20. Arivind Das et al., "The Role of Rural Organizations in Involving the Rural Poor in the Process of Development in Bihar, India" (Paper delivered at the World Conference on Agrarian Reform and Rural Development, Food and Agriculture Organization of the United Nations, Rome, 1979), pp. 96-104.

21. Shaikh Maqsood Ali, "Self-reliance [Swanirvar] Movement in the 1980s — The Social Worker as Change Agent," *Administrative Science Review,* vol. X, no. 2 (1980), pp. 77-108.

22. Sulabha Brahme et al., "Involvement of the Poor in the Rural Development through People's Organizations in Maharashtra, India" (Paper delivered at the World Conference on Agrarian Reform and Rural Development, Food and Agriculture Organization of the United Nations, Rome, 1979), pp. 98-106; 123-147.

23. Van Heck, *Participation of the Poor,* pp. 30-31.

24. Cheema, et al., *Rural Organizations,* p. 29.

25. *Ibid.,* pp. 85-89.

26. Po, "Rural Organizations and Rural Development," pp. 340-41.

27. Das et al., "The Role of Rural Organizations," pp. 96-111.

28. Brahme et al., "Involvement of the Poor," pp. 107-147.

29. *Ibid.*

30. M. Nurul Haq, "The Role of the People's Organization to Involve the Poor in Rural Development: A Country-Study on Bangladesh" (Paper delivered at the World Conference on Agrarian Reform and Rural Development, Food and Agriculture Organization of the United Nations, Rome, 1979), pp. 76-88.

31. Hollnsteiner, "Mobilizing the Rural Poor," pp. 398-403.

32. Haq, "The Role of the People's Organization," pp. 76-88.

33. Brahme et al., "Involvement of the Poor," pp. 107-147.

34. Haq, "The Role of the People's Organization," pp. 76-88.

35. Cheema et al., *Rural Organizations,* pp. 56-57.

36. For a detailed discussion of the functioning of FOs and their impact on the socioeconomic status of farmers, see Barnard Van Heck and Gunter Dresrusse, *Towards Adequate Farmers' Organizations in Malaysia,* mimeographed (Kuala Lumpur: Farmers' Organization Authority, 1975).

37. Dennis F. Hodsdon, *The Federation of Free Farmers* (Geneva: International Labour Office, 1979), pp. 12-18.

38. Kuldeep Mathur, "Administrative Institutions, Political Capacity and India's Strategy for Rural Development," in *Approaches to Rural Development in Asia* (Kuala Lumpur: Asian Centre for Development Administration, 1975), p. 31. For an analysis of constraints on the emergence of organizations of the poor that could safeguard their interests, see D. Bandhopadhyay, "External Impediments to the Growth of Organizations of the Rural Poor in India," in *Organization of Peasants in Asia,* Workshop Series Report V (Bangkok: Friedrich-Ebert-Stiftung, 1974).

39. Gan Wan Yee, *Characteristics of Members and Non-Members of Some Farmers' Cooperatives in Kedah* (Kuala Lumpur: Farmers' Organization Authority, 1977).

40. Hodsdon, *The Federation,* pp. 36-37.

41. For a discussion on membership and management of NUPW, among other organizations, see Charles Gamba, *The National Union of Plantation Workers* (Singapore: Eastern Universities Press, 1962); K.S. Nijhar, "Wage Structure in the Rubber Estates in West Malaysia" (Ph.D. diss., Australian National University, April 1971); and K.K. Kumaran, "The Twenty-Five-Year March of the Plantation Workers Union from 1946 to 1970" (Petaling Jaya: National Union of Plantation Workers, 1970).

42. Cheema et al., *Rural Organizations,* pp. 81-85.

43. Das et. al., "The Role of Rural Organizations," pp. 96-111.

44. Brahme et al., "Involvement of the Poor," pp. 107-147.

45. Haq, "The Role of the People's Organization," pp. 76-88.

CHAPTER 8

DECENTRALIZING INTEGRATED RURAL DEVELOPMENT ACTIVITIES

John D. Montgomery

Decentralization is more an art than a science. It follows its own aesthetic principles (described in manuals by organization theorists who do not have to administer it), but in practice, reality keeps interfering with its logic. Its complexities multiply as it touches different functions and levels of action. It affects its players in different, even contradictory, ways. Making it "work" requires balanced judgment and consideration of the needs of many actors.

The result is that almost nothing is completely decentralized. Even when a government decides to deconcentrate or devolve specific public functions, that decision is rarely fixed for long. There is an ebb and flow in the history of decentralization: Power that is legally devolved to local authority is hard to recapture if the political leadership at the center later changes its mind, while power that is trans-

Author's Note: The author gratefully acknowledges his indebtedness to his colleague John M. Cohen, whose exhaustive inventory of propositions related to integrated rural development is cited herein; to Robert E. Klitgaard, David Leonard, Dennis Rondinelli, and Shabbir Cheema, for helpful comments on a draft; and to his research assistant Samuel Carradine, for his literature search leading to the preparation of case studies used to test some of the ideas developed in this chapter. For errors of observation and interpretation of the vast experience now being accumulated in rural project management, the author reluctantly but firmly assumes responsibility.

ferred from the capital city to field offices of a national ministry can be recovered by simply changing administrative procedures. The reality of decentralization changes almost as readily as its rhetoric.

Nevertheless, experience does accumulate into wisdom. Some activities are almost impossible to carry out effectively through decentralized procedures: strategic national defense, for example, as compared with border protection and tactical maneuvers; or agricultural price and subsidy policies in contrast to infrastructure support functions. Decentralization, viewed as an administrative measure or as a means of developing local political capabilities, has its own inner logic. There are certain activities that nearly always succeed best when decentralized, that is, when major responsibilities are left to local officials. Outstanding examples include special, site-specific projects located in rural areas where routine standardized procedures do not apply. Among these projects, integrated rural development activities nearly always involve the decentralization of at least some decision-making functions to field offices and project managers.

Integrated rural development (IRD) is usually taken to mean a decentralized program that delivers a combination of goods and services to small farmers in a designated region. What distinguishes it from other government operations in the rural sector is that it brings diverse functions together administratively in order to achieve synergies and efficiencies that are not likely to occur as a result of their mere coexistence in the region. The administrative tasks in IRD include scheduling inputs and services to coincide with farmers' needs, achieving economies of scale by eliminating surplus activities, and making appropriate adjustments in the "package" to accommodate changes in the local situation. The origin of the concept has been traced to the Ford Foundation programs developed in India in response to the 1966 famine and the Comilla project in East Pakistan (Bangladesh), though its antecedents certainly trace as well to the Gazira Scheme in the Sudan.[1]

Most of our present knowledge of IRD comes from internationally financed projects. (See Table 8.1). The experiences reported here are drawn from the record; one can only surmise that they are generalizable to survey national efforts. But even that experience is considerable, and it provides the benefit of comparability across countries whose political and administrative systems are quite varied. International donors have become increasingly interested in integrated projects for reasons of efficiency: They anticipate more effective use of public resources, or greater and quicker impact, when governmental services are brought together administratively.[2] However, these outcomes are hard to document. They remain in doubt both among skeptics who perceive a potential watering down of essential functions and among those who question whether more effective project management alone can bring about an optimal combination of rural services. Even so, because of its sheer plausibility, the enthusiasm for IRD persists: Between 1975 and 1980 about one-fifth of all programs of major international agencies working in Latin American involved IRD projects making up a portfolio of $2 to $2.5 billion in that region alone, a figure that does not include nationally financed programs, especially in Mexico, Colombia, and Brazil.[3]

If experience has not verified the superiority of integrated programs over functionally specific services rendered to a rural community, it has offered even less guidance on making this form of decentralization work. This chapter explores four issues of program design that have been considered at some length by organization theorists, the answers to which pose acute dilemmas to planners and managers engaged in IRD: (1) How much control should an IRD project manager have over the resources and services the project needs to accomplish its goals? (2) What kinds of links or transactions should a project have with central agencies and with other organizations working in the area? (3) What kinds of goals can be appropriately assigned to managers attempting to coordinate IRD functions at local levels? (4) What organizational arrangements are needed at the national level to provide local managers with appropriate support and guidance? Underlying these questions is a fifth, latent, question: How much influence should international donors have in approaching these issues in specific instances?

It is tempting to answer these questions with a patronizing "It all depends" and to proceed to describe with statesmanlike shrugs the ways in which each case is unique and therefore requires intelligent, informed management, baseline surveys, and strong political support in dealing with any of these problems. That answer can always be justified by referring to the complexity of the situation; it is frequently encountered in the literature on IRD. But it does not provide much guidance on how to develop the needed information or to make use of whatever political support is available.

A more satisfactory set of answers would seek to identify expectations for different categories of situations within which similar answers can be suggested with reasonable tolerance of error. The approach this chapter follows is to describe the "actors" or decision

(Text continued on p. 238)

TABLE 8.1 Summary of IRD Cases Cited in This Chapter

Name and Country	Functions	Organization	Consequences
1. Bicol River Basin Development Program, Philippines (1973)	Agriculture, natural resources, infrastructure, social services.	Central "lead agency" supported by interagency council; local manager with planning staff plus local area development advisory council. No special resources. Seconded staff on temporary assignment.	Lead agency proved apathetic; project transferred to Special Projects Office. No line agency linkages. Enlisted private investment and university collaboration.
2. Chilalo Agricultural Development Unit (CADU), Ethiopia (1967)	"Precooperatives"; marketing, research, extension, inputs, roads, credits.	Multilevel independent agency within Ministry of Agriculture. Project director with elaborate staff and independent resources.	Limited efforts at local organization, but independent of local officials. Health services later split off to Ministry of Public Health. Functional linkages to other national agencies also failed. Agency later merged with Extension and Implementation Department of MOA. Heavy expatriate component yielded to local management. Increased productivity in first phase but widened income distribution gap as project continued.

3. Haitian-American Community Help Organization (HACHO) Haiti (1966)	Health-based community development plus roads, agricultural, and irrigation functions.	Independent regional development headquarters with one regional office and four field units. Advisory board representing cooperating agencies. Personnel seconded with "topping-off" payments from HACHO.	Planned local project initiation not actualized because of local apathy.
4. Integrated Community Health Project (ICHP), Nepal	Mobile village health workers as motivaters. Family planning and obstetrical services added later.	Pilot project coexisting with other Ministry of Health activities. Expected to integrate independent functional units under local project directors. Separate staff at comparable salaries but perquisites inferior to MOH personnel.	MOH activities continued independent functions. Logistical breakdowns frequent.
5. Kogoma Rural Development Project, Tanzania (1974)	Organization for infrastructure construction, credit, and training.	Cabinet-rank regional commissioner heading separate agency; decentralized coordinating directors; responsive to village proposals. Personnel seconded without special incentives. Expatriate staff aid. Operations left to line agencies and parastatals.	Cooperatives aborted in favor of operations under Project Management Executive. Materials shortages somewhat offset by village artisanship and labor.

(continued)

235

TABLE 8.1 (Continued)

Name and Country	Functions	Organization	Consequences
6. Lilongwe Land Development Program (LLDP), Malawi	Agricultural production, marketing, credit, land management credit, infrastructure.	District projects under Ministry of Agriculture & Natural Resources. Liaison committee. Coordinated inputs from other ministries and parastatals. Project manager with staff support seconded and supplemented by local and expatriate recruitment. Separate components funded by international donors, using standard administrative procedures. Incentive pay.	Expanding pilot project. Organization proved satisfactory for enlargement of field efforts.
7. Vihiga Special Rural Development Project, Kenya (1970)	Miscellaneous projects combined for village development: infrastructure, credit, and technical assistance, as requested.	Central committee under presidential appointee, with staff in Ministry of Economic Planning and Development. "Response" to district and provincial planning committee requests. Special resources, special treatment of central staff. No incentive to field workers. No local management unit.	Supply flows frequently intercepted.

| 8. Masagana-99, Davao del Sur (Philippines) (1973) | Credit base for transport and processing of rice, integrated with road and infrastructure. | Expanding pilot projects under National Food and Agricultural Council Coordination of 31 agencies plus National Bank and Credit Administration under Secretary of Agriculture Provincial Program Office with coordinating committee. Matrix organization. Local staff incentives. | Extension workers expected to collect loans as well as offer advice, with incentives neglecting service function. Loan repayment decline. Considering transfer of extension to local farmer-leaders. |

SOURCES: 1. "Implementing Area Development in the Bicol," by George M. Honadle (Washington, DC: Development Alternatives, Inc., October 25, 1977); Conference Report no. 2, the University of Wisconsin Conference on Planning in Integrated Rural/Area Development, February 1981; and Dennis A. Rondinelli, "The Bicol River Basin Development Program: Prototype of an Equitable Growth Project," *National Development*, vol. 20, no. 1 (1979): 47-57, and *Spatial Analysis for Regional Development* (Tokyo: United Nations University, 1980).

2. "Rural Change in Ethiopia: The Chilalo Agricultural Development Unit (CADU)," by John M. Cohen, *Economic Development and Cultural Change*, vol. XXII, no. 4 (1974): pp. 580-614; "Participation in Rural Development Project Effectiveness: An Organizational Analysis of Four Cases," by Derick Weston Brinkerhoff (Paper submitted to Harvard Graduate School of Education, 1980); Conference Report no. 2, the University of Wisconsin Conference on Planning in Integrated Rural/Area Development, February 1981, pp. 6-10; William Whyte, "Participative Approaches to Agricultural Research and Development" (Draft #4, Cornell University, May 5, 1981).

3. HACHO, Phase II, October 1976: Evaluation by Carol V. Pfrommer, David D. Gow, G. Donald Judd, and James L. Walker (Washington, DC, October 1976).

4. Kenneth Jaramillo, study prepared at the Kennedy School of Government, Harvard University, May 1980; and Donald S. Charls and Padma Raj Rajbhandari, "Nepal's Community Health Leader Project," *Rural Development Participation Review*, vol. II, no. 1 (Fall 1980): 12-14.

5. Case prepared by the Harvard Business School, Boston, Massachusetts; revised January 1979.

6. *National Rural Development Program (NRDP), Malawi*, World Bank Staff Appraisal Reports, published in 1968, 1971, 1975, and 1978; and Um Lele, *The Design of Rural Development: Lessons from Africa* (Baltimore: John Hopkins University Press, 1975).

7. Project evaluation by Edward D. Harmon and Tom Zolla, USAID, October/November 1974.

237

makers most directly affected by these issues, to define the issues themselves in terms of the alternatives they represent to these major decision makers, and to suggest reasons for predicting decision outcomes in these areas. The chapter presents a description of different styles of decentralized management and concludes with suggested criteria that project designers should consult in applying these generalizations to specific situations.

DECISION MAKERS IN
INTEGRATGED RURAL DEVELOPMENT

There are many general propositions about decentralization describing social regularities and probabilities and codifying existing knowledge for the benefit of social scientists and decision makers.[4] But such propositions are not immediately convertible into policies. They carry different action implications for different observers, depending on their own preferences and the institutional or ascribed values they represent. These differences can produce conflicts in decision making, such as those between international donors and national planning agencies or among different jurisdictions or levels of government. In order to move from general propositions to specific policies, therefore, policy makers must identify the prinicipal actors likely to participate in a given set of decisions and assess their relative influence in addressing the issues under consideration. This chapter suggests how such a task might be undertaken in designing IRD programs.

In IRD, the major policymakers are the "planners" (the program designers in national and international agencies), the "central administrators" (heads and staff assistants in national or regional agencies who are given planning and supervisory responsibility for a project), and "project managers" (locally based administrators in charge of operations in a region or district). These three actors may be considered prototypical in the sense that despite their individual variations in skill and outlook, they possess distinct characteristics as groups. There is for each a consistent set of preferences that bridges the shifting policy context of their activities. These three "ideal types" are recognizable enough to explore the implications of their imputed preferences, respectively, in light of selected social science propositions.

Most IRD decisions are neither purely *routine* nor generally *crisis-oriented*. Unlike routine operations, IRD involves identifiable decisions made at specific times by known persons; unlike the crisis situation, a decision to establish, fund, and manage a project of this type takes place over a prolonged time period and in the absence of threat.[5] IRD decisions reflect role perceptions much more fully than do decisions that are created by crises or purely personal choices. The major assumptions of this model of recurrent decision making are thus recognizable in the real world, even though they may not describe all actions and decisions in a given situation. The plausibility of these assumptions can be judged as they are presented in greater detail and tested by reference to case studies of the IRD experience in underdeveloped countries.

The Actors

The three sets of actors whose preferences are generalized here are not, of course, homogeneous groups, though their institutional roles are similar. At central levels, the *planners and designers* are usually staff members acting on behalf of an international donor or a national planning agency. They are responsible for establishing an IRD project and for recommending its organizational structure, its functional definition, and the terms of its financing. Their relationship to IRD is somewhat static: They can influence policy only at the outset, when a program is being funded or set into operation, or during the process of review and evaluation leading to refunding decisions. Thus they are primarily interested in structural relationships and their probable outcomes. Increasingly they participate in decisions about procedures, personnel and procurement policies, and relationships to other agencies and organizations, because these factors are now known to influence project success as much as structure does. A case history, for example, will show that all of these functions were discharged by World Bank planners in establishing the famous IRD project at Lilongwe[6] and its subsequent renewals and expansions; their decisions were made in collaboration with national planners from Malawi, and both groups had full access to field reports and subsequent evaluation studies. Their viewpoints proved to be quite similar.

Central administrations are representatives of national or regional supporting agencies, including both staff and line members working out of the capital city where statutory and budgetary responsibility for the project are located. In a few cases, these actors may be divided between a "national" and a "subnational" agency, in which case their perspectives would diverge as an additional set of bureaucratic jealousies or jurisdictional rivalries might be introduced. They share a "central" perspective with the planners, but their principal decisions are made on a more continuous basis than those of program design, since they have to be involved in the initial plans for geographical and organizational siting and are responsible also for funding and supply arrangements for the project. Their responsibilities include supervision of technical and administrative operations as well as backup support. They are also concerned with establishing routines for linking field operations with the central office: supplies, communications, policy guidance, feedback, and procedures for identifying unusual circumstances requiring nonroutine decisions. Their role vis-à-vis the project management is somewhat ambivalent, since they must collectively (1) respond to its requests for supplies and (2) initiate or review changes in policy or operational procedures. This ambivalance is an inherent part of the center-field relationship and is not peculiar to IRD projects. These actors are likely to be the same decision makers for both new and continuing operations. In Lilongwe, for example, the Ministry of Agriculture and Natural Resources (MANR) established a unit to support it and each of the other field projects, which included a coordinating committee as well as operating agencies of MANR.

The *project management* is perhaps the least homogeneous actor of all, since the number of decision makers involved may range from one director to a large number of specialists, staff advisers, and fieldworkers in supervisory roles. One case history — Chilalo — shows a project director in command, with four section heads and chiefs of twenty-three subunits and departments. Coherence in the positions this "actor" takes is ascribable to the fact that each decision maker acts for the unit and attempts to view it integrally (though the concentration of authority obviously varies, as between those functions under direct project "control" and those coming from other agencies that have to be "coordinated"). Project managers' success depends on their personal persuasions and leadership, since the actual use to which they can put project resources is often a function of decisions made by other participants over whom they have little control. Thus, the unity of viewpoint assumed for this level of analysis is probably a better reflection of reality than for the other two actors. (See Table 8.2.)

Other actors in the decision making environment of integrated rural development can be decisive sometimes, but their roles are

TABLE 8.2 Characteristics of Actors in IRD Decision Making

Actors	Organizational Location	Mission	Resources	Zones of Influence	Primary Instruments
Planners, designers	— International donors; national planning offices	Demonstrate cost-effectiveness of project design; maintain flow of decisions affecting development inputs; "move money"	Access to budgetary allocation; bargaining leverage; review and evaluation	Political and policy elites; budget makers; administering agency leadership	Program agreements; national, sectoral, or project plans; evaluation
Central administrators	— Secretariats; Comptroller and Finance, Personnel, and Supply directorates; Functional offices	Maximize accepted indicators; influence policies of other agencies whose activities affect outputs	Functional expertise; funds, personnel, material; statutory authority; policymaking; discretion; communications system	Political leadership; horizontal links; vertical authority; organized client community	Directives; clearances, approval, and review documents
Project managers	Field offices; special units of regional governing authorities; parastatal agencies; special project offices	Increase production, income, or physical welfare of client groups; influence behavior of other local actors to advance project goals; maintain and increase momentum continuity of appropriate services and functions	Delegated functional responsibility; assigned funds, personnel, materiél; "borrowed" or "coordinated" services involving other units; for exchange relationships; access to local leadership; area expertise	Supervisors in vertical authority; independent agencies and units in region; local government; voluntary local individual clients or organizations	Visible, delivered goods and services; commitments; records

probably not sufficiently comparable or standardized to permit the kinds of policy generalizations we seek. They include political leaders who call unexpectedly for changes in the course or in the administrative leadership of a project; private entrepreneurs who provide goods and services to the same publics being served by the project, perhaps at terms preferable to those available through government channels; and social institutions, nongovernmental organizations, and local officials, all of whom possess the capacity either to divert or to reinforce agencies engaged in IRD.

For purposes of the present analysis, these decision makers are contextual; they are taken as part of the active environment with which policymakers have to deal. They are assumed to be "constant" in the system because policy analysts always have to consider their activities as inputs in the decision-making processes.[7]

Role Stability

This chapter makes use of behavioral assumptions about these three actors, extrapolated from organization theory.[8] It imputes goal priorities for the participating agencies in terms of three major factors: mission, influence, and resources. It assumes a rationality that policymakers and administrators display on behalf of their organizations. Individuals will deviate from such rationalities on occasion, but they usually realize that they are doing so and justify the actions as special cases.

Organizations that have a strong and specific mission will tend to make use of influence and seek resources to advance it. They will not seek to enlarge their functions if the additional goals involved would attenuate the existing sense of mission, and they will not seek additional resources if managing them would distract attention from the primary mission. Organizations with diffuse, changing, or unspecified missions, on the other hand, will seek to influence agencies performing related functions and will seek additional resources to do so. In seeking to expand their resources, they will not suffer from the sense of ambivalence that affects organizations with a stronger sense of mission.

These two categories of organizations (those with "strong" and those with "diffused" missions) suggest different roles with respect to the actors' use of influence: Organizations with a strong sense of mission seek to "control"; those serving diffuse purposes are satisfied with "coordination." The "control" model has also been associated with instrumental goals, such as autonomy, agency-based morale, and stability of purpose, while "coordinating" units recognize their responsiblity to, and over, multiple centers, and their staff morale depends on pride in the performance of novel or unconventional services.

These organizational characteristics imply different roles for the three actors. Designers and planners as a group tend to view their own mission as precise, try to avoid contaminating it with operational responsibilities, and prefer no larger a resource base than is necessary to their function. Central support agencies usually have diffused missions, seek to influence policy at operating levels, and guard their resources jealously. Project managers may either have precisely defined technical or economic targets or see their mission in terms of their clients or special publics. In either case, they are mission-oriented. Because of their position in the hierarchy, they seek resources more than influence in defining their subgoals or subordinate purposes. Their missions may be precisely defined, but their functions are diffuse.

These variations refine the popular assumption that all organizations seek to maximize influence, expand goals, and enlarge budgets. The bureaucratic dynamic is more complex because the roles played by actors at different levels of authority are not necessarily identical or easily reconciled.

ISSUES AND CHOICES

Defining the primary actors in the typical IRD program is only a first step in predicting the dynamics of decision making. Their preferences have to be inferred from their behavior in the face of specific categories of choices or decisions. The outcomes are not always easy to predict, since they depend on the extent to which the actors perceive the differences in perspective among themselves and their respective capacities to confront and resolve them. But their positions in specific issues are predictable, and failure to differentiate these perspectives explains many of the errors and ambiguities of IRD project design and implementation.

The four issues selected for this analysis both illustrate the contrasting positions of the three actors and suggest possible ways of minimizing their potentially harmful consequences.

How much control should an integrated rural development project have over resources and services needed to accomplish its goals?

Designer Preferences

Planners in international agencies take a uniform position on this issue.[9] They are aware of the consequences of inadequate support to a field project: interruptions in the delivery of services that are needed to produce the desired functional integration, failure to meet project deadlines, and the decline in staff moral.[10] Recognizing the problems of trying to operate on the basis of borrowed resources, planners prefer to assign central funds directly to the project in order to guarantee delivery of essential goods and services. In this way they can enhance the prospect that a project will have the desired impact during the lifetime of a grant or loan, thus reducing their own responsibility for any susbsequent shortfall while at the same time demonstrating the donor's good faith to the cooperating government. International projects tend to be "front-end loaded," with maximum resources available at the beginning (when they are least likely to be effectively used) and declining relative to need as the project unfolds.

Even acting on the basis of these insights, however, an international donor can rarely provide all of the resources needed by an integrated rural development project. Its planners, therefore, have to take additional steps to assure that adequate logistical support will be delivered by the host government itself. Since their influence is greatest at the early stages of project negotiations, they will include in the intitial contract specific provisions for support from other agencies. This strategy means that they must offer whatever incentives they can to the host government to provide "counterpart" support from its own resources, guaranteeing by contract, if possible, that the project managers will receive what they themselves cannot provide.[11]

Contracts defining expected host government contributions to project operations are hard to interpret and difficult to enforce. International donors often suggest, therefore, the inclusion of one or two expatriate managers or experts in the system, not only because their specialized knowledge is deemed an asset, but also because that presence can help assure that the host government is living up to its obligations.

All of these design decisions accommodate the institutional needs of donor agencies: They maximize the prospects of quick success by reducing the uncertainties of implementation under adverse field conditions, and they give national and political leaders evidence of their commitment while extracting promises of cooperation and support that are expected to continue after the contract or agreement is negotiated and signed.

Central Administrators' Preferences

The perceptions and preferences of the second actor in integrated rural development differ in important respects from those of the donor agency. The host government's central planners share the donor's capital-city, macro-level view of the project as a symbol of national commitment, but they recognize the threat that such symbols pose to ongoing operations: the risk that special treatment or favoritism given to internationally funded projects will alienate the managers and technicians working in conventional services. Cohen argues that

> the more isolated the project design principles from the national policy position of the country, the more difficulties will arise in obtaining and maintaining integration over services normally performed by independent bodies.[12]

Any effort to exempt special IRD projects from the vicissitudes of a poor field supply system is likely to impose relative privations on the activities that are not so favored, given the situation of scarcity that prevails in all rural development contexts. Thus, central administrators are much more skeptical of the "special treatment" approach than are international planners.

For similar reasons, central planners resist the introduction of expatriate personnel, who are viewed as outrageously costly, ignorant of local law and custom, and ambiguous in their loyalties. Again, Cohen points out that "hiring foreign expatriates to fill top level positions complicates local bureaucratic procedures and processes and impairs the ablility of a project staff to obtain and maintain the integration of administrative services."[13]

The most important bargaining resource in the central planners' position is time: their capacity to outwait the international donors. They may share the latter's desire for quick, conspicuous impact, but they know they will have to live with a project long after the donors have turned to different projects and other countries. They can agree to "front-loaded" projects with the expectation that whatever assets are assigned to a project will remain in a country; but they do not expect to continue providing special treatment to a project after the national attention has drifted away. They occupy an ambiguous intermediate position between the donor's quick-fix perspective and the field manager's recognition that his or her career may involve a long-term commitment to IRD operations. Even their most generous impulses toward a fledgling infant project can gradually turn to a neglectful indifference as other responsibilities claim their attention.

Project Managers' Preferences

The third prototypical actors — the project managers — are much less interested in immediate impact, except as an attention-getter, than they are in staying power. They need support form local leaders, for both personal and project-related reasons. Such support is not automatic even if the project succeeds, since these local leaders are differentiated among themselves. Their expectations from the project have to be balanced off against each other and against demands both from the public and from higher authority. The local politics of project management require that the resources assigned for successful operations be discreetly deployed with these elites in mind: Land has to be purchased or added for project activities with a keen eye to the disposition and helpfulness of the owner; equipment has to be used so that other agencies and organizations derive some benefit from it if their cooperation is required in the future; and project services have to be sited and delivered with due regard to the social structure of the village, even though the intended beneficiaries are among its most underprivileged elements.

These considerations compel project managers to define efficiency of resource use in terms that are often distinctly different from those presented in international agreements and project papers. These managerial dilemmas and the characteristic responses have not been observed extensively in the literature describing IRD operations, but field studies challenge some of the most widely accepted principles of conventional personnel management.[14]

Project managers also have to provide benefits to the general public through the policies they adopt, including employment opportunities and dependable delivery of services. These considerations, incidentally, require a time perspective longer, in fact, than that of either of the other decision makers involved in project design. The commonplace notion that central planners have a broader horizon or a larger view than local managers does not apply in integrated rural development, if indeed it has any validity at all. Local managers have to live with their decisions, and they develop an actute personal interest in a project's performance. Their careers are at stake whether they decide to remain with an assignment until its success has become a major part of their life work or they use it as a stepping stone to a better assignment after a year or two in the field. In either case, their perspective outlasts that of the project designers and negotiators, and it is important to them that whatever equipment, supplies, and services they need for daily operations are provided continuously and on time.

The effects of these contrasting perceptions can be observed in the histories of project successes and failures that are so often attributed to logistical issues. The importance of dependable logistics is illustrated by an evaluation of the Vihiga project, where staff morale was reported to have suffered because of poor management practices, ill-defined objectives, uncertainties in the delivery of supplies and equipment, and delays in reimbursement of out-of-pocket expenses. On the other hand, giving special treatment to a project to avoid these uncertainties can be a source of trouble later if it violates the expectations of local elites. For example, the provision of special vehicles to Ethiopia's CADU generated resentment from local government officials who were not so favored. Unfortunately, the project never was able to turn this resource into a bargaining chip to induce cooperation, and the separateness of the project was sharpened by the disparity in the facilities available to the local management.

Special treatment is often necessary to recruit effective managers for IRD assignments. In one project in Nepal, it was difficult to recruit top-level specialists because the pay scale for the Integrated Community Health Project never exceeded that offered by the line agencies, although the risks were greater, and the sense of professional rewards less, than in more conventional assignments. Even where staff expectations are modest, it may be necessary to offer special inducements to local staff workers to compensate for low staff morale caused by logistical failures. The Vihiga project also illustrates this dilemma.

Experience with expatriates does not necessarily disqualify their use as project personnel of last resort, but they must be assigned with discretion. The advantage of expatriates' expertise is to some extent neutralized at the project level by their unfamiliarity with host government procedures and by latent bureaucratic resentment over their special position in the system. In some recent instances, however, foreign managers have been used for the very reason that local personnel were unwilling to accept the hardships of an IRD assignment, while extraordinary incentives were available for international sources to draw expatriates to the field. The use of expatriates in the Lilongwe project illustrates an unusual, but, in the end, successful assignment of international management technicians. The dilemma of placing foreigners "in charge" of local staff was resolved by assigning them advisory functions, especially international management; the project continued to suffer from dependence on the indigenous support system, however, until special logistical procedures were set up. Over the life of the project, major efforts were mounted to strenthen central management services as the project administration was transferred to local hands. Similarly, expatriate managers in the Vihiga Project, supplied by an American university, were reported in a field evaluation to be ill prepared to function in a decision-making role, because they confused the lines of authority in an already complicated situation of coordination, although they were able to perform some liaison functions. In the Kigoma Project, another situation in which expatriate advisors were asked to perform largely managerial functions, they were unable to operate effectively except in rare cases where the resources available to the project were supplied entirely from internal support systems.

What kinds of linkages should a project have with central agencies and with local organizations?

Designer Preferences

Loan officers in international agencies want the system to provide an uninterrupted flow of resources from their own coffers to the hands of officials concerned with the purchasing of goods and services needed by a project. They prefer a project design that affords minimum delay in reviewing requisitions from the field or, later, in procuring physical and human resources for project use at fair market costs. They want assurances from the field that these inputs are arriving in adequate quantity and timely fashion. For these purposes they perceive central agencies as pass-through devices, "expeditors," so far as prompt movement of these inputs is concerned, but "auditors" when it comes to exercising care that they are provided economically and used properly. They are aware of some tension between these two functions, but regard them as normal aspects of relations between the center and the field.

Donors have a parallel concern over continuous flow of information between field and center reporting progress and obstacles (the justification of continued support or renewed guidance), presenting data on returns or productivity effects, and showing changes of direction that might be useful in planning further investments. Their own need for free access to the project site and its internal records is generally accepted, even by governments that are otherwise suspicious of investigations and audits. They even want to be able to provide information and technical assistance to project technicians as the spirit moves them or as relevant new knowledge becomes available.

The implications of this need include organization preferences for clearly defined project boundaries, both administrative and physical.[15] Clarity in these matters improves the exchange of information about project operations and strengthens the role of both central coordinating groups and local officials.[16]

Central Administrators' Preferences

At first sight, it would appear that central administrators would be sympathetic to these donor preferences: They gain in the clarity of their jurisdiction and the legitimacy of their demands for information because they respond to the obvious needs of international agencies. Regular reporting is often included explicitly, and always implicitly, in project agreements. But there are also contrary currents in these relationships, especially in the donor's expectation that funds will flow promptly to the field with a minimum of review and procedural clearance. The need for expediting responses to requests from internationally supported projects amounts to an invasion of some of the most carefully guarded perquisites of central agencies, the exercise of discretion in assigning resources to field operations. Tensions develop easily over differences in the attention devoted to these projects, especially as they become differences in treatment. Probably no single issue divides central administrators from international donor preferences more than that of the lines of communication and other transactions with the field.[17]

But there are other differences in the perspectives of these two actors. Coexistence with various levels and agencies of government and managerial styles complicates life for central administrators but not for international donors. Cohen contends that "the more reliance project managers have to place on different providers of activities and services spread among national, provincial, and local levels, the more critical is the need to devise strategies for coordination."[18]

Project Manager's Preferences

As IRD projects mature and gain in managerial independence, a form of decentralization emerges naturally. National agencies tend to turn their attention elsewhere and encounter difficulties in reacting quickly to any unexpected developments in the field. Local managers pursue their advantage by routinizing their increasing discretion. In the end, significant changes can emerge in the social consequences of project operations: local elites or the public begin to participate in decision making, further complicating the functions of management.[19] If private enterprise begins to profit from successful project activities, sensitive ideological problems arise because central bureaucratic and political leaders may have markedly different preferences about the private sector.[20]

The differences in perspective among these three actors are organizational imperatives, not just personal differences, although their manifestations sometimes become heated as the issues affect daily operations. Channels can become almost sacred. The desire of international donors for full access deprives the national bureaucratic guardians of their priestly role. Project managers find the possibility of using the donor representatives for protection against their own superiors almost irresistible, unless their own future salvation may be jeopardized by such heresy. Sharing knowledge about project experiences invites a sharing of decisions and disturbs the natural order of things as seen from the bureaucratic perspective.

The sharing of responsibilities in integrated rural development involves not only international and central actors, but also a number of local leaders and organizations whose participation can contribute to a project's success. The focal point of these attitudes is, of course, the project manager, who is often perceived as a relatively minor personage until the significance of the de facto decentralization, the transactions and exchanges among lcoal operating agencies, and the growth of private entrepreneurial activity are recognized as by-products of the project's activities.

The implications of these transactions can be traced in the World Bank experience with the Lilongwe project, where the coordination of different levels of government involved a series of structural changes, including the integration of political and administrative units to support the effort. The project management decided to work through village committees to establish formal liaison between regional administrative units of the project and local government offices. As the market began to play a larger role in the project's activities, the use of the village committees was sidetracked and officials took over. An inverse example occurred in the Vihiga project, where the exchange of intergovernmental information was stymied at the outset because central officials were unwilling to relinquish decision-making responsibility and declined to set up a project management unit in the field. The result was a record of logistical failure that affected the performance of the project.

Organization theorists recognize the problems caused by these diverse viewpoints and urge a fuller sharing of information as a means of reducing conflict. Cohen contends that

> the more information the project management provides to independent units whose activities and services it seeks to organize, the greater are the prospects of a shared viewpoint, and the greater is the probability of gaining the desired cooperation, assuming that the information is similarly interpreted by decision makers in the units involved.[21]

But the assumption that shared information contributes to more effective cooperation presupposes shared purposes. In the absence of that condition, and especially when the bargaining situation prevails, information is treated as a scarce resource and rationed to those whose need is greatest. Information sharing does not contemplate that millenium at which all books are opened, but the more limited, utilitarian concept that knowledge sometimes facilitates action.

Sharing information, in short, is not always standard practice. The information available to international donors will necessarily be limited, once the planning stages have passed, since details of an operation, its resources, and the public responses to it are still in the future. Central administrators, by the same token, also resist bringing project managers into the information-sharing pool, since their participation will tend to divert their own staff members from other obligations and priorities. But project managers will tend to seize every opportunity to advise other agencies and governmental organizations of their own objectives and needs, hoping to discover common purposes and opportunities for exchange of services. Exchanging information thus involves the investment of managerial time that is valued differently among the intended participants.

Linkages that improve information sharing do not always contribute to success in integrated rural development. Plans to coordinate information failed in both Bicol and CADU, where such exchanges were deemed threatening because they emphasized management failures but produced no basis for self-correction. In HACHO the absence of incentives to exchange information resulted in very weak basis for collaboration. Differences in perspective on material transactions are not necessarily reduced by increased exchanges of information, which can equally well increase frustrations and resentments. Sometimes concealment is the best defense in a poor bureaucratic situation.

What kinds of goals can be appropriately assigned to managers attempting to coordinate IRD functions at local levels?

Designer Preferences

"To will the end is to will the means." International planners have to assign specific goals to a project, both to develop a case for supporting it and to establish a basis for measuring its progress. Precisely defined benefits simplify the task of predicting profitability, and they also make it possible for managers on the spot to monitor their own performance. But such precision has to be couched in short-range terms to make measurement feasible; often the goals refer to intermediate processes such as rate of expenditure or distribution of agricultural inputs rather than to the developmental change the project is intended to bring about. If the efficient use of these resources is assumed and the expected public response taken for granted as well, relatively simple calculations provide the justification for undertaking and continuing the project so long as its "absorptive capacity" meets expectations.

Once the international donor expresses its goals with such precision, however, it exposes the project to potential jurisdictional struggles, especially if the focus on intermediate processes resembles the functions and responses of existing agencies.[22] The unique claims an IRD project has to special organizational treatment are reduced to the extent that its functions are defined in standard operational terms that could also describe the activity of an existing agency — a condition that is often necessitated by the international donor's procedures. Standardizing outputs thus simplifies the donor's definition of project functions but complicates the subsequent relations with agencies in the host government that are performing parallel functions.

Central Administrators' Preferences

The national agencies responsible for managing development activities related to a proposed project are expected to provide auxiliary supports from their own sources if the project's immediate goals coincide with their own mission. But as these goals converge, the central agencies involved will demand participation in the project design, even if the donor's internal procedures call for such planning to follow international standards. "The larger the role played by the central government in the formulation of a project," Cohen argues, "the greater is the probability that strong budgetary and staffing support will be extended to the project."[23] Thus, while much recent experience argues against premature specification of goals in IRD, the donor becomes trapped by his own requirement for precision, which in turn induces the cooperating national agencies to participate in the designing of a project in order to co-opt its approaches, absorb its resources, and thus enhance the performance of their own missions.

Project Managers' Preferences

In the field, where the primary responsibility for meeting project goals is lodged, the need for clear-cut authority is directly proportional to the clarity of the assigned objectives.[24] Ambiguity of purpose relieves administrators of accountability for their shortcomings, but when orders are clear and precise, careers are at stake when they are not carried out.

Increasingly, international donors are beginning to depart from the use of intermediate goals as targets and indicators of project performance. Social change — that is, responsive investment on the part of project beneficiaries — is also becoming an important dimension of international appraisal. A project that does not produce "development" is no longer necessarily considered a success, even if it yields benefits or profits in traditional terms. When such goals are made explicit, they present new challenges to the local manager to involve the public in certain operating decisions of the projects.[25]

The longer time perspective local managers have toward project objectives increases their suspicion of the precise, short-term goals preferred by international donors in defining the project's viability and used by central administrators to establish their own claims in matters of design and support.

Goal definition in public programs is sometimes regarded as an exercise in futility, since the actual effects of government actions are so much more likely to depend on implementation and subsequent social developments than on initial perceptions. But in international development projects, adherence to defined objectives is taken as something like an end in itself: It reinforces donor commitment, provides leverage that central administrators can exert over field managers, and gives the latter direct access to the donor if the project needs someone to run interference against other agencies' ambitions. The more precise the definition of objectives, the greater the need all actors have for access to information and the greater the prospect that different time perspectives and conflicting objectives of the three actors will become explicit. Vaguely defined project goals obscure these realities unless, or until, an event occurs that forces redefinition and clarification of objectives.

Unless the definition of goals assigns clear responsibilities among the participating officials (which it rarely does), subsequent events reveal a struggle for control over resources. Both central and local administrators recognize the need for showing results and the importance of gaining control over activities in order to do so. This struggle tends to ignore second-generation consequences and side effects of project activities because the immediate consequences are the primary concern of all actors except in the unusual cases, such as those involving careers that depend on long-term project successes. Donor concerns over goal achievement sometimes produce an extremely close involvement with ongoing operations, as in the case of the Lilongwe project, where the World Bank established an evaluation unit to measure performance and offered precise calculations of rates of return on the basis of three on-site appraisals.

The clarity of goals specified in the Integrated Community Health Project in Nepal illustrates the conflict generated when the standardization of project outputs duplicated those of an existing agency: The proposed expansion was blocked by the Ministry of Public Health. Even in the pilot phases of that project, the Ministry of Health did not permit its own functions to merge with the integrated efforts. In 10 of the 23 districts where ICHP operated, the traditional services were also available.

As international attention turns to the needs of the poor "special" (as opposed to "general") publics, important changes in bureaucratic behavior are enjoined.[26] Special incentives for that purpose may be needed to overcome the "cognitive distance" between bureaucrats and the public.[27] Assigning new service targets to staff members is a function that can best be performed by managers who have direct control over task definition, reward and incentive structures, and promotions. But such changes in the local incentives may conflict with other national standards: In the Masagana 99 program in the Philippines, the offering of bonus payments to extension workers on the basis of loan collections (which was intended to improve the viability of further credit activities) diverted the staff from their primary tasks of helping the rural poor. In the end, both the incentive system and the credit system had to be adjusted because of these conflicting goals.

When the specification of goals is accompanied by changes in administrative conventions, sharp divisions appear in the preferences of the three major participating elements in the decision-making process.

What organizational arrangements are needed at the national level to provide local managers with appropriate support and guidance?

The alternatives available to project designers for providing central support and guidance systems are at least four in number: (a) to assign field operations to an existing agency that is already dominant or can be relied on to perform the essential technical or administrative functions; (b) to divide responsibilities among several independent central agencies under the coordination of one of them; (c) to establish a permanent coordinating committee under the chief executive to integrate the national support functions; or (d) to create a special agency for very large projects or for activities that are expected to multiply beyond the capacity of an existing ministry or department to oversee. The propositions that have been advanced to provide guidance on these alternatives are:[28]

(a) *On using the dominant agency:* The more adequate the core set of services provided by a project's own ministry or agency, the greater the probability that it can gain timely access to other essential services through coordination with independent bodies beyond its control.

The more an integrated rural development project is organized within the existing government system, the higher the probability some of its activities or services will take hold in the local area, even if the larger project fails.

(b) *On dividing the responsibility:* The less an IRD project is viewed as a possible national program and the more area specific and small-scale it is, the less central levels of organization will resist transferring control of the integrative functions to the project management unit.

The more control a given organization is asked to transfer in its technical (as opposed to its administrative) functions, the greater its resistance will be to integration efforts by project administrators.

Special incentives are required to induce independent organizations whose activities and services are beyond the control of project administrators to cooperate with overall project needs.

(c) *On using coordinating committees:* The more information project management provides to independent units whose activities and services it seeks to organize, the greater the prospects of a shared viewpoint and the greater the probability of gaining desired cooperation, assuming that the information is similarly interpreted by decision makers in the units involved.

The larger the role played by the central government in the formulation of a project, the greater the probability that effective administrative mechanisms and procedures facilitating coordination, control, evaluation, and operational flexibility will be included and supported.

The more integrated projects are supported by the center and the more linked they are into the national plan, the greater the probability they will get increased domestic financial support when their special funding sources are ended.

The more the central government is involved in the conceptualization and design of an integrated rural devlopment project, the less the likelihood that the program will be viewed as the product of a power-hungry ministry or an activity foisted on a country by political or economic donor adventurism.

(d) *On creating a separate national agency:* The more project designers perceive central units as inefficient, understaffed, technically incompetent, or developmentally conservative and the more they worry about blockages or opposition in the local government system, the more they will see clear administrative advantages in establishing a separate agency, despite all the new administrative problems that it raises.

The more separate a unit and the less linked it is into established government structures, the less likely it is to get domestic financial support when, or if, its donor funding or particular national support ends.

The more independent and "showcase-designed" an integrated project, the more other government units will act to see it fail or to discredit it, increasing the project's administrative problems.

The larger the amount of funding provided by donors and the more inadequate the national and local government appears, the greater the tendency for the donor to attempt creating a special unit that can circumvent the local government system, use expatriate specialists, and be granted the control necessary to obtain and maintain key activities and services.

Designer Preferences

A conflict arises between the long- and short-term effects of an organizational decision. A project is better served when a separate national agency is set up to support it, but this expectation applies only so long as large elements of its funding come from international or other special sources. When those sources dry up, so too does the special agency, unless it has developed its own patrons and constituents. Donors no longer expect successful demonstrations alone to change the behavior of strong independent organizations, and therefore they are beginning to avoid introducing the separate agency approach in order to reduce the embarrassment caused by the sudden death of their projects when they withdraw.

Among the other three choices, donors like the simplicity of the dominant agency approach if they cannot have a special agency; at the same time, they fear that an innovative project loses visibility if its funds are channeled through an existing powerful agency and it is treated merely as an augmentation of a current activity. Their preferences tend, therefore, to waver between the divided responsibility and the coordinating committee models, the former being superior for its logistical capacities, but the latter easier to deal with because it situates final responsibility in the national chief executive, who is readily accountable under international agreement. The predicted ranking of prefereneces of international donors would then be for models c, d, and b, with model a as the least preferred. National designers would rank their preferences a, c, b, and d.

Central Administrators' Preferences

The first choice among central administrators is for the dominant agency assignment, because it introduces the least challenge to existing procedures and channels. Like international donors, central administrators regard the special agency as an unwise choice because of its probable short longevity and its threat to their own operations, at least by implication. (Why set up a special agency if existing agencies are adequate?) As between the divided responsibility model and the coordinating committee approach (which may become necessary if strong rivalry between possible patrons rules out using a dominant agency), central administrators greatly distrust the latter; they opt for division of responsibility among likely agencies, each of which derives some support from the new activity. Thus, the predicted ranking of preferences is a, b, c, and d.

Project Managers' Preferences

A special agency is much easier for a project manager to deal with for unconventional or experimental activities than is a dominant existing agency, but it has poor prospects for longevity, and career uncertainties are associated with the offline assignments it implies. These concerns lead to a preference for the coordinating committee approach under strong leadership from the chief executive. The alternative of shared responsibility is distrusted because it does not provide by guaranteed services or a clear delineation of functions among the participating agencies. The predicted preferences of project managers, then, are c, a, d, and b.

Project managers have little or no voice in the structure of national organizational support for integrated rural development. Confusion over the potentialities of these organizational devices and over the preferences of different constituents has led to more frequent reorganization of IRD centers than is usually found elsewhere, even in the highly volatile context of internationally supported projects. The direction of change tends to be away from the weaker forms of central support, though there is also a mild trend toward decentralization of specific functions, especially those in which local committees are permitted to participate in decision making. The Lilongwe project was the first supplied by lead agencies — the Department of Agriculture and the Ministry of Economic Affairs — where it was regarded as a "foreign body" and something of an irritant. It was then transferred to the Ministry of Agriculture and Natural Resources, which established a liaison committee including all cooperating agencies, which in turn committed itself to absorbing the personnel and functions of the program as external aid was withdrawn. The Chilalo Agricultural Development Unit in Ethiopia was establshed as an independent agency within the Ministry of Agriculture, but after an unsuccessful effort to integrate health activities with its field operations it transferred those functions to a separate program under the control of the Ministry of Public Health. But it later lost its own independent status and was attached to the Ministry of Agriculture's Extension and Project Implementation Unit. The Bicol project in the Philippines started with one dominant agency (the National Irrigation Administration) given the leading role at the center, but it too was reorganized under an interagency council headed by the Minister of Agriculture when the NIA failed to lend its authority to the planned functional integration. Another effort to make IRD a separate national agency failed in Tanzania, where the Kigoma project director was given cabinet rank but lacked the logistical infrastructure and administrative clout to provide service to the field, ending up with a version of the divided responsibility model by which several strong agencies agreed to maintain the supply links.

Perhaps the best indicator of the effectiveness of these alternative national models would be a logistical performance test. Few such evaluations exist, but a survey of rural health projects in Nepal showed that the divided responsibility model supported only 10 percent of the ICHP posts adequately, while 67 percent of the malaria posts supplied through the Ministry of Health met that criterion. Central organizational arrangements are often heatedly debated at the early stages of project design, but the evidence suggests that the real question is whether whatever arrangements do gain ascendancy can succeed literally in delivering the goods. Perhaps the preferred ranking on the "efficiency" score would be 4, 1, 3, 2: a sequence that corresponds to the preferences of none of the principal actors. (See Table 8.3.)

CONCLUSION:
MODELS OF MANAGEMENT

Decentralization for rural development operations requires planners to assign appropriate functional responsibilities to each of the three principal actors with due regard to their particular needs. Since their preferences diverge in all four of the arenas of choice considered here, the course of wisdom is to consider tradeoffs among them in light of their expected consequences. In weighing these consequences, planners should consider both the probability of success in meeting project goals and their long-run implications for the administrative system as a whole.

The Possibility of Compromise

The anticipated preferences of the three actors are summarized in Table 8.4. They are sometimes complementary, sometimes contrasting, and sometimes conflictual. But their valence is also different for the three levels: Ordinarily the donors/designers are intensely interested in organizational issues and goal assignments, the central support administrators are concerned primarily with logistics, and the project managers tend to be so heavily dependent on resource arrangements that they are usually willing to compromise on other issues in order to gain needed access to them. Thus, decisions made in dividing these functions among the principal actors involved are not

TABLE 8.3   Preferred Models for Guidance and Logistical Support Systems

	Donor Ranking	Central Agency Ranking	Local Management Ranking	"Efficiency" Ranking
Dominant agency	1	1	2	2
Divided responsibility	4	2	4	4
Coordinating committee	3	4	1	3
Separate agency	2	3	3	1

necessarily winner-take-all, zero-sum situations. They are complex but not hopeless. There is room for negotiation. For their part, all three actors seek to minimize uncertainties that might threaten their primary missions. They prefer uncertainty only as the alternative to a serious and certain setback. To reduce uncertainty they need to exercise control over the elements they consider essential to success. Thus, the bargaining situation involves efforts by each actor to avoid the loss of such control and to promote arrangements that extend his or her range of influence. When control is denied, as in the case of shared resources or nonparticipatory decision making, each actor seeks ways to coordinate the desired element with other, better controlled inputs. Many disputes in decentralization involve the tension between contested control and attempted coordination. Planners should be aware of these nuances in assigning functional responsibilities to the three primary actors in IRD.

Two Contrasting "Models"

Control and coordination have slightly different meanings at different levels of responsibility. Just as the preferences and needs of these

TABLE 8.4 Actor Preferences on Four Issues

	I. Designers	II. Central Support Administrators	III. Project Managers
1. Resources	Assign special resources; contract special services; use expatriate staff	Equalize and standardize assets gradually; resist reliance on expatriates	Resist "quick fixes"; develop local base; stabilize flow of services and benefits
2. Transactions	Speed flow of resources; clarify boundaries; encourage prompt reporting	Maintain clearance procedures; observe channels	Maximize discretion; develop local participation encourage direct donor communications
3. Goals	Assign precise goals	Negotiate jurisdictional issues	Demand measured authority; maintain fluid goals
4. Organization	Develop strong agency	Develop central coordinating authority	Guarantee central responsive posture

three prototypical actors differ in the functional areas described in Table 8.3, so their managerial functions diverge as they seek to control essential resources and policies and to coordinate the services and activities that have to be supplied by other organizations. The two major organizational strategies used to bring about the integration of rural development services rely, in short, on control and the coordination functions as their dominant managerial style.[29] The control function is associated with "line" administration, that is, the exercise of authority hierarchically — the familiar vertical pattern that is thought to produce efficient uses of the organization's internal resources. The coordination model is typified by special attention to horizontal relationships, particularly those involving different line agencies or functions serving a common or shared mission. It is thought to produce efficient use of resources available to more than one organization.

The Mixed Model

These models are rarely encountered in their pure form; most IRD projects are mixtures of the two, and most managers make a clear distinction between the two functions in their daily lives. But in theory the two models call for different choices at different levels of decision making, since the structure, resources, and managerial styles appropriate to each differ fundamentally. A true control model is one in which all decisions required for project operations are assigned to the manager or director. In the pure coordination model, nothing is; the project resources are dispersed among several independent agencies, which are expected to cooperate in applying them to project objectives. Contrasting features of these two extremes are suggested in Table 8.5.

Planners considering the mixture of functions to be decentralized in establishing an IRD project should therefore incline toward (1) assigning resources to the project management or a unit as close to it as possible; (2) specifying as precisely as possible the procedures to be used by central support administrators, basing them carefully on existing linkages but setting up standards of promptness that correspond to the best practice of the responsible agencies; (3) specifying multisectoral project goals that conform to prevailing norms currently followed in the technical agencies performing similar functions in other rural areas; and (4) placing primary logistical responsibility in a dominant agency that already possesses adequate communications

TABLE 8.5   Contrast Between Control and Coordination Models of Integrated Rural Development

Issues	Control	Coordination
Resources	Budget-based	Derived through negotiations
Linkages (managerial styles)	Command	Bargaining
Goals (operating responsibility)	Direct	Indirect
Organization (structure of major relation-ships)	Vertical or hierarchical	Horizontal or cooperative
Functions	Sectoral	Diffuse

and supply links to the region in which the project is to be located. The first and second ˹.inciples observe the rules of the control model; the third and fourth call for management skills in coordination, especially at the local level. These basic design features would correspond to the predicted mixture of preferences and priorities of the three actors without jeopardizing the prospects of the project of threatening the administrative system in which it is to operate.

Interim Validation Checks

Empirical validation of this recommended design is still lacking. But some preliminary tests can be inferred from existing data. Studies of the integrated rural development experience do not favor either of the two organizational models so far as actual performance is concerned. There is, in fact, little usable information that would permit an objective evaluation of rural development programs at all, whether integrated or not, to say nothing of yielding a comparison between the outputs of the managerial strategies of control and coordination. Any attempt to compare their utility must therefore rely on internal measures, such as staff quality, motivation, and service delivery.

The quality of staff depends on successive recruitment in the first instance. It is not easy to attract project managers with capacities that match the unusually demanding requirements of integrated rural development.[30] In theory, the management pool available for assignment under the control model is not significantly different from that available for a coordination assignment. The difference is whether the project itself is compelled to follow standard personnel practices or is to be given special treatment so far as pay, career opportunities, and other incentives are concerned. Since the control model is based on hierarchic principles and attempts to follow normal government procedures where possible, its incentive structure is related to career rewards more than to short-term financial gains or prerequisites. Its comparative advantages are that the parent agency can assign its best managerial talent to an integrated rural development project if it wants to do so, and that such assignments may be made part of a defined career pattern. (The "best bureaucrats" in the system may be able to avoid the assignment altogether, however, if it is sufficiently uncomfortable.) The coordination model, on the other hand, places the heavier burden on the bargaining skills of the local manager; and it tends to function outside government routine. Thus, it is more likely to have to offer higher immediate rewards to its management and to seek to recruit "risk takers." The difference is sharp enough to constitute an important element in the designer's choice between the control and coordination approach. Coordination needs better and perhaps more unconventional managers. If it has powerful political support, the coordination model is more likely to be able to recruit them from existing domestic resources; if not, the control model is a more likely source of experienced managers. For example, it was difficult for the Integrated Community Health Project in Nepal to recruit top-level specialists, because the pay scale did not offer incentives beyond those available to the line agencies, which could provide other forms of incentives, such as career advancement and rotation.

By the same token, the attempt to use expatriate managers as substitutes for local staff members becomes slightly more difficult in the control model, where familiarity with the procedures, personnel, and routines of the government is essential. The coordination model also requires some such expertise, but it is more tolerant of expatriate managers, because so many administrative decisions are actually made by the paticipating agencies rather than the project headquarters. Thus, in cases where foreign expertise is necessary in a managerial role, the coordination function is less likely than that of control to introduce procedural difficulties, though the margin of advantage is very slight. Foreign experts perform better as advisers than as managers in either setting; but if they become very conspicuous because of their numbers, or if they are required to serve as top decision makers, the coordination model seems slightly preferable.

Still another device that can be used to supplement the limited supply of managerial talent is to recruit local personnel to serve as staff members. Attracting these potential employees depends more on the flexibility and special procedures available to management than on the project structure. Assuming that the coordination model is less closely linked to routine procedures than is the control model, it can offer higher pay and speedier action. But if, as already suggested, it has shorter longevity and a lower prospect for eventual absorption into ongoing operations, it would offer less of a career option in terms of eligibility for promotions and varied assignments. Only a large IRD project would be likely to have such prospects; but a large project is the least likely to have to depend on coordination for its essential services. Either model permits recruitment of local staff for labor and semiskilled positions; the coordination model can probably offer better pay, but the control model is likely to provide better career prospects for locally hired personnel. For example, even though the pay scales offered to village-level workers in Nepal's Integrated Community Health Project were equal to those applied in other projects, recruitment suffered because of the arduous nature of the task: Workers had to walk from village to village to discharge their functions.

Similar experiences were encountered in the Philippines, where an attempt to provide project managers with control over their own staff members in the Masagana 99 program failed to improve performance because only negative incentives (transfers or fines) were available at their descretion.

Still a third requirement of local project management is to maintain high staff morale, which is itself dependent on the cumulative effect of good performance. Projects that are not well served by their supporting agencies rarely perform adequately and thus suffer further costs when morale declines because of discouragement and resentment over failure to meet expectations. The control model is generally considered the more efficient — that is, indeed, the chief reason for its existence. It takes a well-managed coordinating agency to overcome the disadvantage of having few resources at its own dispositions. On this score, the control model is the better able to offer the incentive of association with "success." For example, staff morale in the Vihiga project, using the coordination model, was reported to have suffered because of poor management practices and ill-defined objectives, uncertainties in the delivery of supplies and equipment, and delays in reimbursement of out-of-pocket expenses.

The two models also offer different advantages in providing terms of service that could contribute to strong morale. Usually special incentives are needed to compensate for the lack of amenities and for

TABLE 8.6   **Comparative Ratings of Control and Coordination Models for Providing Staff Incentives**

Issue	Control	Coordination	"Manageability"*
1. Recruitment	1	1	0
2. Expatriate management	−1	1	2
3. Local staffing	1	2	1
4. Efficiency	2	−1	3
5. Terms of service	2	1	1
6. "Special public"	2	−1	3
Net Total (Comparability)	7	3	

NOTE: 2, advantageous position; 1, little advantage on this issue; −2, disadvantaged position; −1, little disadvantage.

*Issues on which the two models differ are deemed more "manageable" from the viewpoint of project designers than those on which the two models come off about equal.

the frustrations arising from failure to achieve consensual standards of efficiency.[31] Either model can provide good terms of service and adequate supervision. The control model, which is preferred by international donors because of its presumably greater accountability and efficiency, may yield additional (that is, foreign) resources that could contribute to good physical conditions of work, thus offsetting the fact that the coordination model may be more able to free its own staff from the exigencies of bureaucratized routines because of their presumably more flexible style of operation. In lieu of direct budgetary support, the Philippines' Masagana 99 project was able to authorize the national coordinating agency to offer incentives (including training opportunities and motorcycles for local transportation) for the benefit of freed staff workers.

Preferences and Outcomes

Table 8.6 explains why designers and planners tend to prefer the control model: It can more readily offer incentives to staff members for better performance. It is at some disadvantage in the use of expatriate personnel, and it may not have as much leverage in obtaining local staffing as the coordination model, but on all other criteria it has the greater scope for managerial action to motivate staff behavior. The issues listed in the first column do not, of course, exhaust all of the managerial methods available for staff motivation. But the other devices considered by organization theorists to to be most closely related to improved performance (such as task definition by peers and assignments to production teams) would, on the whole, be easier to introduce under the control than under the coordination model.[32] The third column, on "manageability," is intended to suggest the extent to which decisions made at the project level can influence the incentive structure in either direction. There is variability among them; decision makers who have to deal with such issues ought to be aware of the extent to which they can be resolved by good management under one setting or the other.

The art of decentralization has to accommodate the needs of all actors, from local managers concerned with the morale and performance of their staff members to national and international planners and supporting officials. There is rarely a solid, homogeneous commitment to decentralization that makes continuous, fine adjustments to keep the system functioning smoothly. Decentralization is a state of dynamic equilibrium, responding to different challenges at each level of decision making. It offers few certainties except assured succession of opportunities and risks. True artistry in its management lies is knowing which is which.

NOTES

1. John M. Cohen, "Integrated Rural Development: Clearing Out the Underbrush," *Sociologia Ruralis,* vol. XX, no. 3 (1980): 198-199.

2. Robert E. Klitgaard, *On the Economics of Integrated Rural Development* (Cambridge: Lincoln Institute of Land Policy and John F. Kennedy School of Government, Harvard University, July 1981).

3. Estimates by Thomas F. Carroll in an unpublished paper for the InterAmerican Development Bank, December 1980.

4. A propositional inventory was prepared in connection with this study by John M. Cohen, "Integrating Services for Rural Development," Baselines for Discussion no. 5 (Cambridge: Lincoln Institute of Land Policy, Harvard University, 1979). Subsequent notes in this chapter refer to specific propositions in Cohen's study.

5. For discussion of routine decisions, see Graham T. Allison, *Essence of Decision, Exploring the Cuban Missile Crisis* (Boston: Little, Brown, 1971), Ch., 3; crisis decision making is defined by Glenn D. Paige in *The Korean Decision* (New York: Macmillan, 1968) and tested by Charles F. Hermann in *Crises in Foreign Policy: A Simulation Analysis* (Indianapolis: Bobbs-Merrill, 1969).

6. The projects cited in this chapter are summarized in Table 8.1. A more complete description of these case histories is in preparation.

7. The importance of these actors as part of the environment of IRD is emphasized by the experiences of fieldworkers reported in John D. Montgomery and

Masihur Rahman, *The IRD Experience: Views from the Field* (Cambridge: Lincoln Institute of Land Policy, Harvard University, 1981).

8. See M. Aiken and J. Hage, "Organizational Independence and Interorganizational Structure," in *Complex Organizations and their Environment*, ed. M. B. Brinkerhoff and P. R. Kunz (Dubuque: William C. Brown, 1972), pp. 367-394; J. K. Benson, "Interorganizational Network as a Political Economy," *Administrative Science Quarterly*, vol. 20 (June 1975): 229-249; P. M. Blau, *Bureaucracy in Modern Society* (New York: Random House, 1950); M. Halperin, "Why Bureaucrats Play Games" *Foreign Policy*, vol. 2 (Spring 1971); D. Katz and R. L. Khan, *The Social Psychology of Organizations* (New York: John Wiley, 1966); G. E. Konglan, R. D. Warren, J. N. Windelpleck, and S. K. Paulson, "Interorganizational Measurement in the Soical Service Sector," *Administrative Science Quarterly*, vol. 21 (December 1976): 675-687; H. A. Landsberger, "The Horizontal Dimension in Bureaucracy," *Administrative Science Quarterly*, vol. 6. (December 1961): 299-332; P. R. Lawrence and J. W. Lorsch, *Organization and Environment* (Boston: Harvard Graduate School of Business Administration, 1967); E. Litwak and L. F. Hylton, "Inter-Organizational Analysis: A Hypothesis on Coordinating Agencies," *Administrative Science Quarterly*, vol. 6 (March 1962): 395-420; J. A. March and H. A. Simon, *Organizations* (New York: John Wiley, 1958); R. N. Osborn and J. G. Hunt, "Environmental and Organizational Effectiveness," *Administrative Science Quarterly*, vol. 19 (June 1974): 231-246; H. G. Rainey, R. W. Backoff, and C. H. Levine, "Comparing Public and Private Organizations," *Public Administration Review*, vol. 36, no. 2 (March/April 1976): 233-244; and A. H. Van de Ven, A. L. Delbecq, and R. Koenig, Jr., "Determinants of Coordination Modes Within Organizations," *American Sociological Review*, vol. 41, no. 1 (February 1976): 322-338.

9. As already indicated, most IRD projects reviewed in the literature are supported by international development agencies. These project designs tend to display a donor bias, but many purely national efforts are based on these designs because the planners' preferences are similar.

10. See Cohen, "Integrating Services," Propositions 2 and 107.

11. *Ibid.*, Proposition 69.

12. *Ibid.*, Proposition 28.

13. *Ibid.*, Proposition 109.

14. Development Alternatives, Inc., "Integrated Rural Development: Making It Work?" Draft Report to the Agency for International Develoment (Washington, DC: Development Alternatives, Inc., 1980), Proposition IV.

15. See Cohen, "Integrating Services," Propositions 35 and 37.

16. *Ibid.*, Propositions 6 and 36.

17. Robert E. Klitgaard, "On Assessing a Gift Horse," *International Development Review* (Focus: Technical Cooperation), no. 4 (1975).

18. See Cohen, "Integrating Services," Propositions 61 and 68.

19. *Ibid.*, Proposition 16.

20. *Ibid.*, Proposition 25.

21. *Ibid.*, Proposition 60.

22. *Ibid.*, Proposition 1.

23. *Ibid.*, Proposition 53c.

24. *Ibid.*, Proposition 55.

25. Development Alternatives, Inc., "Integrated Rural Development," Propositions IV-30 and V-17.

26. See Milton J. Esman and John D. Montgomery, "Administering Human Development," Staff Working Paper no. 403 (Washington, DC: World Bank, July 1980).

27. See Robert Chambers, "Rural Poverty Unperceived: Problems and Remedies," Staff Working Paper no. 400 (Washington, DC: World Bank, July 1980).

28. Cohen, "Integrating Services."

29. Many organization theorists use the term "coordination" as the rough equivalent of "integration" in the sense used here (that is, the rendering of different public services as joint inputs to common goals of rural development). The terms "vertical" and "horizontal" are usually substituted for "control" and "coordination" in such cases. See, for example, Andrew H. Van de Ven et al., "Determinants of Coordination Modes."

30. Cohen, "Integrating Services," Proposition 103.

31. Development Alternatives, Inc., "Integrated Rural Development," Proposition IV-32, found that "much of the inactivity and low work output of staff can be understood as a rational response to a combination of terms of service, living conditions, working conditions, and supervision, leading to underrealization of their potentials."

32. Katz and Kahn, in *Social Psychology of Organizations,* pp. 296-425, discuss such relationships.

CHAPTER 9

INTERORGANIZATIONAL LINKAGES FOR DECENTRALIZED RURAL DEVELOPMENT
Overcoming Administrative Weaknesses

David K. Leonard

Rural development requires a new type of decentralization. What is needed is not power for either central government or local organizations, but complementary strength in both. Central government agencies, intermediate organizations and local groups all possess resources and capabilities that are needed by the others. The challenge is to link these institutions in such a way that their weaknesses are counterbalanced and their comparative advantages are used. A contribution can thereby be made to development that neither local nor national organizations could achieve alone.

There are two features of rural development programs for which decentralization is particularly required. First, the implementer needs adaptability. Knowledge of how to achieve rural development is incomplete, and project implementation constantly produces unexpected consequences. Rural development requires major doses of incrementalism; one learns as one proceeds what works and what

Author's Note: This chapter has grown out of a collaborative research project with Dale R. Marshall, Jose Garzon, Stephen Peterson, Sven Steinmo, Richard Edelstein, and Victor Magagna and incorporates many of their views. The research was funded by the U.S. Agency for International Development under a cooperative

does not. Those managing the project must be able to adapt to the lessons of its experience.[1]

Second, implementation of rural development programs usually involves the incorporation of community participation. A considerable body of literature stresses the advantages of participation.[2] It is necessary to mobilize local resources, and it facilitates the collection of the information that is needed to adapt a program to local conditions. As rural development frequently involves the promotion of social change, active involvement of the community is generally necessary in order to bring about its transformation. Local participation may begin to build the public demand structure for a service, which will lead to its continued funding.

Despite the need for decentralization to achieve rural development, there are substantial barriers to its adoption. The intermediate-level organizations to which responsibility ought to be decentralized and the local groups whose participation should be sought are most often lacking in finances and administrative capacity. Generally, intermediate and local organizations are therefore forced to look to the center for these resources. It should come as no surprise that in their review of the rural development experience of sixteen Asian states, Norman Uphoff and Milton Esman concluded that one of the prerequisites for rural development is a strong system of local organizations together with effective links to compatible national agencies that can support them.[3]

A few examples may help to illustrate the point. The preliminary processing of coffee requires a small processing and drying factory. Large estates will have their own, but the operation of one is impossible for a smallholder. The Kenyan experience suggests that the optimal factory serves about 2,000 small growers. Any economies of production that would come from a larger unit are more than offset by transport costs for the growers. Such factories have become the basic unit of cooperative organization in central Kenya and are managed

agreement with the University of California (AID/DSAN-CA-0199). The chapter has benefited greatly from extensive critical comments on an earlier version by John Cohen, Norman Uphoff, Janice Jiggins, Walter Oyugi, Preston Chitere, David Korton, and others. Portions of this article originally appeared in David K. Leonard and Dale R. Marshall, eds., *Institutions of Rural Development for the Poor* (Berkeley: Institute of International Studies, University of California, 1982). Reprinted with permission. Portions of it are also published in D.K. Leonard and D.R. Marshall, *Decentralization and Linkages in Rural Development* (Berkeley: Institute of International Studies, 1983).

independently of one another. Nonetheless, these primary societies have difficulty retaining competent accountants; hence they turn to the district cooperative union for these services. Similarly, the international marketing of the coffee produced is far beyond the resources of even a district union. This function is performed by a national cooperative organization. Coffee smallholders thus are served by a three-tier cooperative system, each level with its distinctive competence and linked to the others in a complementary manner.

Effective primary education systems also depend on at least three levels of organization. At the level of the classroom, the participation of parents is a tremendous asset in motivating the children and assisting them with learning. Second, the construction and maintenance of school facilities is usually done better and quicker when it is handled at a local or intermediate level. On the other hand, the development of curricula, the setting of qualifying examinations, and other functions closely related to the professional aspects of education are almost always best handled at the national level.

Another example concerns the interdependence of the community health worker and the M. D. in rural health care. There are a variety of economic and social reasons that paramedical personnel are generally more appropriate than doctors as the basic providers of health services and education in the developing world. But these community health workers will tend to be ineffective it they are not closely supported by M. D.s in the larger medical system. Each has an appropriate role and scale of operation.[4]

Finally, the construction and maintenance of rural roads involves links between community organizations and intermediate levels of subnational government. The local group is needed to organize voluntary labor for construction and to oversee or provide maintenance. It also can make extremely helpful contributions at the planning stage in order to ensure the optimal fit between local use and road layout.[5] On the other hand, the engineers to design the road and the earth-moving equipment to do the heavier construction work must be found in supralocal organization. Rural works projects function best when each is communicating with and is in support of the other.[6]

The preceding examples simply reemphasize the ideal of partnership between central and local organizations in rural development. Thus, this chapter focuses both on the division of responsibility between them and on the nature of their interorganizational linkages. It is concerned with the transactions among local participatory organizations, the national government, and the subnational governments and field offices that mediate between them. *Linkages are the mechanisms by which one organization is tied to or attempts to influence another.* Note that this use of the term "linkages" is synonomous with interorganizational relationships. Although organizations that mediate between the state and the poor are important, it is not they but their ties to the state that are referred to as linkages — financial and technical assistance, regulatory controls, influence, and the like.

IDENTIFYING TECHNICAL AND ADMINISTRATIVE CAPACITY

The most commonly given reason for not decentralizing a function is that the lower organization lacks administrative or technical capacity. But capacity for what? Incapacity is rarely a generalized condition that applies to all conceivable tasks. Most intermediate and local organizations are good at some things and dismal at others. The problem is to identify which is which, to use the strengths, and to figure out how to compensate for the weaknesses.

To implement a program effectively, an organization must be more than well intentioned; it must also have the capacity to translate those intentions into reality. Administrative capacity, be it at the center or in a local organization, is an elusive concept, for it involves more than the presence of skilled personnel. True, the organization has to be able to recognize the existence of problems and opportunties that affect it and to identify the solutions that will be appropriate to them. It also must have the ability to manage the personnel and materials required for implementing the solutions. These abilities do involve technical and managerial skills.

In addition, however, the organization has to produce a decision to act, to sustain the legitimacy of that decision against internal and external challenges, and to mobilize the human and material resources needed to execute the program chosen. These attributes are "political." They derive from the interaction of leadership and institutional history.

Over time, agencies acquire customary clienteles, upon which they rely in the ubiquitous battles for budgetary resources and for assistance in doing their work. If a particular program evokes opposition among an agency's historical clientele, its administrators are unlikely to pursue it vigorously, even if the activity has support in the larger political system. Thus, agricultural extension services that have developed strong symbiotic relations with well-to-do progressive farmers in the promotion of export agriculture have real difficulty in creating new networks oriented toward less-advantaged, subsistence producers.[7]

Equally powerful are the internal patterns of recruitment and institutionalization that determine the professional orientation of an agency's decision makers.[8] Professional training and organizational experience tend to instill a commitment to the value of certain types of activities, methods of doing them, and ways of analyzing when and where to do them. These technologies, methodologies, and decision-making modes often have significant implications for benefit distribution. For example, most contemporary Western medical practice is oriented toward and attaches high prestige to high-technology, hospital-based, curative medicine. Agencies dominated by these types of doctors will find it difficult to give priority to the types of promotive, preventative, and paramedical medicine that mean the most to the health of the rural poor. On the other hand, health practitioners trained in public health have a different orientation from the rest of the medical profession and value precisely the types of service the disadvantaged most need. Where an agency has traditionally had its dominant functions in public health and has had relatively little to do with mainstream medical practice, its recruitment patterns and organizational socialization are likely to produce an orientation that effectively helps the poor.

A similar illustration is provided by the engineering profession. A civil engineer's training is best used and his or her prestige is most enhanced by large, capital-intensive projects. The labor-intensive road-building projects that best benefit the poor are technically undemanding, are professionally unrewarding, and may even involve specifications that are "substandard" in the industrialized countries toward which engineering education is oriented. Agencies dominated by engineers who have not been resocialized will tend to upgrade and recapitalize labor-intensive public works projects.[9]

Leadership is the art of using and manipulating the organization's institutional heritage to make decisions, legitimate them, and mobilize resources for their execution.[10] Poor leadership may have difficulty acting even within the confines of its institution's history; good leadership is able to expand on it creatively. In either case, an organization will lack the capacity for certain types of actions and will have adequate capacity for others.

Organizational effectiveness, then, is based on a number of capacities: (1) problem and opportunity identification, (2) solution identification, (3) decision making and conflict resolution, (4) decision legitimation, (5) resource mobilization, and (6) implementation management.[11] These involve technical, managerial, and leadership skills as well as a favorable institutional heritage. All three types of skills will be appropriate for some types of programs of actions and inappropriate for others.

Programs or program components have a number of critical features that must be matched with the capacities of an organization if effective implementation is to be achieved. The first is technical. If a program is based on a particular technology, the organization will need to have personnel with that technical skill, be able to obtain them, or be assured of access to them through technical assistance. This attribute is important and obvious. Consequently, it frequently dominates consideration of appropriate organizations for program implementation. Sometimes this emphasis is unfortunate, for if the skill is generally available in the society, it is one of the easier capacities to add to an organization. The attention given to it then may preclude attention to attributes that are harder to provide.

The second attribute is that of scale. For reasons of efficiency or technology, a program component may need to be operated with a certain size of unit. An irrigation system built around a hydroelectric dam has a vast scale of operation compared to one using a tube well and pump. A hospital requires a much larger clientele to be efficient than does a clinic. The organizations constructing macadam arterial roads must be much larger than those providing maintenance or building dirt feeder roads. The implementing organization must be able to operate effectively at the particular levels of scale required, be they large or small. Many organizations are simply too small or limited in geographical scope to undertake projects with large-scale requirements; others lack the capacity to operate at the village level required by some technologies. A program frequently has some components that have large economies of scale and others that are best managed by small or local units. Then one needs to find a single organization with both capacities or to share the components between small organizations and a large one, with linkages between them.

The third attribute is the complexity of the administrative process required. Programs that call for a single set of tasks to be executed by a group of workers under the immediate supervision of a single superior are administratively simple. Those that involve several work units that are independent and uncoordinated with one another are somewhat more difficult, but still fairly simple. Those that require the closely coordinated action of several different operations, either in sequence or simultaneously, are administratively complex. A much higher level of managerial expertise and experience is needed for the latter than for the former types of programs.[12]

The fourth program attribute is the contributions that it requires from extraorganizational actors. A smallholder tea program will need to have feeder roads built and maintained in order to get the leaves to the factories promptly. If the implementing organization is an agricultural one, will it obtain the necessary services from a public works department? A preventive health program would need the cooperation of villagers to have latrines built and used. Note that the tea program depends on the use of influence over a government agency, while the second relies on standing with the village community. The ability of the organization to elicit the appropriate forms of cooperation is part of its administrative capacity.

The fifth attribute is related to the preceding and might even be seen as an extension of it. This is the magnitude of resources, largely financial, needed for the program. The more money needed to run a program, the greater must be the ability of the organization to raise uncommitted funds. If the program is managed by a national agency with international donor financing, will that agency successfully fight for an increased share of the national budget when the overseas aid ends? If the program is a pilot one, does the organization have potential access to funds, not just for the first stage but for the expansion as well? If the program is to be run by a local organization but financed by a central agency of some kind, is there the possibility of a meaningful local matching contribution? Either local commitment or independence tends to be lost if there are no matching funds.

There are other attributes of specific programs which draw on administrative capacity. The preceding list covers the most important ones, however, and is sufficient to illustrate the kind of analysis needed in assessing administrative requirements.

THE ALLOCATION OF FUNCTIONS BY ORGANIZATIONAL PRIORITIES

Organizational units will tend to give priority to different aspects of a service sector. Thus, it is best to allocate primary responsibility for a task to that entity which treats it more seriously. Organizational value propensities are distinct from their technical capacities, although they sometimes are related. When the necessary technical capability to perform a task is to be found in more than one organization, even if it is only minimal in one of them, it generally is best to allocate that function to the unit that gives it the higher priority.

In education, for example, local school committees, in comparison with the levels above them, tend to be more concerned with physical plant facilities and manifest results, especially on standardized examinations. The educational professionals at the intermediate and particularly at the national levels, on the other hand, generally care more than the locals do about standards, curriculum development, and diffuse educational objectives. This suggests precisely the kind of division of responsibility between local school committees and superordinate units that has been adopted in most countries. The local community plays a major role in financing school buildings and can be trusted to press for teachers who will produce success by the more obvious educational indicators. At the intermediate and national levels, the educational professionals set standards (and thus determine who can be hired as "qualified" teachers) and define a great many of the success indicators (that is, write the exams) on which communities rely. These higher levels also are best suited to the demanding support role of curriculum development.

With respect to health, local communities are likely to care most about the *availability* of *curative* health practitioners and pharmaceuticals. Elites and M.D.s tend to give priority to the quality of curative medicine, at the expense of quantity, if necessary. Public health professionals are oriented, by training, to the promotion of healthful living conditions, to preventive medicine, and to the wide distribution of health services. These latter issues are the ones that actually have the greatest impact on health status. Thus, the interests of the rural poor are generally better served the greater the extent to which public health professionals are able to define the nature of the health care system and to influence the allocation of resources within it. However, it is very rare for public health practitioners to control a national medical system. Usually the most they can do is to gain overall responsibility for rural health. There they can set program parameters such that there are adequate means for wide distribution. For example, the drugs that rural health centers are permitted to stock can be limited to the most critical, relatively inexpensive ones. This increases the likelihood that the poor will have access to the pharmaceuticals they most need. Otherwise the few would be likely to receive expensive drugs and the many, none at all. Similarly, the training requirements for community health workers can emphasize the development of health promotion and preventative skills, so as to socialize them toward the benefits these offer. Within the parameters of such a system, the demand of local communities for wide availability of curative services and the drive of M.D.s for high quality are functional. Thus, local governments and communities can be given responsibility for financing their facilities and M.D.s can be allocated the role of supporting the work of paraprofessionals and handling referrals.[13]

Unfortunately, the literature on health care systems does not indicate whether this combination of guidance by public health professionals and a strong drive to expand the system is more likely to be found among intermediate local governments or national rural health services. Elected rural local governments have a history of pressing for the wide distribution of static health facilities and of doing battle with urban interests for the resources to support them. These intermediate organizations may be less receptive to the professional guidance needed to maintain a public health orientation, however. Further research is needed on this point.

The allocation of functions between local and intermediate cooperatives and the state poses somewhat different issues. Accounting is a nearly universal problem for cooperatives.[14] In the large and intermediate cooperatives, there is the danger of misallocation of funds by the leadership. In small cooperatives and alternative local organizations, the members usually lack accounting skills. Thus, the books are badly kept or are turned over to local elites — again raising the danger of misappropriation and perhaps forcing the poor to accept elite leadership unnecessarily. Only in cooperatives with a membership that is both fairly sophisticated and relatively homogeneous is accounting not a weak point. In recognition of this problem, the involvement of external agencies in cooperative bookkeeping is widespread and appropriate. Intermediate cooperative organizations usually have their accounts audited by or under the supervision of the state. The weaker primary cooperative societies and alternative local organizations generally are wise to obtain bookkeeping services from district cooperative unions or field officers of the state — both of which are intermediate organizations. Ths division of labor has several advantages. Those providing financial monitoring are in organizations that are more removed from the opportunities of profit from mismanagement; the state and secondary cooperative organizations often depend for their income on the performance of primary societies; accounting and auditing are provided at organizational levels, where those skills are usually more easily found; and the assumption by an intermediate organization of the inherently bureaucratic accounting responsibilities permits the local organizations to be more informal and therefore more accessible to control by their poorer members.[15]

Appropriate control is a service to the local organization's constituency, and it is important to provide it *only* for those areas where the service is needed. Effective control is based on four requisites: First, it depends on social distance. Where the controller is close to the people being monitored, he or she is likely to become a part of the problem as well. Where the center needs both to control an organization and to have good feedback from it, separate control and support agencies are implied. In the case of financial controls, this can be done through the retention of private firms or separate government departments for auditing. The second requisite for effective controls is some political backing. If a problem is identified but nothing is done about it, the monitoring is for naught. Part of the problem in the Kenyan cooperative movement has been political protection for leaders identified by the Department of Cooperatives as having misappropriated funds. Third, controls must be accompanied by a deconcentration of authority to administratively competent field agents. Otherwise adaptability, and the entire rationale for a decentralized structure, is lost. Taiwan does this deconcentration well in monitoring its farmer associations.[16] Often the problem with controls is not that they exist but that the contollers have inadequate flexibility and discretion themselves. Fourth, external controls generally should be seen as a service to the organization's constituency, protecting it from its own internal weaknesses. Otherwise the controller loses sight of the purpose for which the organization exists and destroys its ability to function.

In assessing external controls, special attention must be given to the needs of local organizations. These serve as a link between the formal governmental system and the face-to-face community. This tie between the formal and informal structures of society is what the state most needs from these local organizations. Generally there is tension between the strength of the link to government and the tie to the community. Studies of primary health care and irrigation organizations particularly stress the need for local organizational autonomy.[17] In general, the greater the need for a close tie to the face-to-face community, the more important it is to loosen government controls. To the extent that control is needed, it often can be achieved indirectly through the intermediate organizations that provide services to the local ones. Thus, Taiwan is able to guide local irrigation associations through its control over the intermediate, supply-providing farmers' associations.[18] Usually intermediate organizations need less autonomy to preserve their downward links, as they already are more removed from the community.

When controls become too extensive, any local sense of responsibility for the organization is lost and with it much of the ability of the organization to function well. One cannot define when controls become too tight in the abstract, for the issue is more subjective than objective. Some cultures, such as those in East Asia, expect high degrees of state control and will continue to feel responsible for a local organization under levels of external supervision that would quite discourage other peoples. "Too much control," then, is a culturally relative concept, but the point at which it is reached can be determined by observing organizational behavior in the society concerned.[19]

ASSISTANCE LINKAGES

Despite the need for controls in some areas, the basic relationships in decentralization should be ones of assistance. Program failure due to administrative incompetence or a weak resource base at the intermediate and local levels is all too common. Assistance linkages are vital in overcoming these shortcomings. The need for the center to maintain a service orientation and to provide assistance beyond simple finances to intermediate and local organizations is the great decentralization lesson of our generation.[20]

One of the advantages of assistance over control linkages is that they facilitate the internationalization of the basic value orientations of a program at the local level. This emerges clearly from the U.S. experience with poverty programs. Central controls set up resistance and create an adversary relationship. Training, professional advice, and the like are (properly) seen as assistance, are more readily accepted, create less psychological resistance, and have a socializing effect on local program content. Thus, assistance linkages often produce more results among resistant organizations than do controls.[21]

Despite its advantages, an assistance orientation is not an easy one for the center or intermediaries to maintain. It is costly for the unit providing it. Even nonmaterial forms of assistance impose heavy personnel and administrative burdens. While assistance internalizes costs for the providing organization, controls externalize most of the expenses and impose them on the receiving organization. Of course, the superordinate organization must still bear the expenses of administering the controls, but most of the costs are borne by the subordinate one, creating the illusion for those above that controls are cheaper than assistance. For the system as a whole, however, they may actually be more expensive, for resources then are spent on interorganizational conflict as well as on getting the job done. Controls *are* frequently needed, but often assistance is the better alternative and is discarded for reasons of false economy alone.

A footnote concerns the subtle boundary between control and assistance linkages. Certain forms of assistance have the potential for turning into controls — supply channels, marketing services, professional advice and services, and the like. The clearest signal that the assistance may be turning into a control is the desire of the providing organization to monopolize it. The program designer and institutional analyst want to pay special attention to this transition and be sure that it is appropriate. Controls may well be needed, and then their being clothed in the form of an assistance monopoly makes them more palatable. Where they are not truly necessary, however, this transformation of assistance lowers the effectiveness of the service system by imposing hidden, indeterminate cost and by reducing the redundancies in service channels that are so vital to organizational effectiveness.

There can be too much to a good thing. Assistance linkages can be enfeebling instead of supportive. When an organization is provided with too much assistance or receives it too fast, it becomes overwhelmed, and the locality's administrative capacity and sense of responsibility are destroyed. The rural roads program in Ayub Khan's Pakistan illustrates this problem particularly well.[22] Emergency relief programs and large international donors are more likely to provide enfeebling assistance than are other central organizations. Their good intentions may need to be checked on occasion, in the long-term interests of development.

Technical Assistance Linkages

There are several ways central organizations can provide assistance to weak intermediate or local ones. The most popular have been training and technical assistance. Training is generally seen as the long-term solution to the problem, and personnel are provided on loan for a limited period to overcome the immediate staff shortage. This device is extremely popular with international donors, but it is practiced within developing countries as well. For example, the national government of Malaysia has seconded members of the Federal Civil Service to some of the weaker state governments.

Dale Marshall has examined the evidence on the effectiveness and impact of technical assistance in the U.S. poverty programs. She found that through its use it is possible to compensate for low administrative capacity in the recipient organization in the short run and to build its competence in the long term. Close supervision and evaluation by a committed, competent central or intermediate unit can be an extremely effective form of assistance to a weak local or intermediate organization. Nonetheless, such assistance is not easy for the superordinate body to provide. It makes intensive use of the provider's administrative and personnel resources; an assistance orientation has to be kept in the forefront; the temptation to invade the recipient organization's autonomy must be resisted; and resources have to be committed to long-term, low-visibility efforts of diffuse impact even when immediate, readily apparent, focused results are being rewarded. These are demanding requirements, and many central agencies have difficulty meeting them. One of the more difficult, but important, forms of international aid is that which institutionalizes a central organizational capacity to assist local and intermediate organizations. Donors have found it hard both to help local organizations and to teach national central agencies to do it too. This is one area in which American domestic experience may be especially helpful. In the War on Poverty, the sole function was to provide technical assistance to weak local bodies.[23] This model deserves further study for possible replication elsewhere.

The technical assistance model just described is based on the presumption that the local or intermediate organization will eventually develop its own trained staff. An alternative model is needed when this assumption does not apply. Sometimes discrete, decentralized governments offer career opportunities that are too limited by themselves. Good professional staff are reluctant to join them since they are afraid of being stuck in a small organization for the rest of their careers. The creation of a single national cadre from which local, senior civil servants can be drawn then helps to overcome this barrier to recruitment. The Indian Administrative Service is a particularly famous example of this model of seconding national staff to state government use. This example also illustrates the danger that national assistance with personnel can have an element of control built into it when it is permanent and concerns the most senior, policymaking staff. National cadre schemes that provide for the seconding of teachers or accountants are less threatening to the autonomy of local policy in this regard.

Both technical assistance models do assume that administrative strength exists somewhere in the system and that administrative capacity can either be developed in the assisted organization or loaned to it permanently. When these assumptions are not warranted, technical assistance is not the appropriate response.

Linking Apportioned Functions

The Case

Another strategy for dealing with administrative shortcomings is to move the more complex functions to those organizations or levels that have the capacity to handle them. Some organizations never will be able to develop certain forms of competence. Even in Brazil and India, where there is a large supply, doctors resist working in rural clinics, and their services are unavailable in the more remote villages.[24] Similarly small, rural cooperatives find it very difficult to retain adequate accountants for their needs.[25] In circumstances of this sort, it is unwise to assume that these shortcomings can be remedied. If they are approached with professional training programs, the organizations will simply lose their staff once they are qualified. Instead of pouring resources into a bottomless training bucket, one should move the function in question to an organization that *can* retain the relevant professional and then construct a link between it and the needy local organization. Thus, many local cooperatives have their accounting provided by district-level intermediaries.[26] Sometimes the demand for accountants is so great that no public organization can retain an adequate supply of trained ones. This is the case in Kenya today. Then methods of linking public and cooperative bodies to the services of private accounting and auditing firms have to be created.

The linkage method has gained wide acceptance of late for dealing with technical weaknesses, especially for the local level. Primary health care systems have abandoned the attempt to place highly qualified medical staff in villages and are using them as the trainers, supervisors, and backup for those who are willing to work there.[27] Linkages are being used within administrative hierarchies as well. The Training and Visit system, which the World Bank is promoting for agricultural extension services, is a good example. It uses sub-professionals as the farmer-contact agents and backs them up with very close management by professionals at the intermediate level. These professionals assume the full responsibility for the assembly of information, the design of technical packages, and the adaptation of recommendations.[28] Somewhat similar methods have been proposed for extension via paraprofessionals as well.[29]

The Caveats

This author argued for such administrative methods himself in an earlier work.[30] Nonetheless, precisely because of the growing popularity of linking apportioned functions, it is wise to express three cautions about it. The method is quite demanding of the superordinate organization; it is not new and is difficult to maintain; and it poses real problems for maintaining local adaptability.

First, moving the more complex functions up a level in the organization system reduces the technical demands on those at the base, but it more than proportionately increases them at the new level of responsibility. It requires greater professional skill to perform a technical task for someone else and then to help that person put it to use than it does to do it for oneself. Thus, an organization that uses linkages to support subprofessionals will be larger than those using only professionals. The former may even use almost as many professionals as the latter. Their justification is not so much that they conserve professional staff as that they make technical skills indirectly available in rural areas where professionals are unwilling to live and provide for more intensive staff interaction with villagers. Thus, in Madhya Pradesh (India) the World Bank's Training and Visit system for agricultural extension uses one professional at the district level and below to support every four subprofessionals working with farmers. When the system was introduced, it required a 38 percent increase in the *proportion* of professionals employed.[31] Linking apportioned functions can relieve local shortages of skilled personnel, but it still requires substantial numbers of professionals in the larger support system.

Second, the support of local subprofessionals by professionals at the central and intermediate levels is not new. The idea is evident in the educational systems developed in the colonial era. The role of the school inspector began as a monitor of instruction and examinations, to ensure minimal academic standards. As educational systems in the developing world expanded rapidly, trained teachers were in short supply, and inspectors often assumed new roles. They came to serve as local curriculum consultants and to provide instructional advice and training for teachers, as well as continuing to act as agents of control. This combination of functions is similar to that of the professionals in the primary health care and Training and Visit extension systems. The historical experience with the educational inspectors sounds a note of caution. The inspectorates have generally been understaffed and hampered by poor transport. In most countries reviewed, a school was fortunate to receive one visit a year, far less than needed. Given the pressures on inspectors' time that arise from their inadequate numbers, their control functions have tended to supplant their support ones.[32] The point is not that the apportioning of linked functions does not work; it does. Rather, it is necessary to warn that for it to work properly, an investment of personnel and resources in support services is demanded that is hard to sustain. To do so requires foresight, attention, and effort.

Third, the apportioning of linked functions poses problems for maintaining local adaptability. One of the attributes of professionals is that they have sufficient expertise to adapt their knowledge to local conditions. Good subprofessionals know the standard technical solutions but lack sufficient understanding of their basis to alter them when they do not work. The professionals not only have to develop and initiate the solutions for the subprofessionals to apply; they must also constantly seek signals of problems that the subprofessionals may be unable to recognize. Such feedback is difficult to maintain, for the professionals have to overcome adminstrative distance to receive the error messages. Hence, one of the reservations often expressed about the Training and Visit system of agricultural extension is that it will not be adaptive and will lead to the mindless application of inappropriate technical packages.[33] Doctors have a similar concern about misdiagnosis and misplaced simple cures in primary health care systems. The problem is serious and real. The ideal solution is to have professionals at the base of the system — but their unavailability was the origin of the apportionment of functions in the first place. Feedback and adaptation sysems have to be designed and receive constant, high-priority professional attention instead.

The linking of apportioned functions is an attractive response to irremediable administrative weaknesses at the local and intermediate levels. It does depend on administrative strength at the center, however. There also are dangers of malfunction associated with it, and attention is required to avoid them. Nonetheless, it frequently is the best solution available.

Redundant Linkages

For Problem Solving

The solutions to administrative weakness examined so far have presumed that compensating strength is available at the center or from an international donor. Are there responses to administrative problems that would reduce their impact rather than shift them elsewhere? One is to build redundancy.

Especially when dealing with essential services or their component parts, organizational effectiveness — not efficiency — is the first criterion of performance. The important point is to do the job. Only after that is assured does attention turn to lowering the costs of doing it. "Efficiency" dominates the vocabulary of organizational virtues, and it is easy to forget that its importance is subordinate to that of effectiveness. This is especially important with regard to poverty programs, where failures may mean loss of life or the exposure of change-oriented poor to retaliation by local elites, whom they have been encouraged to challenge. No single mechanism is fail safe, be it a machine or an organization. Thus, protection against failure is needed in backup systems, in redundancy.

Redundancy is important first when the solution to a problem is unclear. It then permits multiple approaches, with the chance that at least one will succeed. Rural development efforts are classic examples of "messy problems," ones in which the path from the present to the goal, and sometimes even the exact goal itself, is controversial or unknown.[34] Multiple, redundant assaults on these "messy" problems greatly increase the probability that one will succeed.[35]

For Service Effectiveness

The preceding principles have implications not only for program design, where they suggest multiple strategies in the trial stages, but for organizational structure as well. When a program is tied to a single set of nonredundant organizations, it will fail if any one of those units fails. In the Sudan, for example, the entire governmental health system is dependent on the Central Medical Stores for its pharmaceutical supplies. When that one unit recently lost its capacity to keep essential drugs and vaccines cold, most of the rest of the medical system was rendered impotent — no matter how well it was being run.[36]

It generally is dangerous in development design to reduce functional redundancies in organizations. Take the example of cooperative organizations in East Africa. These began as a highly dynamic response to oligopolistic private marketing enterprises.[37] After a time, some of them began to falter. To ensure their survival and to improve their efficiency, they were granted monopoly rights over the marketing of certain export crops in their areas. Once this was done, both the state and the peasant producers became highly dependent on these co-ops. Farmers were reduced to the choice of using them or withdrawing from export production. Their "exit" options, to use Albert Hirschman's term, became more limited. The state was rendered even more dependent, however; it needed the foreign exchange revenues of these crops; it could not afford to let the co-ops fail. An unfortunate dynamic was thereby released. Since the state could not afford to let a co-op fail, signs of weakness were met with new central controls. The peasantry then felt progressively alienated from "their" co-ops. They no longer controlled them; the state did. An institution that needed *responsible* local involvement to function well lost it.[38] This downward vicious cycle probably would have been broken if organizational redundancy had been permitted. Competition between co-ops (as in the United States) would have caused the weaker co-ops to disappear and would have made stifling government regulations unnecessary. In this way, two important linkage priniciples could have been maintained: that the local organization be permitted some significant autonomy and that the credibility of withdrawal of central support be retained as a sanction. When there is no organizational redundancy in a critical sector, the center cannot withdraw and must instead exert control to protect its dependency.[39]

Stephen Peterson's examination of the literature on agricultural marketing and input supplies suggests that organizational redundancies may be easier managerially and cheaper in resources than creating reliable organizations. In a resource-scarce environment, agricultural services seem to be more reliable when provided by competing organizations. We need careful empirical research on this point. "Common sense" appears to suggest the opposite — that when skills are short they should be concentrated in a single organization to assure their most efficient use. Thus, country after country has created parastatal or cooperative monopolies at various levels in its agricultural sectors. The weaker a country's administrative resources, however, the more likely these monopolies will break down, resulting in negative consequences for production. Contrary to "common sense," competition (be it between private or public units) is less demanding of scarce administrative talent. The market is itself an administrative mechanism, but one that does not use administrators.[40]

One of the advantages of having structural redundancy is that failing organizations can be permitted to die. It is important to make reasonable efforts to assist weak organizations, but when these efforts are unsuccessful it is best to let such organizations collapse. When malfunctioning organizations are kept alive by unending infusions of assistance, there are four negative consequences:[41] (1) The society must continue to endure poor performance in an organization from which it presumably needs good service. (2) The organization acts as a continuing, unproductive drain on central and local resources. (3) The example of assistance provided to an ineffective organization acts as a disincentive to others to perform well. (4) As long as the malfunctioning organization is kept alive, it inhibits the rise of an alternative, stronger one. Administrative problems often are institutionalized in a particular organizational structure. An alternative organization operating in much the same functional area might well not have the same problems. Indeed, the collapse of a malfunctioning organization can be a positive learning experience for a community. The causes for its failure will be remembered and are less likely to be repeated in the next attempt. Organizational death helps to teach society how to administer, and it releases scarce administrative resources to those agencies and groups that can use them more productively.

Redundancy also has its virtues looking upward in the organizational hierarchy. From the point of veiw of the peasant, the existence of two or more local organizations providing a service (even if one is more conveniently located) assures him that he can alter behavior to depend on them, for at least one of them will be there when he needs it. He can grow a market crop knowing that if the co-op collapses or becomes exploitative, there is another one or a trader to turn to instead. The local organization also benefits from being linked to more than one central agency. If resources run down in one program area, then it can rely more heavily on those in another. When redundant channels of support are available, dependency on the center need not end in loss of autonomy.[42] With upward and downward redundancies, strong interdependencies can be created among organizations without tight control by one over the other and with less danger that administrative weaknesses will cause the collapse of the whole service chain.

Administrative Simplification

The final response to administrative and technical weaknesses is to reduce the complexity of the program or its components to the capacity of the units that will implement them. The research of the Berkeley Project on Managing Decentralization has indicated six maxims that can be followed in reducing complexity and administrative demands:[43]

(1) Single-function organizations are less complex than multiple-function ones.

(2) Small units are less complex than large ones.

(3) The greater the number of hierarchical levels, the larger the complexity.

(4) The market is administratively simpler than a hierarchy.

(5) It is much more difficult to administer benefits that are targeted for a specific clientele than those that are general.

(6) When administrative capacity is in doubt, simplicity outweighs all other virtues in organizational and task design.

As trite as these maxims are, they frequently are ignored and their application would reduce the administrative problems of rural development. For example, they lead to a new look at large, integrated rural development programs. It is one thing to argue that rural development requires many institutional components and that integration is therefore needed in analysis, planning, and policymaking. It is another to create an *administratively* integrated, multifunctional program in an administratively weak environment. If the effective operation of each component is made dependent on the others, there is a high probability that the whole program will not work. This has happened with the World Bank's Integrated Agricultural Development Project in Kenya. It seems preferable to make components independent of one another — even at the cost of performance *potential* — in order to increase the probabilty that *actual* performance will meet minimum standards.

CONCLUSIONS

Weaknesses in administrative and technical capacity are a serious impediment to decentralization. However, if rural development is to be achieved there must be adaptive decision making near the local level and possibilities for popular participation. Linkages between an administratively strong national government and weak intermediate and local organizations can be used to overcome this problem. By apportioning functions to those organizations that have the commitment and competence to perform them and by providing central assistance to decentralized entities, the weaknesses of both can be counterbalanced and their comparative advantages highlighted.

NOTES

1. Bruce F. Johnston and William C. Clark, *On Redesigning for Rural Development: A Strategic Perspective* (Baltimore: Johns Hopkins University Press, 1982), Ch. 1.

2. Norman T. Uphoff, John M. Cohen, and Arthur A. Goldsmith, *Feasibility and Application of Rural Development Participation: A State-of-the-Art Paper* (Ithaca, NY: Center for International Studies, Cornell University, 1979); Norman T. Uphoff and Milton J. Esman, *Local Organization for Rural Development in Asia* (Ithaca, NY: Center for International Studies, Cornell University, 1974); Lenore Ralston, James Anderson, and Elisabeth Colson, *Voluntary Efforts and Decentralized Management* (Berkeley: Project on Managing Decentralization, Institute of International Studies, University of California, 1981).

3. Norman T. Uphoff and Milton J. Esman, *Local Organization,* xi-xii.

4. Sven Steinmo, "Health Care Linkages in the Third World," in *Decentralization and Linkages in Rural Development,* ed. D. K. Leonard and D. R. Marshall (Berkeley: Institute of International Studies, University of California, 1983).

5. Judith Tendler, *New Directions for Rural Roads* (Washington, DC: Agency for International Development, Office of Evaluation, 1979).

6. Jose M. Garzon, "Small-Scale Public Works, Decentralization and Linkages," in *Decentralization and Linkages in Rural Development,* ed. D. K. Leonard and D. R. Marshall (Berkeley: Institute of International Studies, University of California, 1983).

7. H. U. E. Thoden van Velzen, "Staff, Kulaks and Peasants: A Study of a Political Field," in *Government and Rural Development in East Africa: Essays on Political Penetration,* ed. L. Cliffe, J. S. Coleman, and M. R. Doornbos (The Hague: Martinus Nijhoff, 1977).

8. Sven Steinmo, "Health Care Linkages."

9. Judith Tendler, *New Directions,* pp. 42-44.

10. Warren Ilchman and Norman Uphoff, *The Political Economy of Change* (Berkeley: University of California Press, 1969).

11. The criteria are largely derived from John P. Powelson, *Institutions of Economic Growth: A Theory of Conflict Management* (Princeton, NJ: Princeton University Press, 1972).

12. For more on the complexity of coordination and its organizational implications, see James D. Thompson, 2*Organizations in Action* (New York: Mc Graw-Hill, 1967), pp. 54-61.

13. Sven Steinmo, "Health Care Linkages."

14. Stephen B. Peterson, "The State and the Organizational Infrastructure of the Agrarian Economy," in *Decentralization and Linkages in Rural Development,* ed. D. K. Leonard and D. R. Marshall (Berkeley: Institute of International Studies, University of California, 1983).

15. Stephen B. Peterson, "Limited Local Organizations: Supporting the Agricultural Development of the Poor," in *Decentralization and Linkages in Rural Development,* ed. D. K. Leonard and D. R. Marshall (Berkeley: Institute of International Studies, University of California, 1983).

16. Benedict Stavis, *Rural Local Governance and Agricultural Development in Taiwan* (Ithaca, NY: Center for International Studies, Cornell University, 1974).

17. Sven Steinmo, "Health Care Linkages"; Stephen B. Peterson, "The State and the Organizational Infrastructure."

18. Benedict Stavis, *Rural Local Governance.*

19. For more on expectation levels and the related idea of relative deprivation, see Peter Blau, *Exchange and Power in Social Life* (New York: John Wiley, 1964).

20. See also Milton J. Esman and John D. Montgomery, "The Administration of Human Development," in *Implementing Programs of Human Development,* ed. Peter T. Knight (Washington, DC: World Bank, 1980).

21. Dale Marshall, "Linkage Lessons from U.S. Poverty Programs," in *Decentralization and Linkages in Rural Development,* ed. D. K. Leonard and D. R. Marshall (Berkeley: Institute of International Studies, University of California, 1983).

22. Rehman Sobhan, *Basic Democracies Rural Works Programme and Rural Development in East Pakistan* (Dacca: Bangladesh Bureau of Economic Research, University of Dacca, 1968), p. 89.

23. Henry C. Finney, "Problems of Local, Regional and National Support for Rural Poor Peoples' Cooperatives in the United States: Some Lessons from the War on Poverty" Reprint no. 142 (Madison: Institute for Research on Poverty, University of Wisconsin, 1975).

24. H. M. Penido, "Health Objectives in Brazil," in *Health Objectives in Developing Countries,* ed. E. C. Long (Durham: Duke University Press, 1965), pp. 38-40; D. Banjeri, "Social and Cultural Foundations of the Health Services of India," *Inquiry* (1975): 73.

25. Stephen B. Peterson, "The State and the Organizational Infrastructure."

26. *Ibid.*

27. R. A. Smith, *Manpower and Primary Health Care* (Honolulu: University of Hawaii Press, 1978).

28. Daniel Benor and James Q. Harrison, *Agricultural Extension: The Training and Visit System* (Washington, DC: World Bank, 1977).

29. R. D. Colle, M.J. Esman, E. Taylor, and P. Berman, *Paraprofessionals in Rural Development* (Ithaca, NY: Center for International Studies, Cornell University, 1979).

30. David K. Leonard, *Reaching the Peasant Farmer: Organization Theory and Practice in Kenya* (Chicago: University of Chicago Press, 1977).

31. World Bank, "India: Madhya Pradesh Agricultural Extension and Research Project," Report no. 1442a-IN (Washington, DC: World Bank, May 2, 1977), annex 2, p. 5.

32. N. R. Inamdar, *Educational Administration in the Zilla Parishads in Maharashtra* (Bombay: Popular Prakashan, 1974); International Institute for Educational Planning, *The Organization of Education in the Sankhuwa Sabha District of Nepal: Draft Final Report* (Paris: UNESCO, 1978); International Institute for Educational Planning, *The Organization of Education in the New Halfa District of the Democratic Republic of the Sudan: Working Draft* (Paris: UNESCO, 1979), International Institute for Educational Planning, *Problems of Education in Latin America* (Paris: International Institute for Educational Planning, UNESCO, 1979).

33. Max K. Lowdermilk, "Promoting Increased Food Production in the 1980's: Approaches to Agricultural Extension in Different Production Systems" (Paper delivered at the Symposium on Promoting Increased Food Production in the 1980's (Washington, DC: World Bank, January 5-9, 1981).

34. Johnston and Clark, *Redesigning Rural Development,* Ch. 1.

35. For the origin and best elaboration of these ideas, see Martin Landau, "Redundancy, Rationality and the Problem of Duplication and Overlap," *Public Administration Review,* vol. 29 (July/August, 1969): 346-358.

36. Medical Services Consultants, Inc., *Report of the Health Sector Assessment Team-Sudan* (Washington, DC: USAID, 1977); United States Agency for International Development, "Sudan Health Sector Support Project Paper," no. 650-0030 (Washington, DC: USAID, 1980).

37. Goran Hyden, ed., *Cooperatives in Tanzania: Problems of Organization Building* (Dar es Salaam: Tanzania Publishing House, 1976).

38. Goran Hyden, "Government and Cooperatives," in *Development Administration: The Kenyan Experience,* ed. R. Jackson, D. Hyden, and J. Okumu (Nairobi: Oxford University Press, 1970); Goran Hyden, *Cooperatives in Tanzania,* pp. 17-19.

39. Martin Landau and Richard Stout, "To Manage is Not to Control: The Danger of Type II Errors in Organizations," *Public Administration Review,* vol. 39, no. 2 (1979): 148-56.

40. Stephen B. Peterson, "The State and the Organizational Infrastructure."

41. Stephen B. Peterson, "Limited Local Organizations."

42. For a South Korean example, see Frances E. Korten and Sarah Young, "The Mothers' Clubs of Korea," in *Managing Community Based Population Programmes* (Kuala Lumpur: International Committee on the Management of Population Programmes).

43. Stephen B. Peterson, "Limited Local Organizations."

CHAPTER 10

DECENTRALIZATION AND DEVELOPMENT
Conclusions and Directions

G. Shabbir Cheema and Dennis A. Rondinelli

The essays in this volume confirm that during the past three decades governments in developing countries have attempted to implement a variety of decentralization policies. Some have been comprehensive in scope and designed to transfer development planning and management responsibilities to local units of government. Others have been more narrowly conceived; they simply deconcentrated or reallocated administrative tasks among units of the central government. In most countries decentralization policies have taken four forms. Governments in countries such as India, the Sudan, and Tanzania sought to devolve or delegate decision-making authority to local governments or administrative units; others — as in Brazil, Argentina, Venezuela, and Mexico — assigned specific planning and management functions to semi-autonomous organizations. Almost all governments in East and North Africa and Southeast and South Asia deconcentrated some development functions to provincial or district administrations. Decentralization in a few developing nations has taken the form of debureaucratization: Functions previously performed by governments were transferred to voluntary organizations or the private sector.

The motivations for decentralizing planning and management in Third World countries were also varied. In some, the desire of the national elite for greater political legitimacy spawned attempts at decentralization, while in others the policies were enacted in response to pressures for greater participation in decision-making by ethnic, regional, religious, or tribal groups. In most countries where it was tried, decentralization was seen as a way of improving the efficiency of planning and management within the central bureaucracy and was often enacted in reaction to the stultifying slowness with which central ministries responded to pressing social and economic problems. In their analyses, Mathur, Rondinelli, Nellis, and Harris show that political and administrative leaders in each of the countries examined in this book had their own particular reasons for promoting decentralization. In a few countries, international assistance agencies brought pressures on national governments to decentralize planning and management functions as a way of dealing with the serious and growing disparities in income and wealth among regions. In more than a few countries, decentralization may have been seen as a convenient way for national leaders to rid themselves of responsibility for regional and local development problems by transferring them to local units of government or to private organizations.

Whatever the motivations for the decentralization policies that were enacted in developing countries over the past few decades, all of the studies in this volume point to the wide gap between objectives and results. Only in those countries where decentralization was defined more narrowly and the scope of policies was limited to reallocating functions among units of the central government did developing countries achieve their intended goals.

In this chapter an assessment of the impact of decentralization policies in developing countries is offered and an attempt is made to highlight some of the critical factors that have affected the capacity of developing country governments to implement decentralization policies. Suggestions are made for improving the design and implementation of development programs, and a framework for formulating implementation strategies is outlined.

THE IMPACTS OF
DECENTRALIZATION POLICIES

Policymakers, planners, and development administrators in the Third World continue to express dissatisfaction with the way decentralization policies have been implemented, and studies in this volume document the disappointing results of attempts in most countries to decentralize planning and management functions. In most cases, central governments initiated, introduced, and heavily publicized decentralization policies only to see them falter during implementation.

The studies of decentralization policies in this volume reveal a kind of schizophrenia in developing countries about the desirability and feasibility of transferring powers and responsibilities from central ministries to other organizations. While local administrative organizations were given broad powers in some countries to perform development planning and management functions, adequate financial resources and qualified personnel to carry them out were often withheld. Field offices of central ministries, provincial planning and administrative units, and district and local development committees were established in most countries in Asia and Africa, yet central government officials have been reluctant to assist them. Local officials have been hesitant to use their discretion, and even in routine matters local officials continue to look to central government ministries for decisions. In their desire to minimize political conflicts, governments in Third World countries have discouraged the growth of community and nongovernmental organizations needed to support and carry out decentralization policies. Thus, even when opportunities were created for greater involvement in decision making by local groups, the intended beneficiaries often lacked the organizational capacities to take advantage of them.

As Rondinelli's analysis (Chapter 4) of decentralization in Kenya, Tanzania, and the Sudan shows, development planning and administration remain highly centralized after a decade of persistent attempts at decentralization. Harris (Chapter 6) illustrates how the proliferation of central government bureaucracies in Latin America has expanded their power at the expense of local governments. Despite the apparent concern for decentralization in Asia, Mathur observes (Chapter 3), the results there also have often led to creation of a stronger dependence of local governments on the center. In some cases, innovative programs were created without linking them to established organizations and sources of political and financial support. In others, authority was delegated without giving local organizations the flexibility to perform new functions in ways that met local needs.

Nellis's studies of Algeria, Libya, Tunisia, and Morocco (Chapter 5) show that performance and impact have not matched the goals of their decentralization policies. Control over financial resources continues to be centralized; local and regional organizations continue to have severe shortages of qualified personnel. As Friedman argued in Chapter 2, local governments in most Asian countries still function as bureaucratic instruments of the center rather than as generators of alternative values, preferences, and aspirations. Local organizations thus cannot easily nurture political development; they act merely to extend centrally established priorities and controls. Local leaders are seen by central government officials as communicators of national government priorities and solicitors of support for national policies.

Despite these limitations, however, there have been some positive results of the decentralization policies that were enacted during the 1970s and early 1980s. First, the access of people living in previously neglected rural regions to central government resources and institutions has been increased, if only incrementally, in much of Asia and East Africa. Second, the introduction of decentralization policies has increased the capacity of local bureaucratic and political leaders in some countries to put pressure on central government agencies and thus to obtain larger amounts of national resources for local development. Third, the administrative and technical capability of regional and local organizations may be slowly improving in many Latin American and Asian countries, although usually not fast enough to perform the functions formally assigned to them. Fourth, new organizations have been established in Asia and Latin America at the regional and local levels to plan and manage development. In Latin America, as Harris notes, these include regional development agencies, departmental development corporations, parastatal institutions, and semi-autonomous organizations. In Asia provincial development planning committees have been created in Thailand, state-planning units in Malaysia, regional development councils in the Philippines, provincial development planning boards in Indonesia, and special-purpose development organizations in Pakistan and India. Finally, regional and local-level planning is now increasingly emphasized as an important component of national development strategy, bringing new perspectives and interests into the decision-making process.

The success of decentralization policies has varied among the countries examined in this volume, and the factors affecting the success or failure of policy implementation can be examined within the four broad categories listed by Rondinelli and Cheema in Chapter 1: the capabilities of implementing agencies, interorganizational relationships, resources for program implementation, and environmental factors.

CAPABILITIES OF IMPLEMENTING AGENCIES

Ultimately, decentralization can be effective only when agencies and actors at the regional and local levels have developed the capacities to perform effectively the planning, decision-making, and management functions that are formally granted to them. As Leonard points out in Chapter 9, their effectiveness as participants in a decentralized system depends on the ability of local organizations to (1) identify development problems and opportunities; (2) identify or create possible solutions to development problems; (3) make decisions and resolve conflicts; (4) mobilize resources; and (5) manage development programs and projects. Thus, the essential features of a program for decentralizing development functions to regional or local organizations must be matched with the capacities of implementing agencies if the programs are to be carried out successfully. Where administrative capacities are weak, actions must be taken to increase, expand, or strengthen them.

In his description of the Central Tunisia Development Project, Nellis documents the gaps between policy and implementation that appear when the capabilities of local agencies are weak. The Tunisian government created the Central Tunisia Development Authority (CTDA) as a semi-autonomous body to transform one of the poorest regions of the country. It was empowered to plan, coordinate, and implement development projects in agriculture, health, and social services. However, the organization could not carry out its decentralized functions because of its weak leadership and the shortage of qualified personnel. Thus, in its initial years of operation, the Planning Ministry rejected eight out of nine activities proposed by CTDA, presumably on technical grounds.

One of the dilemmas facing governments attempting to implement decentralization policies is that central government officials take the initiative, usually under pressure from other groups, to decentralize authority, but then negate that authority by refusing to transfer financial, administrative, and technical resources to local agencies. Rondinelli's discussion (Chapter 4) of decentralization in Kenya, the Sudan, and Tanzania shows the crucial effects of shortages of trained manpower on the success of decentralization policies in those countries. National ministries, public corporations, and other central government agencies attracted the most skilled technicians and the best-educated managers, leaving a chronic shortage of talent at the local level. Leadership and management training courses for local officials were not adequate. In the Sudan, he points out, there were severe shortages of competent administrators even within the central ministries before decentralization policies were enacted. Decentralization, and the continuing "brain drain" to oil-producing countries, exacerbated already serious staffing problems. Thus, for example, the ability of provincial administrators to use the extensive authority to provide health services that was transferred to them during decentralization was limited by inadequate numbers of trained staff, especially in the Southern Region of the Sudan.

In Asia, too, administrative support and local capabilities for implementing decentralization are inadequate. As Mathur points out in Chapter 3, personnel structures and practices encourage qualified and ambitious managers to gravitate toward the center. Those who are assigned to the local levels see such duty as temporary until they can find posts in a central ministry. Those who remain in local administration are often frustrated by low salaries, slow advancement, and low morale. Civil service structures in most Asian developing countries encourage high turnover at the local level; in some districts in India, Mathur observed, six or seven changes occurred in project officers in the Drought Prone Area Program within a period of three years. In a highly centralized civil service system, he argued, local agencies are commonly viewed as "data feeding units" rather than as decision-making organizations.

In Latin America the efforts to transfer planning and management functions to local governments have not been matched with those for strengthening their administrative capabilities and, as Harris notes, administrative reforms have had only limited success: Local governments can perform only a few of the many tasks delegated to them. Cheema observes that in Asia functions are often delegated to voluntary organizations without taking their administrative capacities into consideration.

The inadequate technical and managerial skills in local agencies also limit their political influence. In most developing countries, citizens tend to look to the center rather than to local organizations for resources and approval for community projects. The morale of local administrators remains low and their skills remain weak; eventually many lose their commitment to local development activities.

Another factor severely inhibiting the successful implementation of decentralization policies has been the inability of local agencies to coordinate and integrate their activities with those of central ministries. Coordination is often weaker at regional and local levels than at the center. Proliferation of government agencies has led to compartmentalization and lack of complementarity, further weakening the administrative capacities of local agencies.

INTERORGANIZATIONAL RELATIONSHIPS

Successful implementation of decentralization policies requires some degree of coordination among national, regional, and local agencies. To achieve complementarity among levels of administration, viable linkages must be established and maintained among them. Planning, implementation, and evaluation procedures must be standardized so that agencies at different levels of government can coordinate common activities or those that have impacts on each other. Functions must be allocated in a way that takes advantage of the strengths of agencies at different levels of government.

The importance of linkages in policy implementation was demonstrated clearly by David Leonard in Chapter 9. He argues that supporting linkages must be created between central government and local agencies to overcome weaknesses in administrative capacity at lower levels of government. The creation of such linkages, he contends, is likely to produce more positive responses to national development priorities from local and regional agencies than central regulations and controls. There are several ways central government agencies can provide assistance to weak local administrations: by providing training facilities; by seconding personnel from central agencies to meet pressing staff shortages at the local level; by supervising and assessing local projects and providing technical assistance when problems or weaknesses appear; and by creating a single national cadre to supply personnel to agencies at provincial, district, and local levels.

Leonard also notes some of the limitations of creating assistance linkages: The conditions necessary for supporting local agencies may not exist, as was the case in Tanzania; some assistance linkages may ultimately become control mechanisms, thereby increasing local dependence; and once the linkages are created, it may become more difficult for local agencies to establish and maintain flexibility and discretion in decision making.

Establishing viable linkages among agencies at different levels of government is often hindered by the diversity of interests, perceptions, and needs of the various "actors" in the development process, that is, of the designers of development programs in international assistance organizations, planners and administrators in central management support agencies, and field project managers. As Montgomery argues (Chapter 8), project designers within central planning ministries and international funding institutions seek an uninterrupted flow of resources for purchasing goods and services. They perceive the role of central agencies as expeditors of these inputs. These agencies also seek a continuous flow of information between the field and the center. Planners and administrators in the central management support agencies, on the other hand, prefer to exercise their own discretion in assigning resources to field operations. This often leads to tensions between central government agencies and the staffs of international funding organizations in the implementation of foreign-funded development projects. As projects are implemented, the role of local project managers becomes more important; they bring new and different perceptions of needs to the decision-making process and attempt to protect their discretion and flexibility. Montgomery identifies the kinds of problems that arise from these conflicts during project implementation, and Nellis's study of the operation of the Central Tunisia Development Authority highlights the difficulties encountered by decentralized agencies in carrying out their functions within this system of interorganizational relationships. The intervention of foreign donors also complicates these relationships, for, as Nellis observes, the intervention of U.S. aid officials in the work of CTDA led central ministry officials to view the agency as an expensive and inappropriate "American idea" for doing regional development.

Thus, closely related to the question of how to establish viable linkages among levels of government is the question of how to allocate functions appropriately among them. Within any particular sector, such as agriculture or education, some activities are more effectively performed at the center, while others are more efficiently carried out at regional or local levels. As Leonard suggests, local school committees tend to be concerned with physical facilities, and professionals at the regional and national levels are usually more concerned about educational standards, curriculum development, and national educational objectives.

Another important issue that is identified in nearly all of the chapters in this book concerns the kinds of goals and tasks that can be appropriately assigned to local administrators and, especially, to managers of rural development projects. This issue is closely related to the question of which organizational arrangements are most suitable for implementing decentralized programs and projects. In his analysis of internationally funded development projects, Montgomery describes the complex and sometimes conflicting views of various actors on these issues. International donors usually prefer to create autonomous organizations to implement projects because they are often free of the political, financial, and administrative constraints that shackle regular government agencies. Also, their activities are easier to monitor and the results of their work are often easier to evaluate. Administrators in national ministries naturally prefer that authority be granted to them so that they can have greater control over the allocation of resources and hold project managers accountable for their use. Project managers also attempt to obtain as much control over resources as they can. Thus, unless goals are clearly defined and responsibilities are unambiguously assigned, a struggle over resources may create severe problems during the implementation of development projects.

Appropriate organizational arrangements must also be made at the national level to provide local managers with support and guidance. All of the authors of chapters in this book recognize that decentralization involves a combination of central control and local autonomy and that even in highly decentralized government systems, central agencies must play important roles in facilitating and guiding the use of national resources at the local level. Several organizational alternatives have been used to implement decentralized programs: (1) an existing line agency of the national government, (2) field agencies of a central ministry, (3) regional or provincial government agencies, (4) several independent agencies under the coordination of a "lead agency," (5) permanent coordination committees under the direction of the chief executive, (6) special-purpose development agencies, or

(7) semi-autonomous project management units.[1] Each of these alternatives has advantages and disadvantages, and the choice of organizational arrangements must depend on the nature of the program to be implemented and the goals and objectives to be achieved.

Montgomery notes in Chapter 8 that different actors in the development process have different perceptions of which organizational arrangement is most appropriate. International donors usually prefer autonomous project management units or coordinating committees, while national planners and administrators prefer projects to be implemented through existing ministries, lead agencies, or coordinating committees. Central support agencies prefer their own organization or a lead agency to be given responsibility; if they cannot obtain control they seek to have responsibilities divided. Local managers usually prefer a coordinating committee or dominant agency.

Rondinelli's assessment of decentralization in East Africa demonstrates how ambiguity in the design of decentralized programs and weaknesses in the capacity of central administrative agencies to support and assist decentralized units adversely affected implementation in Kenya, Tanzania, and the Sudan. Similar problems were identified by Nellis in his study of North Africa and by Harris in his review of the experience in Latin America. Uncertainty about the extent and purposes of decentralization and ambiguities in assigning roles and responsibilities to organizations at various levels of government undermined the success of policies in most of these countries.

Mathur observes how the constraints in administrative procedures in Asian countries inhibited cooperation among agencies in implementing decentralization. Although many decentralized institutions have been created, departmental loyalties usually impede coordination and cooperation at regional and local levels. Government functionaries from various departments tend to work in isolation, pursuing their own interests or responding to those of their departmental superiors.

RESOURCES FOR PROGRAM IMPLEMENTATION

The inadequacy of financial resources has been one of the most critical factors obstructing successful implementation of decentralization policies in many of the countries examined in this volume.

Harris points out that in Brazil the proportion of total tax receipts of municipal governments has been declining. Tax reforms have favored the federal government over states and municipalities. In Mexico, the financial imbalance is even greater; the total annual budgets of all state and local governments is less than 10 percent of the federal government's annual budget. Similarly, in Argentina and Venezuela, decentralization policies have not been followed up with steps to enhance the financial capability of regional and local administrative units. Thus, in much of Latin America local governments can hardly cover their basic operating costs, let alone take on new functions and responsibilities.

Analysis of the Asian experience comes to a similar conclusion. In most cases, local governments remain financially dependent on central governments either because they are not authorized to levy sufficient taxes to perform their tasks or because they are unable to collect authorized taxes. In Malaysia, for example, state governments are reluctant to grant additional revenues to local governments, making local administrative units more dependent on the center. Local governments are usually unable to valuate property regularly and to recover funds from those who default on local tax payments. Even in India, where "democratic decentralization" was introduced in the 1950s, most local governments continue to be financially dependent on grants from higher levels of government. Thus, local governments remain weak. While in theory more extensive powers have been given to local units of administration in these countries, the inadequacy of resources to perform their new responsibilities has undermined the intent of decentralization programs.

In East Africa, as Rondinelli points out, all of the countries had serious national economic problems, limiting their capacity to provide financial assistance to the local administrative units to which they deconcentrated or devolved development planning and management functions. High levels of poverty and low levels of administrative capacity prevent local governments in rural areas from significantly expanding their revenue base.

The low levels of political support at the center in most Third World countries have also undermined decentralization policies. Nellis contends that the self-interest of the elite precluded the possibility of significant decentralization in the North African countries that he examined, even though national leaders have taken occasional steps toward decentralizing responsibilities in response to pressures from intellectuals, middle-level officials, and regional political groups.

Mathur's analysis of the Asian experience shows that most central political and administrative leaders have not enthusiastically supported decentralization and that many feared that it would lead to regional, ethnic, communal, or religious fragmentation. Even in countries such as Tanzania and the Sudan, where decentralization was advocated by strong presidents, political support was not widespread enough among other national and regional leaders to overcome difficulties during implementation. President Nyerere in Tanzania and President Nimeiry in the Sudan had to apply strong and continuous pressures for nearly a decade before programs could be carried out, and in both countries obstacles to effective implementation still exist. Rondinelli argues that, in most cases, decentralization is supported strongly by national political leaders only when it generates more support for central government policies in rural areas or allows them to maintain their influence over local activities. In some countries the central bureaucracy was able to use programs of deconcentration and delegation to extend their control and influence in rural areas. Rather than creating a more effective partnership between national and local governments, they increased the penetration of central authority into the countryside, where knowledge of and support for national development policies had previously been weak.

The reluctance of central administrators to transfer functions to local agencies has also been an impediment to the implementation of development policies. Decentralization has usually been perceived as a threat to the influence of central ministries; thus, they frequently attempted to sabotage it. The studies by Mathur, Rondinelli, and Nellis note that central government officials often do not have much faith in the abilities of their own subordinates, who are commonly perceived to be incompetent and therefore incapable of making decisions effectively.

The lack of widespread political support for decentralization in Asia is substantiated by Cheema's analysis of voluntary organizations. He finds that despite the proliferation of voluntary groups, their overall impact on rural development has been, and continues to be, minimal. Most governments are not willing to tolerate the politicization and conflict that independent, nongovernment organizations are likely to create in rural areas, and thus, only those voluntary organizations that have been created by the government or that assist central government agencies in implementing their programs are likely to survive and grow.

One of the crucial issues that needs to be resolved in the design of decentralization policies or in the early stages of implementation is the degree of control that local organizations, especially integrated rural development projects, should have over resources. This is particularly significant in the case of projects funded by international development organizations. As Montgomery again points out, the perception and preferences of the actors involved are usually conflicting. Planners in international agencies prefer to assign funds directly to project implementation units to facilitate the procurement and delivery of goods and services and to achieve agreed-upon goals expeditiously. Administrators of central ministries are usually against giving special treatment to such projects and argue that such preferential treatment alienates managers of other programs. Even when central government officials are forced to agree to such an arrangement, they usually withdraw special privileges after international funding ends. Project managers have direct responsibility for providing services and therefore prefer arrangements that provide continuous or timely flows of resources, equipment, and supplies.

THE ENVIRONMENTAL CONTEXT

The implementation of decentralization policies seems to be strongly influenced by the environment in which interactions among organizations take place. The experiences of the developing countries examined in this volume illustrate some of the constraints on effective management of decentralized programs: political structures and styles, characteristics of the local power structure, resource constraints, and access to physical infrastructure.

As the studies by Friedman, Mathur, and Nellis clearly show, the implementation of decentralization policies has both administrative and political dimensions. Indeed, the characteristics of the political system and political styles in a country can fundamentally affect how decentralization is defined and influence how implementation is pursued. As Friedman points out, the political ideology in many countries creates a rationale for local government that limits it to eliciting compliance with national priorities rather than establishing local organizations as instruments for wider participation and political development.

In most developing countries, landownership is inequitably distributed and a majority of the rural poor is usually landless. In such situations, vested local interests attempt to sabotage those aspects of decentralization that affect landownership or distribution. Rondinelli notes that traditional local elites were usually opposed to or gave only passive support to government efforts to bring younger leaders into community decision making or to establish new local administrative structures or planning procedures in East Africa. Cheema's analysis shows that in Asia the lack of involvement of the rural poor in voluntary organizations is due partly to the inegalitarian power structure, which gives a dominant position to the rural elite.

As noted earlier, resource constraints have inhibited successful implementation of decentralization in nearly all cases examined in this book. The limited financial, technical, and managerial resources available in developing countries to support local organizations undermine decentralization and reinforce the weaknesses in local organizational structure.

Nellis argues that sociocultural traditions are another environmental constraint on successful implementation of decentralization. He found in North Africa, and Rondinelli discovered in East Africa, that traditional deference to authority, reluctance of lower-level officials to disagree openly with superiors or officials in central ministries, and vestiges of colonial behavior create conditions under which the staffs of decentralized organizations are reluctant to use even the limited authority granted to them. Cheema notes that in Asia the style of decision making in many of the voluntary organizations that he studied was paternalistic. Most of the voluntary organizations were created by the central government, and ministry officials often held dominant positions in them.

The capacity of decentralized units to carry out their assigned responsibilities has also been adversely affected by the limited physical infrastructure, such as transport and communications, in rural areas. Rondinelli argues that the lack of infrastructure and the restricted access to services and facilities in rural areas of Tanzania, Kenya, and the Sudan are not conducive to interaction among local development committees and administrative units and between them and central government ministries. Thus, it is difficult for central ministries to create supporting linkages and for decentralized units to interact with each other at the local level or within regions. Relatively little attention has been given in the design and implementation of decentralization policies to the spatial and physical requirements.[2]

IMPROVING THE IMPLEMENTATION
OF DECENTRALIZATION POLICIES

The studies in this volume illustrate many of the constraints that have frustrated the efforts of governments in Third World nations to implement decentralization policies and programs. Although the analyses have identified some of the most important obstacles, it must be emphasized that the particular combination and significance of these factors in influencing the outcome of decentralization vary from country to country. The studies also reveal that despite limited success in implementing these policies, governments in developing countries are continuing to decentralize development planning and management responsibilities, not only because political groups seeking new roles for regional and local units of administration continue to bring pressure on them, but because they have discovered that the overconcentration of decision making and management responsibilities at the center can lead to inefficiencies and delays in carrying out centrally conceived development plans.

The gaps between the goals of decentralization and the results of policy implementation in the Third World remain wide. In several cases, however, relatively successful decentralization has taken place, which implies that there do exist factors and conditions in these countries that are conducive to the achievement of decentralization objectives. Our argument is that the implementation strategy for decentralization should attempt to maximize the impact of support factors while at the same time minimizing the constraints. We contend that the reality of the situation in developing countries is such that an incremental implementation strategy clearly articulated and continuously implemented in stages over a longer period of time would both be politically feasible and lead to meaningful results.

The chapters in this volume indicate that most, if not all, of the variables identified in Chapter 1 affect the success or failure of decentralization policies in developing countries and that these factors must be considered more carefully in the design and execution of those policies in the future. The planning of decentralization can be guided through the kinds of analyses depicted in Figure 10.1:

(1) *Determining the Desired Scope of Decentralization.* Too often, governments in developing countries enact decentralization policies that are vague and amorphous in their purposes, goals, and

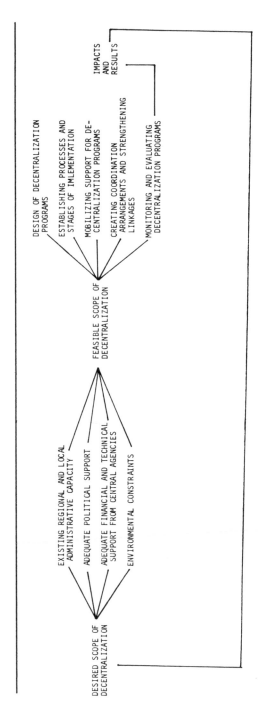

Figure 10.1: Implementation Strategies for Decentralization Policies

scope, leading to confusion among political leaders, administrators, and citizens as to what is intended and how it is to be achieved. Stronger distinctions must be made in decentralization laws among the various forms of decentralization, and clearer policy statements are needed as to whether the central government is seeking to promote devolution, debureaucratization, delegation or deconcentration. The objectives of decentralization policies also need greater clarification. As Rondinelli and Cheema point out in Chapter 1, the objectives can range from simply attempting to promote greater efficiency in central administration by relieving top decision-makers of responsibility for routine matters to eliciting widespread participation in development policy-making by devolving functions to local governments or transferring them to the private sector.

(2) *Assessing Existing Regional and Local Capacities.* The studies in this book show that too often governments in developing countries have decentralized planning, decision-making, and management functions without considering the capacities of local or regional organizations to absorb them and carry them out efficiently. Some countries have delegated or devolved functions *en masse,* without taking into account that state, provincial, district, or local organizations in different parts of the country have different levels of administrative capacity, different amounts of resources, and different levels of commitment to decentralization. Policy planners and analysts must more carefully allocate functions among levels of administration and tailor them to the needs and capacities of organizations in different parts of the country. The literature of development administration offers a variety of methods and approaches for assessing the planning and management capabilities of governments and private organizations. An assessment of regional and local capacities should precede decisions about the scope of decentralization and the allocation of functions.[3]

(3) *Determining Political Support.* Before decisions are made on the appropriate scope of decentralization policies and on the allocation of functions, greater attention must be given to determining the extent of political support and opposition to various forms of decentralization among national political leaders, high-level administrative officials, field staff, local elites, and leaders of local interest groups.

(4) *Estimating Financial and Technical Support Capacities of Central Agencies.* Equally important in improving the implementation of decentralization strategies is gauging the capacity and desire of officials in central administrative agencies to give the financial, technical, and managerial support to decentralized organizations. Where capacity or desire is weak, plans must be made to reorient central ministries to new roles and change the reward, incentive, and punishment structures within the civil service to create greater support for decentralization.

When decentralization policies create new roles and resources for central agencies as well as reallocate their functions and responsibilities, they may generate greater acceptance and more enthusiasm within the central bureaucracy for implementing them.

(5) *Reviewing Environmental Constraints.* Some account must also be taken of the potential obstacles to decentralization arising from existing political structures and styles, traditional cultural or behavioral characteristics, national economic conditions and trends, the present state of development in various regions, and differences in organizational capacities among levels of government. Although precise measurement and comprehensive analysis are unlikely to be possible in most developing countries, consideration of potential effects can lead to more carefully designed and executed policies. A broad reconnaissance of the political and social environment in which proposed decentralization policies will be implemented is needed to inform judgment about feasible alternatives.

(6) *Delineating A Feasible Scope of Decentralization.* The appropriate degree and forms of decentralization in any particular country at any given time should be determined not on the basis of abstract theory, but by careful analysis of existing regional and local capacities, available political support, the willingness and capacity of central agencies to provide needed financial and technical assistance, and the ability to create environmental conditions that are conducive to successful policy implementation. Strategies must be devised for overcoming environmental and technical constraints.

(7) *Designing Specific Decentralization Programs.* After a feasible scope of decentralization is determined, policies must be translated into programs, and organizational arrangements must be

designed for transferring planning and management functions. Experience with decentralization in the countries examined in this book suggests that a combination of arrangements is needed and that different arrangements are appropriate for different regions and levels of government. Among the alternatives examined here were creation of semi-autonomous agencies, restructuring of local governments, establishment or strengthening of field agencies, creation of local and provincial planning committees and administrative units, transfer of planning and management authority to state, regional, provincial, district, and municipal governments, and the decentralization of budgeting procedures.

(8) *Identifying Stages and Procedures of Implementation.* Experience indicates that decentralization can be implemented most successfully if the process is incremental and iterative. Those aspects or programs that are least likely to be opposed and for which there is adequate administrative capacity should be expanded as political support and administrative competence increase. Greater attention must be given to building administrative capacity from the "bottom up" as well as from the "top down" and to finding ways of using and strengthening existing organizations and traditional decision-making procedures in rural areas. Policy implementation, in many cases, must be experimental. Pilot and demonstration projects may be needed to test and substantiate the ability of local government to assume greater responsibility.[4]

(9) *Mobilizing Support.* Support for decentralization policies must be deliberately and carefully mobilized among leaders in central ministries and departments, state, provincial, district, and local units of administration, autonomous and regional agencies, political parties, and interest groups that will be affected by those programs. The mass media, training and public information programs, and political bargaining must be used to forge a base of support for decentralization policies if they are to be implemented successfully. In most countries, changes must be made in civil service systems to provide incentives and rewards for those officials who promote development at the local levels.

(10) *Creating Coordinating and Assistance Linkages.* If decentralization is to be effective, means must be found of reorienting

central administrators' perception of their roles from control and direction to support and facilitation. In the early stages of decentralization, strong support and guidance are needed from central agencies to increase the administrative capacity of local organizations. But central agencies must also be prepared to withdraw to a facilitating and coordinating role once local capacities have increased. If the purpose of decentralization is to provide more discretion at the local level to meet unique local needs and to generate innovative solutions to development problems, then the role of central ministries must change from one of directing development efforts to one of absorbing and integrating local programs into national development policies.

(11) *Specifying Monitoring and Evaluation Procedures.* The implementation of decentralization policies must be seen as a continuing process of modifying government structure and procedures as conditions become more conducive to incremental expansions in their scope and application. The ability to adjust and adapt depends on effective monitoring and evaluation procedures that gauge the pace and impact of decentralization and from which information can be derived to make policy changes in an appropriate and timely fashion.

Much more needs to be known about the experience of individual developing countries with designing and implementing decentralization policies, and the expansion of knowledge needed to refine implementation strategies depends on more extensive comparisons of national experiences. The implementation of decentralization provides a rich and rewarding research agenda through which development scholars, policy analysts, and practitioners can contribute to the task of refining and improving the process of implementing decentralization policies in developing countries in the future.

NOTES

1. For a discussion of alternative organizational arrangements, see George Honadle and Rudi Klauss, eds., *International Development Administration: Implementation Analysis for Development Projects* (New York: Praeger, 1979); G. Shabbir

Cheema, "Establishing Local Development Units: A Strategy for Institutional Reform in Asia," *Public Administration Review,* vol. XIX, no. 1 (1981); Dennis A. Rondinelli, ed., *Planning Development Projects* (Stroudsburg, PA: Dowden, Hutchinson, & Ross, 1977); G. Shabbir Cheema and S. Ahmad Hussein, "Local Government Reform in Malaysia," *Asian Survey,* vol. XVIII, no. 6 (1978); and R. N. Haldipur and V.R.K. Paramahamsa, eds., *Local Government Institutions in Rural India* (Hyderabad: National Institute of Community Development, 1970).

2. For a detailed discussion, see Dennis A. Rondinelli and Kenneth Ruddle, *Urbanization and Rural Development: A Spatial Policy for Equitable Growth* (New York: Praeger, 1978); Dennis A. Rondinelli, "Spatial Analysis for Regional Development: A Case Study in the Bicol River Basin of the Philippines," *Resource Systems Theory and Methodology Series,* no. 2 (Tokyo: United Nations University, 1980); Walter Stohr and D.R.F. Taylor, eds., *Planning from Above or Below?* (London: John Wiley, 1981).

3. Gabriel U. Iglesias, "Implementation and the Planning of Development: Notes on Trends and Issues Focusing on the Concept of Administrative Capability," in *Implementation: The Problem of Achieving Results* (Manila: Eastern Regional Organization for Public Administration, 1976).

4. See Dennis A. Rondinelli, "Designing International Development Projects for Implementation," in Honadle and Klauss, *International Development Administration,* pp. 21-52.

ABOUT THE AUTHORS

G. Shabbir Cheema is Development Administration Planner, United Nations Centre for Regional Development, Nagoya, Japan. He received his Ph. D. from the University of Hawaii in 1973 and has taught at Government College, Pakistan, the University of Hawaii, and Universiti Sains Malaysia. His areas of interest are development administration, rural development, and regional and local planning. Dr. Cheema has undertaken field research in the People's Republic of China, Malaysia, and Pakistan. Author of articles in professional journals and books, his latest publication is *Institutional Dimensions of Regional Development* (Singapore: Maruzen, 1981).

Harry J. Friedman is Professor of Political Science at the University of Hawaii and formerly taught at Michigan State University and the University of Pittsburgh, where he received a Ph. D. in 1956. He has served as a consultant and visiting professor at the Pakistan Academy for Rural Development and the University of the Philippines College of Public Administration, and has conducted field research in India during two separate visits. He is the author of a module, *Local Government in Third-World Asia* (Morristown, NJ: General Learning Press, 1973); "An Overview of Other Asia," in Donald C. Rowat (ed.), *International Handbook of Local Government Reorganization: Contemporary Developments* (Westport, CT: Greenwood Press, 1980); and other articles on rural local government, administration, and development in Asia.

Richard L. Harris is a member of the Politics Board and the Coordinator of the Mexican Studies Program at the Santa Cruz campus of the University of California. He was formerly the Assistant Director of the Project on Managing Decentralization at the University of California, Berkeley. Over the last fifteen years, Professor Harris has taught, conducted field research, and served as a consultant in various parts of Latin America and Africa. He is also a Coordinating Editor

317

for *Latin American Perspectives,* a quarterly journal on Latin American political, economic, and social affairs.

David K. Leonard is Associate Professor of Political Science at the University of California, Berkeley. He has worked for over ten years in various parts of Africa, most recently as a management adviser to Kenya's Ministry of Livestock Development. His publications include *Reaching the Peasant Farmer: Organization Theory and Practice in Kenya* (University of Chicago Press, 1977).

Kuldeep Mathur is Professor at the Indian Institute of Public Administration New Delhi. He has been on the faculties of the Universities of Rajasthan and Himachal Pradesh and has also served as Deputy Director (Research), HCM State Institute of Public Administration, Jaipur. He obtained his master's degree from Rajasthan University and a Ph.D. from the University of Hawaii under an East-West Center Fellowship. His articles and papers have appeared in various journals, and his books include *Bureaucratic Response to Development* (1972), *Administrative Response to Emergency: Scarcity Administration in Maharashtra* (1975), *District Administration* (1976), *Monitoring and Evaluation of Rural Development Programmes in Asia* (co-editor, 1980), and *Bureaucracy and New Agricultural Strategy* (1982).

John D. Montgomery, Professor of Public Administration at Harvard, is author of *Forced To Be Free* (1957), *The Politics of Foreign Aid* (1962), *Technology and Civic Life* (1974), and other studies of international development. He has been a consultant to the United Nations, the World Bank, the Agency for International Development, and several foreign governments.

John R. Nellis is Professor of Development Planning and Public Administration at the Maxwell School of Citizenship and Public Affairs of Syracuse University. He obtained his Ph.D. from Syracuse University. He has taught public administration, political science, and international affairs at Carleton University, Ottawa; served as Assistant Representative for North Africa of the Ford Foundation; was a research fellow at the Institute of Development Studies at the University of Nairobi, Kenya; and was an evaluator of the rural development program of Tanzania. He has served as a consultant to the United Nations Development Program, the International Development Research Centre, the Ford Foundation, the United States Agency for International Development, and the Canadian International Development Agency, and has worked in Morocco, Algeria, Tunisia, Upper Volta, Nigeria, Kenya, Tanzania, Uganda, Lesotho, Botswana, and Swaziland. He is the author of a number of books and articles on development strategies, rural development, and the administration of development.

Dennis A. Rondinelli is Professor of Development Planning at the Maxwell School of Citizenship and Public Affairs, Syracuse University. He received his Ph. D. from Cornell University. He has taught at the University of Wisconsin and Vanderbilt University and served as a senior fellow at the East-West Center in Honolulu, Hawaii. Dr. Rondinelli has been a consultant to development projects in Asia, Africa, and Latin American and has served as an adviser to the U.S. Agency for International Development, the United Nations Centre for Regional Development in Nagoya, Japan, and the World Bank. He has published numerous articles on various aspects of international development policy and urban and regional development planning, and is author, co-author, or editor of seven books on development policy, planning, and administration.